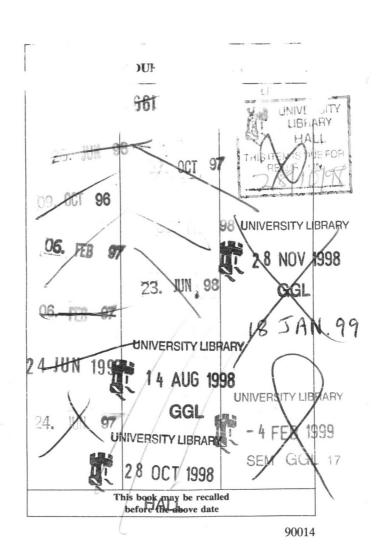

What Works:
Reducing Reoffending

UNOTT

The Wiley Series in Offender Rehabilitation

Edited by

Clive R. Hollin

*Youth Treatment Service and
The University of Birmingham, UK*

and

Mary McMurran

*Rampton Hospital, Nottinghamshire
and The University of Birmingham, UK*

Young Offenders and Alcohol-Related Crime
Mary McMurran and Clive R. Hollin

What Works: Reducing Reoffending
Guidelines from Research and Practice
Edited by James McGuire

What Works: Reducing Reoffending

Guidelines from Research and Practice

Edited by

James McGuire
The University of Liverpool, UK

JOHN WILEY & SONS
Chichester · New York · Brisbane · Toronto · Singapore

Other Wiley Editorial Offices

John Wiley & Sons, Inc., 605 Third Avenue,
New York, NY 10158-0012, USA

Jacaranda Wiley Ltd, 33 Park Road, Milton,
Queensland 4064, Australia

John Wiley & Sons (Canada) Ltd, 22 Worcester Road,
Rexdale, Ontario M9W 1L1, Canada

John Wiley & Sons (SEA) Pte Ltd, 37 Jalan Pemimpin #05-04,
Block B, Union Industrial Building, Singapore 2057

Library of Congress Cataloging-in-Publication Data

What works : reducing reoffending : guidelines from research and
    practice / edited by James McGuire.
        p.   cm. — (The Wiley series in offender rehabilitation)
    Includes bibliographical references and index.
    ISBN 0-471-95053-X — ISBN 0-471-95686-4 (pbk.)
    1. Recidivism—Prevention.   2. Criminals—Rehabilitation—Great
Britain—Case studies.   I. McGuire, James.   II. Series: Wiley
Series in offender rehabilitation.
HV6049.W48   1995
364.3'6—dc20   94-44564
                                                                        CIP

British Library Cataloguing in Publication Data

A catalogue record for this book is available from the British Library
ISBN 0-471-95053-X (cased)
ISBN 0-471-95686-4 (paper)   1000502808

Typeset in 10/12 pt Century Schoolbook by
Mathematical Composition Setters Ltd, Salisbury,
Printed and bound in Great Britain by Bookcraft (Bath) Ltd.

This book is printed on acid-free paper responsibly manufactured
from sustainable forestation, for which at least two trees are planted
for each one used for paper production.

Contents

Part III: Practice, Research and Programme Delivery

About the Editor

James McGuire   University of Liverpool, Department of Clinical
                     Psychology, Whelan Building, Liverpool L69 3BX,
                     UK.

James McGuire is a clinical psychologist and lecturer in forensic clinical psychology at the University of Liverpool and Ashworth Hospital. He obtained degrees from the universities of Glasgow, Leicester and Leeds, and has carried out research in prisons, probation services, adolescent units, and special hospitals, on a number of aspects of offender rehabilitation and evaluation of services. He has worked at the universities of Edinburgh, Hong Kong and London and was also for some years involved independently in training, staff development, and consultation in criminal justice agencies.

Contributors

Don A. Andrews	Department of Psychology, Loeb Building, Carleton University, Ottawa K1S 5B6, Canada.
Jack Bush	Correctional Treatment Associates, RR3, Box 6749 East Road, Barre, Vermont 05641, USA.
Tim Chapman	Probation Board for Northern Ireland, Projects Team, 40–44 Great Patrick Street, Belfast BT1 2LT, UK.
David Cooke	The Douglas Inch Centre, 2 Woodside Terrace, Glasgow G3 7UY, UK.
Clive R. Hollin	School of Psychology, University of Birmingham, Birmingham B15 2TT, UK.
Christine Knott	Greater Manchester Probation Service, Oakland House, Talbot Road, Manchester M16 OPQ, UK.
Mark W. Lipsey	Department of Human Resources, Box 90, George Peabody College, Vanderbilt University, Nashville, Tennessee 37203, USA.
Friedrich Lösel	Institüt für Psychologie, Bismarckstrasse 1, Der Universität Erlangen-Nürnberg, D-90471 Erlangen, Germany.
Gill McIvor	Social Work Research Centre, University of Stirling, Stirling FK9 4LA, UK.
Robert Prentky	Joseph J. Peters Institute, 260 S. Broad Street, Suite 220, Philadelphia, Pennsylvania 19102-3814, USA.
Philip Priestley	Peace Close, West Horrington, Wells, Somerset BA5 2ED, UK.
Colin Roberts	University of Oxford, Department of Applied Social Studies, Barnett House, Wellington Square, Oxford OX1 2ER, UK.

Series Preface

Twenty years ago it is doubtful that any serious consideration would have been given to publishing a series of books on the topic of offender rehabilitation. While the notion of rehabilitation for offenders was widely accepted 30 years ago, the 1970s saw the collapse of what we might call the treatment ideal. As many other commentators have noted, the turning point can be pinpointed to the publication of an article titled 'What Works—Questions and Answers about Prison Reform', written by Robert Martinson and published in 1974. The essential message taken from this article was that, when it comes to the rehabilitation of offenders, what works is 'nothing works'. It would be stretching the case to say that Martinson single-handedly overturned the rehabilitative philosophy, but his message was obviously welcomed by a receptive audience. As writers such as Don Andrews have suggested there are many reasons why both the academic community and politicians and policy-makers were more than willing to subscribe to the 'nothing works' philosophy. (Although the evidence suggests that the public at large did not buy completely the need to abandon rehabilitation.) Thus the 1970s and 1980s saw a return to hard sentencing, the predominance of punishment, and the handing out of just deserts to those who transgressed the law of the land. Throughout this period of rehabilitative nihilism a small group of academics and practitioners kept faith with the rehabilitative ideal, led perhaps by Paul Gendreau and Robert Ross, and slowly began to look for new ways to argue the case for rehabilitation. The turnabout, when it came, was dramatic. Through the development of a methodology for statistically reviewing large bodies of research, called 'meta-analysis', unequivocal evidence was produced that rehabilitative programmes did work. The view that 'nothing works' is simply wrong: rehabilitation programmes do have a positive effect in reducing recidivism. The effect is not always large, although sometimes it is; nor is it always present, although on average it is. However, it is there and that cannot be ignored. Since 1990, armed with these findings, there has been a remarkable resurgence of the rehabilitative ideal: practitioners have eagerly attended conferences, seminars, and training courses: researchers are working not to make the case for rehabilitation, but to improve and refine techniques for working with offenders.

This volume brings us up to date with developments in offender rehabilitation and we are grateful to James McGuire for editing this text for the series. We hope that readers will find this a ready source of useful information which will guide both practice and research.

The renewed emphasis on rehabilitative work with offenders means that information on assessment, intervention and evaluation should accrue rapidly over the coming years. We hope that The Wiley Series on Offender Rehabilitation will continue to keep practitioners and researchers abreast of current developments.

Mary McMurran
Clive R. Hollin
December 1994

Preface

In the current media mythology of crime and punishment, there is an underlying semantic dimension that is ever-present, which provides a framework for much of the discourse. This is an imagined continuum between the 'hard' and the 'soft'. The words also neatly polarize the human species into two competing attitudinal camps, the 'realists' versus the 'do-gooders'.

To be a member of the realist school means to be hard-headed, to be able to face the facts. A direct link is depicted between such cerebral 'hardness', and a preparedness to do what is necessary, to take hard action towards offenders. Hence they will be taught lessons, and given their 'just deserts'; approached with less understanding, and more punitiveness. This vocabulary reproduces the imagery of the street; it is pervaded by metaphors of toughness. It recreates the same interpersonal modalities that many offenders have applied in relation to their victims.

Pitted against the realists are a softer-headed, well-meaning, but ultimately deluded group of people. They are typically portrayed as liberal, muddled and idealistic, as having their heads in the clouds, and as wishing to help criminals (perhaps by sending them on exotic journeys), and forgetting about victims. They, more than any other group in society, are purported to be responsible for the deterioration of law and order, through their advocacy of leniency and permissiveness.

The substance of this continuum is not completely irrational. Rather, it contains a mixture of different types of thinking: stereotypical (highly), mystical (partly) and logical (minimally). But most important, it is not even remotely scientific. Regrettably, it leaves our responses to criminal justice in a extremely confused conceptual state.

The aim of this book is to place the question of how to respond to offending behaviour on a rational and empirical footing. It takes as its starting point the not unreasonable assumption, concerning which there is envisaged to be a wide consensus, that a principal goal of working with offenders should be to reduce the likelihood that their illegal or anti-social behaviour will be repeated. This is, arguably at least, the single most highly valued service that could be delivered to victims of crime.

The evidence to be presented in the book indicates that the 'soft–hard' dimension is simply not a useful way to think of criminal justice and that it would be better to completely dispense with it. If we wish the action we take to contribute towards achieving the goal of reduced reoffending, then the question of how hard or soft we are becomes virtually irrelevant. A recommended alternative course of action (and in intellectual terms a more hard-headed one) is to examine evidence. There is now a substantial body of research findings that cut across the 'soft-hard' polarity in the criminal justice debate. This evidence demonstrates the possibility of reducing offence behaviour neither by punishing offenders, nor by being indulgent towards them, but by taking constructive action of specific kinds. The objective of the book is to assemble and consolidate that evidence, and indicate directions for possible future developments in both practice and research.

The book is divided into three parts. The chapters in the first part draw together the present state of research concerning the question of 'what works' to reduce reoffending. James McGuire and Philip Priestley describe in broad outline the context of the debate and the nature of the evidence now available. Don Andrews locates these findings in a general social-psychological understanding of the causal factors which contribute to crime. Mark Lipsey presents results from the largest single integrative review ever undertaken of 'treatment–outcome' research in work with offenders. Finally, Friedrich Lösel sounds a cautionary note, and while acknowledging overall positive results, identifies where we should be sceptical about the details of some of the findings so far reported, and which important types of research remain to be done.

In Part Two of the book, five illustrations are presented of the kinds of developments that are required for effective intervention to reduce rates of recidivism. Christine Knott outlines a large scale community-based programme, aimed at individuals who have committed a wide range of offences, which has obtained positive and encouraging results. Tim Chapman focuses on one specific offence, car theft/joyriding, and illustrates the importance, in designing structured programmes, of carrying out work which takes account of the social and cultural conditions in which offenders live. Jack Bush outlines in detail the processes of teaching and training individuals in methods of self-change to reduce their violence to others. Robert Prentky analyses the contributory factors in sexually assaultive behaviour and stipulates what would be required of comprehensive programmes for them to have an impact on some of the most serious kinds of harmful acts. Finally, David Cooke reports on an innovative project focused on mentally disordered offenders and describes both the nature of the work involved and its end results.

Part Three turns to practical questions of programme delivery and evaluation. It has all too frequently been a major drawback of work in criminal justice settings that very little evaluation has been carried out. Clive Hollin addresses the complex issue of programme integrity and its importance in the design and undertaking of systematic work. Gill McIvor provides a rationale and clear guidelines to practitioners for collecting their own evaluative data. Lastly, Colin Roberts presents a general framework for targeting and selection, provision of resources, and delivery of services to offenders with different risk levels and needs.

Readers will find the word 'treatment' used frequently throughout this book. In the present context, this is a general term used in experimental designs, which may refer to interventions and programme activities of an enormous variety of kinds. It is important to emphasize that this does not derive from the application of a medical model, imply that offenders are 'ill', or that they can be 'cured' by the dispensing of medication or other ministrations which depend in part on the existence of a power differential between the professional and the client. Though by no means an ideal word for referring to the range of work touched upon in this book, there is unfortunately no comparable word with the same generality and flexibility.

There are two main general conclusions of this book. The first is that the findings surveyed here represent a significant contribution to knowledge in the social sciences, though as in every other field much more work remains to be done. The second is that these findings provide practical guidelines which should be of interest to sentencers, practitioners and policy-makers throughout the criminal justice system. In this respect, however, the book cannot be seen as anything other than a beginning. It is hoped that it may be a stimulus both to research and practice, and to wider discussion of the issues with which it deals. Both the publishers and the editor will be grateful for any feedback that readers wish to give concerning the ideas and findings which the book presents.

This book was inspired by a series of conferences, entitled *What Works*, held in Manchester in 1991, 1992 and 1994. I wish to express warm thanks to fellow members of the planning groups for those events: Mike Davies, Jean Hoyes, Jackie Kennedy, Helen McIlvany, Mary McMurran, Gordon Paterson, Ann Power, Philip Priestley, and Beverly Rowson. Thanks also to those who provided administrative and other kinds of support: Debra Cain, Paul Hilton, Katheryn Huyton, Melanie Kettle, Sheila Prentice, Janet Prichard, Elaine Smith, Judith Vaughan and Sheila Vellacott.

James McGuire
October 1994

PART I

The 'What Works' Debate

CHAPTER 1

Reviewing 'What Works': Past, Present and Future

James McGuire

University of Liverpool and Ashworth Hospital, Liverpool, UK

and

Philip Priestley

Peace Close, West Horrington, UK

THE 'WHAT WORKS' DEBATE

The question of how society should respond to those who break its laws is a constantly perplexing one. With steadily increasing crime rates in many countries, a high level of media attention devoted to crime, and escalating public fear and anger concerning it, the controversy over how to deal with offenders has been sustained during recent years at an almost feverish pitch.

The mainstay of official response to those found guilty of offences, in most jurisdictions, is of course punishment. Nowadays, the direct infliction of physical pain is (officially at least) comparatively rare, though it still occurs in some countries. Punishment is now accomplished much more frequently by two principal methods. The first is fines, the exacting of money payments, a very extensively used measure for less serious kinds of offence. The second is imprisonment, the most commonly used penalty for more serious crimes in a majority of societies. The latter has retained a central place in most Western countries for a period of approximately

What Works: Reducing Reoffending—Guidelines from Research and Practice.
Edited by J. McGuire. © 1995 John Wiley & Sons Ltd.

two hundred years. The most severe punishment of all, the death penalty, shows a varying pattern of usage but in 1989 was still being utilized in 100 of the 180 member states of the United Nations surveyed (Hood, 1989).

It has become ever more apparent over recent decades, however, that punitive measures have done little to arrest the increase in crime. It has often been contended instead that in fact they make things worse. It is certainly very difficult, if not impossible, to demonstrate that punishment achieves its desired effect of deterring offenders from reoffending, an argument to be returned to later. But the question of whether or not punishment 'works' must be located in a wider debate over whether any form of response to adjudicated offenders can have an impact on reoffending rates. This general question, of the effectiveness of interventions of any type, is commonly known as the 'what works' debate.

The objective of this book is to assemble the available evidence relevant to this debate. Such evidence, marshalled in the chapters that follow, indicates that it has now been demonstrated that rates of reoffending can be reduced, but not by punitive methods. Rather, the methods that 'work' for this purpose are those that address the factors that have played a causal or contributory role in an offending act, and that would place the offender at risk of reoffending in the future. Across the range of evidence now bearing on this point, a number of features emerge with sufficient consistency for it now to be possible to identify ingredients of effective intervention programmes.

The suggestion that it is possible to reduce reoffending contradicts a well established and widespread assumption about working with offenders. Only a few writers have articulated this view explicitly, but it has nevertheless formed a backdrop to much thinking in criminology, penology, psychology and social work over the past twenty years. This view states that, when we systematically examine attempts to alter or reduce offence-proneness, little or nothing of any kind will be found to work. The origins of this statement are to be found in a number of wide-ranging surveys of research, conducted in the mid-1970s in the United States and in Britain. These reviews sought to draw together all the evidence then existing from 'treatment–outcome' studies in work with offenders.

The phrase 'What Works?' is taken from a much-cited article of that title by Martinson (1974), who expressed his general conclusion in straightforward terms. He believed that his work revealed a ' . . radical flaw in our present strategies—that education at its best, or that psychotherapy at its best, cannot overcome, or even appreciably reduce, the powerful tendency for offenders to continue in criminal behaviour' (Martinson, 1974: 49).

Writing at more or less the same time, Lipton and colleagues (1975) in the United States, and Brody (1976) in the United Kingdom, showed a consensus of pessimism on two broad points. The first was that most research that had been done up to that time was plagued by poor methodology: wide variations in the quality of experimental design made it difficult to draw any clear conclusions at all. The second was that, as far as any pattern could be detected in the studies that were acceptably rigorous in design, there was no evidence that anything could be consistently relied upon to work. In subsequent years this view attained the status of a virtual dogma as far as many people were concerned. Yet we now know that these reviews were partly flawed, and the conclusions drawn from them invalid. On the basis of the evidence presented in the chapters which follow, it will be seen that the contention that 'nothing works' is in need of radical revision.

Despite an accumulation of evidence that contradicts it, however, the belief that intervention is unlikely to be effective is still at the core of thinking of many commentators in the criminal justice field. Even in quite recent years a number of established British experts in this area have continued to endorse the conclusions of the 1970s reviews. They include, for example, Blagg and Smith (1989) and Davies (1990) who, though writing more than 15 years after Martinson's initial (1974) conclusions, still accepted on his authority that there were no legitimate claims to be made regarding effectiveness of any interventions. More recently still, Pitts (1992) declared that ' . . . rehabilitative methods tend, by and large, not to rehabilitate . . . research into the effectiveness of 'methods of intervention' . . .is a doomed endeavour' (Pitts, 1992: 144).

DISSENTING VIEWS

Such authors express what can perhaps be characterized as a 'mainstream' view regarding the likely returns from investment of effort in attempts at 'rehabilitation'. But running beneath this dominant ideological glacier there has been a subglacial stream of dissent. From the outset a number of researchers in the field of offender services expressed reservations concerning the conclusions of the Martinson group, and challenged them in a variety of ways. In North America they included, for example, Palmer (1975) and Gendreau and Ross (1980). The former has been a consistent and vocal critic of the 'nothing works' doctrine and has recently reassembled his arguments against it in book form (Palmer, 1992). Gendreau and Ross compiled a 'bibliotherapy for cynics' and edited a volume of research papers that had reported positive outcomes, directly countering the suggestion that little or nothing worked. The methods described in these reports included: (a) several types of system diversion incorporating structured interventions of various kinds; (b) behavioural and skills-training sessions with delinquent families; (c) family crisis intervention strategies; (d) the 'buddy system', a peer-administered contingency management programme; (e) youth counselling programmes incorporating a range of cognitively oriented therapies; (f) behavioural programmes focused on employment; (g) vocationally oriented psychotherapy; (h) a behavioural role-playing and 'crime-inoculation' programme; (i) role-rotation training; (j) differential treatment programmes in probation settings; (k) the Achievement Place parent training programme; (l) a variety of community-based behavioural and skills-training programmes; (m) interpersonal problem-solving skills training; and (n) 'anti-criminal modelling' and problem-solving training (Gendreau & Ross, 1980). Clearly, research studies with positive outcomes were by no means in short supply.

Also, following on the work of Martinson, Brody and their associates by a gap of a few years, a variety of other workers in the United Kingdom reassessed the arguments and reached conclusions quite opposite to theirs. For example, Blackburn (1980) examined a series of studies carried out during the second half of the 1970s. He subjected them to a standard set of methodological tests proposed by Logan (1972), in which studies were required to satisfy specified criteria as regards use of follow-up periods, matched control groups, and so on. Blackburn unearthed only five pieces of work that met these criteria in full. However, in all of them, reductions in recidivism were obtained amongst treated as compared with untreated groups. This is a far cry from the view that 'nothing works' and that criminal behaviour is not susceptible to change.

At a later stage, McGuire and Priestley (1985) assembled a sizeable list of studies in which promising outcomes had been obtained, and sought to challenge the (by then, widespread and firmly established) view that nothing constructive could be done to alter patterns of offence behaviour.

Equally damaging for the 'nothing works' position was a study by Thornton (1987) in which he reinvestigated a selection of the studies used by Lipton and co-workers (1975) to derive their original conclusions. Contrary to what had been claimed by Lipton and colleagues, a number of these projects had in fact described positive outcomes. Indeed, focusing on those studies that employed psychological therapy as the 'treatment' in controlled experimental designs, almost 50% of the results had demonstrated a positive advantage for therapeutic intervention. In the remainder of the studies, no differences were detectable and in one, therapy yielded a net disadvantage. But, as Thornton pointed out in the wake of his reanalysis, while many questions could still be asked about the exact nature of the gains secured, the one conclusion that was not permissible was that 'nothing works'.

Perhaps the most startling feature of this history is the fact that, in parallel to these diverse criticisms, Robert Martinson, the most widely quoted and publicized of the original group of reviewers, withdrew and revised his own initial conclusions. In 1979, he acknowledged errors in the earlier reviews, and reported on a new survey of research studies from which the evidence was '. . . too overwhelming to ignore' (Martinson, 1979: 252). On this basis he recanted the statements made in his 1974 article. Martinson also cautioned, however, that some interventions could be harmful and that the setting in which they were delivered was of crucial importance. By that stage, however, the 'nothing works' view had become deeply embedded in the thinking of a majority of professionals at most levels of the criminal justice system.

RECENT RESEARCH REVIEWS: META-ANALYSIS AND OUTCOME EVALUATION

On the above grounds alone, by the end of the 1980s there were reasons for serious disquiet regarding the integrity of the view that little or nothing could be done to accomplish the goal of reducing reoffending. Arguments nevertheless continued between proponents and opponents of the view that recidivism could be reduced by 'rehabilitation' (Doob & Brodeur, 1989; Gendreau, 1989; Genevie et al., 1986; Van Den Haag, 1982). However the most compelling evidence in the field of offender 'treatment' derives from another source: from research reviews concerning outcomes of intervention published from 1985 onwards. In the field of comparative outcome research there are two main kinds of research review. The first, traditional format is known as a 'narrative review'. The author will locate and read all the research reports pertaining to the chosen area of work. Having done so, he or she will then attempt to provide a summary or interpretation of the trends amongst their respective findings. Research reviews of this kind play a major role in synthesizing research results. This is indispensable for theory-building and for pointing to unanswered questions and new directions for work. Often, however, it can be a very daunting task. There could be many studies in one area and methodological differences between them may prohibit the drawing of any clear conclusions at all. The sheer quantity may make it difficult to see any pattern within them. Reviews of this kind generally include summary tables of the various pieces of work that have been surveyed.

However, the evidence that now enables us to turn the 'nothing works' conclusion on its head is of a different nature. Since the mid-1980s a number of reviews have been undertaken using the statistical tool of 'meta-analysis'. This method has been developed to facilitate the review process and enable reviewers to combine findings from different experiments (Wolf, 1986). It involves the aggregation and side-by-side analysis of large numbers of experimental studies. The studies included may differ considerably in detail. For example, different outcome measures may have been employed or they may be based on very disparate numbers of subjects. Meta-analysis can also incorporate adjustments for the fact that studies vary considerably in the degree of rigour of their experimental design.

Meta-analysis has been used extensively in fields such as medicine and education to evaluate outcomes of clinical treatments or intervention programmes. Since the early 1980s, it has also been used for the large-scale evaluation of the effects of psychotherapy (Glass et al., 1981; Lambert & Bergin, 1986). In a major review Lipsey and Wilson (1993) present findings from a total of 302 meta-analyses of the effects of psychological treatments, conducted in mental health, occupational and educational settings.

Essentially, the procedure of meta-analysis requires recalculation of the data from different experiments in a new all-encompassing statistical analysis. An obvious problem in attempting to do this is that different studies may have used different methods to evaluate the effects of interventions. In one form of meta-analysis, this is overcome by expressing the changes from pre-test to post-test in 'standard deviation units', which are independent of the precise outcome measure used, and which cumulatively provide a new variable called 'effect size'. In another form, findings are expressed in the form of a correlation coefficient depicting the relationship between expected and observed studies in 'success' and 'failure' categories. In the most thorough meta-analyses (such as that of Lipsey, Chapter 3, this volume) numerous finer adjustments and cross-comparisons are made. These are used, for example, to test whether better, more strictly designed studies obtain different effects from those that are weaker or looser in the way in which they have been carried out.

A number of meta-analytic reviews have now been conducted on recidivism and allied variables in work with offender groups (see Lösel, Chapter 4, this volume). They include the first study of this kind by Garrett (1985), which surveyed 111 papers incorporating a total of more than 13 000 incarcerated young offenders. She found a significant overall effect of treatment on a variety of outcomes including reoffending. A weaker effect was obtained by Gottschalk and colleagues (1987), working on community-based interventions. Whitehead and Lab (1989; Lab & Whitehead, 1988) reported predominantly negative findings in their meta-analysis, and described only a few promising results, but close examination of their review shows that they discarded all studies with a treatment effect size of less than 0.2. This is somewhat bewildering, as most policy-makers would surely be impressed if a reduction in reoffence rates approaching this magnitude could routinely be obtained. Lösel and Koferl (1989) described the outcome of the German 'socio-therapeutic' prison regimes, and reported a modest positive effect with highly recidivistic, long-term offenders. Izzo and Ross (1990) compared programmes that contained a

'cognitive' component with those that did not, and found a marked superiority in terms of reduced recidivism following the former. Finally, the
two most recent and largest meta-analyses of all, those of Andrews and
colleagues (1990) and Lipsey (1992) have obtained consistent, parallel
patterns of results and have drawn together a set of conclusions based,
in Lipsey's case, on no fewer than 397 outcome studies. These were based
on work with offenders aged between 12 and 21, and cumulatively
accounted for a sample in excess of 40 000 clients. Andrews and colleagues
incorporated findings from 150 research reports in their meta-analysis,
and included studies undertaken with adult offenders.

A principal finding of Lipsey's survey was that a total of 64.5% of the
experiments he examined showed positive effects of 'treatment' in reducing
recidivism, scarcely compatible with the proposition that 'little or nothing
works'. Taking all of these meta-analyses together, it can be demonstrated
that the net effect of 'treatment' in the many studies surveyed is, on
average, a reduction in recidivism rates of between 10% and 12%. Though
a positive finding, this may not appear an especially large prize given the
volume of research carried out. Nevertheless, it would probably be seen
as worth obtaining by sentencers, programme managers and the public
alike. Lösel (1993a) has pointed out that evaluations of many medical interventions (such as heart bypass surgery or some cancer treatments) benefit
from a considerable investment of resources, but when examined through
meta-analysis yield no greater an effect than this.

Beyond the average effect size, the detailed findings of meta-analytic
reviews are fairly complex, but it is in this area that much of the real
interest lies. Perhaps the most telling observation is that, like many
average figures, the 'mean effect size' conceals wide variations. Thus there
are studies in which much larger reductions in reoffence rates were
obtained, and others in which recidivism rates actually worsened. Amidst
this variation, some clear trends can be detected concerning the ingredients of programmes with higher or lower levels of effectiveness in
reducing reoffending.

WHAT DOES NOT WORK

Before considering what can be detected in these trends concerning what
'does work', it is salutary to look first at what the meta-analyses tell us
about what does not. Several points emerge as important.

Psychotherapeutic Models

First, the value of classical psychotherapeutic models emerges as questionable at best. Though they may be effective for problems in other areas,

there is little evidence that their continued use in work with offenders is very often rewarded by useful outcomes. This applies also to individual casework counselling, which has long been a subject of scepticism following the reviews of Fischer (1973, 1978). In concordance with this Russell (1990) has reviewed evidence that, when later evaluations of casework have been more encouraging, it is because more structured approaches, such as task-centred or behaviourally based methods, have been adopted within it. This point is exemplified by the work of Reid and Hanrahan (1981) on the outcomes of task-centred casework, and is supported again by reviews of social work effectiveness reported by MacDonald and co-workers (1992) and Sheldon (1994).

Medical Models

Second, interventions based on medical models, including not only medication itself but also such innovations as dietary change, are, in the absence of psychosocial components, unlikely to have any lasting impact in reducing reoffending. In some circumstances (e.g. use of anti-libidinal drugs) such methods may have a place, but only within the context of a more comprehensive programme of work.

Punishment

Third and perhaps most controversially politically, let us examine the effects of punitive measures. Overall, meta-analytic evidence suggests that they have a net destructive effect, in that they serve primarily to worsen rates of recidivism. In Lipsey's (1992a, 1992b) reviews, punishment-based programmes, such as shock incarceration, intense surveillance and similar approaches, on average led to a 25% increase in reoffence rates as compared with control groups. It is worth pausing for a moment to reflect on the nature of this result. The following comments are confined to interpretation of this empirical finding only, and are made without reference to the separate question of whether or not punishment is ethically desirable or justified.

A sentence of imprisonment is imposed, in principle, to deprive the individual of his or her freedom; the experience of restriction of liberty in itself (and it alone) is intended to be punitive. Deriving from it there are assumed to be three main types of outcome: (a) the direct deterrent effect of the experience on the individual's own behaviour, which will encourage him or her to 'reform'; (b) a general deterrent effect, by which the visible use of prison sustains the law abiding behaviour of other citizens, and (c) the immediate result of 'incapacitation' of the individual, so protecting the public at least for the period of the sentence. Prison stands, in a sense, as the ultimate symbol of the power of the state to enforce conformity with the law and maintenance of social order (Garland, 1990). These three justifications by outcome, however, have little empirical evidence to support them.

Specific Deterrence

Concerning the first argument, imprisonment fulfils very few of the criteria known to be necessary for a punishment to be effective as a method of behaviour change (see below for further details on this point). Besides, although most offenders are aware of the possibility of being imprisoned and do not want to be caught, studies of offence motivations or decisions show that the prospect plays little active part in their thinking in the moments immediately prior to an offence (e.g. Carroll & Weaver, 1986; Light et al., 1993; Mayers, 1980). It is not surprising, then, that evaluations such as Lipsey's of the effects of punitive sanctions show them to have a net effect of increasing recidivism (see also Wooldredge, 1988). Reference to Prison Department statistics for England and Wales for 1992 (Home Office, 1994) shows a very high reconviction rate over a 4-year period for offenders discharged in 1987. For young adult males, who commit the bulk of recorded crimes, it was 82%. When more punitive regimes were tested in the 'short sharp shock' experiment of the early 1980s, the results showed them to have no effect on reconviction rates (Thornton et al., 1984). In general, while the possibility that a small number of individuals are deterred by imprisonment cannot be ruled out, this proposition cannot be tested directly, as other factors may have contributed to their desistance from crime. There is certainly little evidence that the deterrent impact of the prison is substantial or even satisfactory.

Deterrence of Others

The second justification, and the question of whether imprisonment acts as a general deterrent, presents a very difficult hypothesis to test. Some of the intricacies of estimating the possible effects of deterrence have been explored by Gibbs (1986). Even where there are significant relationships between changes in crime rates and probabilities of conviction, such findings can be influenced by numerous factors, and their interpretation is difficult (Farrington et al., 1994). That being imprisoned is universally viewed as an undesirable experience does not in itself confirm its impact as a deterrent, given the complex interactions of the factors that influence criminal behaviour. Thus the fact that most citizens, most of the time, are law-abiding could have any number of explanations, even acknowledging criminological evidence that most also at some time break the law, and that illegal behaviour is actually quite widespread. But the most serious penalty of all, death, has not been shown to have any clear-cut effect on rates of serious crime. When comparisons have been made between states with or without official execution, or in which it has been abolished or restored after a period of abstention, no strong evidence emerges of any general deterrent effect (Hood, 1989).

Incapacitation

It is obvious *de facto* that removal of an individual from circulation means that he or she cannot be a danger to members of the public during the period of incarceration. It is less obvious, however, whether marginal increases in the prison population, excluding progressively more offenders from the public arena, can have a measurable effect on the overall crime rate, unless the number so dealt with is very large. This is the conclusion of a detailed analysis of this possibility, using reconviction and other statistics and a specially designed statistical model, reported by Tarling (1993). 'Incapacitation models' take into account a number of factors, including: (a) the rate at which offenders commit crimes; (b) the probability of being apprehended, cautioned or convicted for a crime; (c) the probability of being sentenced to imprisonment having been convicted; (d) the average time spent in custody; and (e) the average residual 'career length' of offenders. Examining a number of studies in which such models have been applied, with reference to England and Wales Tarling (1993: 154) states that ' . . . change in the use of custody of the order of 25 percent would be needed to produce a 1 percent change in the level of crime . . . the incapacitation effect of current levels of imprisonment is not great. Relatively few crimes would be prevented. A general increase in the use of imprisonment, either by increasing the proportion sentenced to imprisonment, increasing the sentences imposed or increasing the proportion of the sentence that offenders spend in custody, would not affect crime levels by any substantial amount'.

Thus to achieve a truly incapacitating effect the resultant prison population would have to increase to a level that would currently be seen as unacceptable both in ethical terms and in monetary costs. Applying this model rather crudely to the United Kingdom, for example, to obtain a reduction in the crime rate of 30%, the prison population would have to increase by a factor of 7.5, to 375 000. Obviously, to secure such a figure there would have to be a commensurate increase in levels of policing. The ultimate consequence of applying this principle, if carried to its conclusion, would be a prisonized, fear-dominated society. Even in monetary terms, the net cost of the required changes would consume a very substantial portion of the country's GNP.

The counter-intuitive effects of punishment contradict common-sense perceptions of its place in the correctional system, and the expectation that people will 'learn their lesson' if they suffer pain and discomfort as a result of breaking the law. However, an examination of the findings of behavioural research on punishment shows that we should not be at all surprised by this result (see for example Barker, 1994; Grant and Evans, 1994; Sundel and Sundel, 1993). Such research clearly establishes several points. First, punishment is an effective method of behaviour change, though principally when the objective is to reduce some form of unwanted activity. Second, on balance, methods of behaviour change based on some form of positive reinforcement work better overall. Third, for punishment to be at its most effective, a series of conditions must be met. They include:

(a) *Inevitability*. When the undesired behaviour appears, it will without exception be followed by punishment.

(b) *Immediacy*. To be most effective, punishment should occur more or less instantaneously following the behaviour to be reduced.

(c) *Severity*. The most effective punishments are those that occur at the maximum possible intensity.

(d) *Availability of alternative behaviours*. Punishment works best when, in place of the unwanted behaviour, other responses can be made and are reinforced.

(e) *Comprehensibility*. With intelligent, reasoning organisms such as human beings, it is also crucial that a punishing experience be understood in relation to the behaviour that has brought it about.

It goes virtually without saying that none of the foregoing conditions is adequately met in the criminal justice system. First, given the low detection rates for most types of crime (e.g. for reported vehicle thefts in 1991 it was 28% (Home Office, 1992)), arrest and subsequent conviction are far from guaranteed. Data quoted in the British Crime Survey yield an estimate that the probability of conviction following a criminal offence is 3%, and only a small proportion of convictions results in imprisonment (Barclay, quoted in Mayhew et al., 1993). To borrow an analogy from Felson (1994), being burnt on a hot stove will make someone very unlikely to touch it again. But if the stove only had this effect once in every few hundred times it was touched, its effects on behaviour would be far less predictable. Second, given the protracted and intermittent nature of legal processing, punishment typically occurs weeks or months after the offending behaviour. Third, other ethical principles to which society subscribes would not allow punishment to be used to its utmost severity in every case. Fourth, many illegal acts are instrumental or goal-oriented.

In the absence of other means to achieve the intended goals, it is very difficult to eliminate them. For the majority of offenders, society provides few alternative means of securing the goals towards which their offending is directed. In any case, a large proportion of them may not have acquired personal resources for accomplishing this task on their own. Fifth, for many offenders, the responses of criminal justice agencies to them appear anything but comprehensible. They may have elaborate belief systems through which they have taken account of the likelihood of punishment, and either discounted it, or built up stronger antisocial attitudes as a result. Furthermore, in an unjust world in which they see other law-breakers escaping punishment, their own suffering is not likely to be interpreted as a signal that they should control their impulses to reoffend.

When all of the above points are summed together, the failure of punishment to have a demonstrable impact on offence behaviour can be seen to be not only explicable, but patently obvious. The notion that punishment can reduce the rate of crime in society is little more than an irrational and unfounded hope. Returning to the results of the research reviews, let us examine instead their more positive findings.

GUIDELINES FOR MORE EFFECTIVE PROGRAMMES

It must be emphasized first that the meta-analytic reviews do not suggest that there is any single, outstanding approach that is by itself guaranteed to work as a means of reducing recidivism. There is no more a panacea in this area than in any other search for solutions to human ills. The cumulative findings of the meta-analytic reviews are of considerable complexity. The following summary is based on the work of Andrews, Lipsey and other meta-analysts, but also takes account of recent narrative reviews by Antonowicz and Ross (unpublished, 1993), Gendreau and Andrews (1991), Gendreau and Ross (1987), Lösel (1993b), MacDonald and co-workers (1992), McIvor (1990) and Mulvey and colleagues (1993). Within these studies a number of principles concerning the design and assembly of effective programmes can be identified.

1. *Risk classification*. In more effective programmes there is a matching between offender risk level and degree of service intervention, such that higher-risk individuals receive more intensive services, while those of lower risk receive lower or minimal intervention. ('Risk' in this sense is defined on an actuarial basis, i.e. based on prior history of offending, and on statistical tables derived from large samples showing subsequent rates of reconviction over time.)

2. *Criminogenic needs*. Following the precepts of Gendreau and Andrews (1991; and see Andrews, Chapter 2, this volume), it is essential to

distinguish between criminogenic and non-criminogenic needs, i.e. we should separate client problems or features that contribute to or are supportive of offending, from those that are more distantly related, or unrelated, to it. This principle underpins direct work on offending behaviour. If the purpose of a programme is to reduce reoffending, there should be a focus within it on criminogenic needs as goals of intervention.

3. *'Responsivity'*. Both clients and staff have a wide range of learning styles; programmes work best when there is a systematic matching between styles of workers and styles of client. But on balance the learning styles of most offenders require active, participatory methods of working, rather than either a didactic mode on the one hand or a loose, unstructured, 'experiential' mode on the other.

4. *Community base*. Programmes located in the community on balance yield more effective outcomes. This is not to dismiss institution-based work, but the findings do imply that proximity to individuals' home environments has a greater prospect of facilitating real-life learning. This point requires clarification and amplification through further research.

5. *'Treatment modality'*. As part of Lipsey's work (1992a; 1992b; Chapter 3, this volume), intervention programmes were divided into those located in statutory (governmental and state) agencies and those located in the 'non-system' (voluntary and private) sector. Across both system-based and externally based programmes, the most consistent pattern of findings to emerge was as follows. More effective programmes were found to be: (a) multimodal (i.e. they recognized the variety of offenders' problems, substantiating what Palmer (1992) has called 'the breadth principle'); (b) their contents and the methods they employed were skills-oriented (i.e. designed to teach clients problem-solving, social interaction or other types of coping skills); (c) they utilized methods drawn from behavioural, cognitive or cognitive–behavioural sources.

6. *Programme 'integrity'*. Effective programmes are those in which the stated aims are linked to the methods being used (see Hollin, Chapter 10, this volume). Adequate resources are available to achieve these aims, and staff are appropriately trained and supported. There is an agreed plan for programme monitoring and evaluation, and these activities take place and are systematically recorded.

It cannot be claimed, on the strength of these findings, that a full answer to the question of how to design effective programmes has been found. There are still many problems to be solved and issues to be addressed, and much more research remains to be done, preferably informed as energetically as possible by direct links with practice. Nevertheless, it is here contended that the above findings represent an important advance in the state of knowledge in this field, and supply at least preliminary indications of more useful and less useful ways in which to work.

The results of Lipsey's meta-analysis are of interest in some further respects. First, the largest single effect size obtained (reducing recidivism by approximately 35%) was for employment-focused programmes in which clients were able to secure 'real' jobs. However, this finding was based on a comparatively small number of studies, and was obtained from research in criminal justice-based (statutory) services only. The corresponding finding for programmes based in non-system services was that employment programmes had a small negative impact. Skills-based, multimodal, cognitive–behavioural programmes emerged more consistently as effective, independent of the organizational setting. Second, loosely defined, unstructured forms of individual counselling, which are the modal form of practice in a large number of criminal justice services, had an effect on recidivism which, though positive, was virtually negligible. Third (recalling the above discussion on punitive methods), deterrence-based programmes, interventions containing strong punitive elements, had a significant negative effect on recidivism and served to increase it by the order of 25%. Thus the mean effect size of 10–12% seen across all programmes is so partly because of the pronounced negative effects of punitive interventions.

COGNITIVE–BEHAVIOURAL METHODS

Amongst the range of intervention methods included in the meta-analyses, those which emerge as offering the most promising outcomes are based on the 'cognitive–behavioural' approach. As its name suggests, this is a form of intervention based on a synthesis of methods drawn from behavioural and cognitive psychology (Hollin, 1990; Meichenbaum, 1977). To illustrate the variety amongst 'what works', some individual studies in this area will be briefly surveyed. The studies cited vary in experimental design: some are controlled experiments, others single case studies. They are focused upon a wide range of antisocial acts. Follow-up periods vary considerably, from 1 month to 10 years. The objective of this exercise is by no means to suggest that all of the questions regarding interventions with offenders have been answered, nor all the problems solved.

Behaviourally based methods.   These have been applied to several types of offence, and consist, for example, of contingent reinforcement (Lawson, 1983; Miller et al., 1974); covert punishment contingencies (Guidry, 1975) and other self-administered contingencies (Epstein & Peterson, 1973); the 'Buddy system' (O'Donnell et al., 1979); self-reinforcement and family contracting (Stumphauzer, 1976); contingency contracts, sometimes used in the context of probation orders (Polakow & Doctor, 1973, 1974; Polakow & Peabody, 1975; Welch, 1985); behaviour modification employing family teaching programmes to reduce stealing and aggression (e.g. Bank et al., 1987; Reid & Patterson, 1976); stimulus satiation for the treatment of fire-setting (Daniel, 1987a); covert sensitization (Brownell et al., 1977; Harbert et al., 1974); shame aversion therapy for the reduction of indecent exposure (Daniel, 1987b); and masturbatory reconditioning (Laws & O'Neil, 1981). More details concerning a number of these methods are given by Morris and Braukmann (1987).

Relaxation and systematic desensitization. These techniques are directed towards a number of offence-related behaviours that are associated with tension and arousal, such as: alcohol problems (Hay et al., 1977; Hedberg & Campbell, 1974; Lanyon et al., 1972; Miller et al., 1974); sexual exhibitionism (Bond & Hutchinson, 1960; Wickramasekera, 1968); chronic kleptomania (Marzagao, 1972); and aggression and violence, including racially motivated hostility, and aggression whilst driving (Evans & Hearn, 1973; Hazaleus & Deffenbacher, 1986; O'Donnell & Worell).

Social skills training. Methods such as modelling and guided group discussion have been used successfully with young offenders (Sarason, 1978) and with emotionally disturbed adolescents (Foxx et al., 1987). So too have role-reversal exercises with 'egocentric' young adults (Chandler, 1973); modelling and coaching with arsonists (Rice & Chaplin, 1979); and negotiation training to help resolve parent–child conflicts within families of delinquents (Klein et al., 1977; this study reported a 50% reduction in recidivism rates for the trained groups over a follow-up period of 3.5 years). Training in heterosocial skills is thought to be an essential component of any effective programme with sex offenders (Crawford & Allen, 1979). Prison pre-release courses based mainly on social skills training and allied methods have also yielded reduced rates of subsequent reconviction for violence (Priestley et al., 1984).

An alternative form of interaction skills training is illustrated in the use of assertion training for purposes such as helping problem drinkers to refuse drinks (Foy et al., 1976), or in anger replacement (Foy et al., 1975; Frederiksen et al., 1976; Rahaim et al., 1980; Rimm et al., 1974).

Self-instructional training. This includes a number of variants such as Anger Control Training, of which there are reports of effective use with adults located in the community (Novaco, 1975), with adolescent offenders (Feindler et al., 1984; Feindler & Ecton, 1986; Feindler & Fremouw, 1983; Lochman et al., 1986; McCullough et al., 1977; Moon & Eisler, 1983); with adult and adolescent psychiatric patients (Bistline & Frieden, 1984; Feindler et al., 1986); with young offenders in secure accommodation (Kaufman & Wagner, 1972); with adult prisoners (McDougall et al., 1987a); and with abusive parents (Denicola & Sandler, 1980; Nomellini & Katz, 1983). Thus its most frequent application has been as a method of reducing 'affective' aggression, but it has also been used as a component of self-control training to reduce stealing and shoplifting (Aust, 1987; Henderson, 1981), behavioural disturbance in adolescents (Snyder & White, 1979), and fire-setting (Clare et al., 1992); while the related method of 'thought stopping' has been used in the treatment of homicidal ruminations (Horton & Johnson, 1977). It has been used in conjunction with social skills training (Deffenbacher, 1988; Deffenbacher et al., 1987), and can also take other forms such as cognitive restructuring (Kolko & Milan, 1983) or problem-solving training (Hains, 1984; Hains & Hains, 1988). Finally, it has been applied in combination with more behaviourally based methods in the treatment of paedophilia using self-control and biofeedback (Laws, 1980).

Training in moral reasoning. Together with reduction of antisocial attitudes, this has been achieved in relation to such problems as racial hostility (Culbertson, 1957), or football violence (McDougall et al., 1987b); and moral education programmes based on the cognitive–developmental theory of Lawrence Kohlberg have been shown to have potential for securing a wide range of changes in juvenile offenders (Arbuthnot & Gordon, 1986; Gibbs et al., 1984; Rosenkoetter et al., 1986).

Multimodal programmes. These incorporate a range of behavioural and cognitive components and have offered one of the strongest prospects of systematic reduction of reoffence rates. One of the most thoroughly developed of these, which originated from Canadian work but has since been adopted in several other countries, is the 'Reasoning and Rehabilitation' programme, a cognitive skills 'training package', first tested in probation services in Ontario, Canada by Ross and colleagues (1988). It has since also been used by Correctional Services of Canada in a number of prisons, employing custodial staff as specially trained 'coaches' who run the programme sessions (Fabiano & Porporino, 1992; Robinson et al., 1991). It is also now being piloted in a number of probation areas and prison establishments within the United Kingdom (see Knott, Chapter 5, this volume; McGuire, 1995; Raynor & Vanstone, 1994). The programme is currently under test at other prison and probation sites at several locations in the United States, Spain and elsewhere.

Other multimodal programmes include 'Aggression Replacement Training', which, as its name suggests, has been used with violent offenders and in particular in work with gangs (Goldstein & Keller, 1987; Goldstein et al., 1986, 1989, 1994). Combined 'Cognitive–Behavioural Therapy' programmes incorporating a range of ingredients and addressed towards a number of separate change 'targets' have been shown to offer the best prospects of reducing reoffending amongst sex offenders (Dwyer & Myers, 1990; Marshall et al., 1992; Miner et al., 1990; Perkins, 1987; Prentky & Burgess, 1990). Similarly, programmes that contain a range of cognitive–behavioural ingredients have also been found to have a significant impact on criminogenic attitudes of drink–driving offenders placed on probation (McGuire et al., 1995).

Mentally disordered offenders. In work with mentally disordered offenders, a cumulative body of research has now indicated that amongst persons suffering from psychotic illness, the strongest risk factors for criminal violence are symptoms such as delusions and hallucinations (Monahan & Steadman, 1994). A number of treatment studies have now been published that illustrate the potential of cognitive–behavioural therapies in the reduction of such symptoms (Chadwick & Lowe, 1990; Fowler & Morley, 1989; Hartman & Cashman, 1983; Lelliott & Marks, 1987; Milton et al., 1978; Tarrier et al., 1993; Watts et al., 1973). Methods employed in these studies have included: belief modification; self-instructions; verbal challenge and confrontation; exposure and response prevention; reality testing; and coping strategy enhancement.

COMMUNITY SENTENCING AS PUNISHMENT

If equivalent discoveries to those discussed in the last few pages were made in any other field, such as agriculture, medicine or technology, it would not be inappropriate to assume that, after a reasonable time-lag, we would see changes in practice as the findings were progressively absorbed and implemented. In criminal justice, however, things do not appear to happen that way. Despite some useful, albeit provisional, research results, which might assist a criminal justice community struggling with unwieldy problems, the consistent trend in policy in many countries has been towards the increased use of punishment.

Thus in both Britain and the United States probation staff have been enjoined to participate in developing practices which place more emphasis on control of offenders than on anything connected with rehabilitation. In the United Kingdom this has been encapsulated in a policy of 'punishment in the community'. But evidence of the counterproductive nature of punitive measures even in probation settings has already come from recent work by Gendreau and colleagues (1993), who reviewed outcome studies of Intensive Probation Supervision (IPS) programmes in North America. These are programmes which involve a range of innovations in probation and parole work, including: markedly increased contact time between supervisors and offenders; home confinement; curfews; random drug testing; electronic monitoring; and in some centres, even a requirement that clients should pay for supervision sessions.

When first conceived, the concept of IPS was proclaimed as having four potential benefits in criminal justice. It was thought (a) that it would provide more options for sentencers, and so add flexibility to their decision-making. It was thus assumed (b) that it would reduce prison overcrowding; and associated with this, (c) that it would cost less not only than custody itself, but would yield savings even over conventional probation orders. Finally, (d) given the expectation that punishment 'works', it was thought that these programmes would reduce recidivism.

As Gendreau and colleagues show in detail none of these promises has been fulfilled in practice. Most IPS programmes, contrary to initial hopes, have had a net-widening effect. They have certainly proved cheaper than incarceration, but given the additional costs of some components (e.g. in Arizona, about US $500 000 was spent on random drug tests alone), they have not represented savings over standard probation supervision. Because of increased rates of technical violation in those being closely supervised, in most cases there has been not a reduction in prison overcrowding, but the reverse. Lastly, though few programmes have been fully evaluated as regards their impact on recidivism, results so far have shown that most IPS programmes have had little impact in this area.

However, the results were not as simple as this. In a small number of these programmes, positive outcomes on recidivism were obtained, but close inspection of these positive results revealed a different factor at work. This was, quite simply, that where programmes had positive effects it was because they contained not more intensive punishment or surveillance, but some form of 'treatment'. Increased staff–client contact was used not simply for monitoring, but for active intervention of some kind. Further, in a number of studies reviewed, distinctions were made between probation officers in terms of the style and quality of supervision they offered. Where this was done, there was a clear difference in outcome (i.e. recidivism) associated (a) with higher-quality supervision, and (b) with a balance being struck between a 'law enforcement' and a 'social work' ethos in the work that had been undertaken.

Parallel findings to these have emerged from the work of Petersilia and Turner (1993), who evaluated the implementation of Intensive Probation and Parole supervision in a number of American states. This was a large-scale study, with a total sample size approaching 2000, examining programmes in 14 jurisdictions across nine states, and using matched samples and random assignment to experimental and control groups. However, there was no evidence that intensive supervision had an impact on any aspect of recidivism. The only significant relationship was between levels of participation in drugs or alcohol counselling, employment and restitution programmes, and subsequent reconviction rates, with the former being associated with a 10–20% reduction in the latter. While Petersilia and Turner state that this may have been a selection effect, it is striking that once again the only positive finding is one which is linked to some form of direct service delivery ('treatment') to clients.[1]

These findings also recall those of one of the meta-analyses cited above, that of Whitehead and Lab (1989). This is the only study from which its authors derived negative conclusions. Their study focused on diversion programmes, and the authors applied a strict criterion of disregarding effect sizes on recidivism of less than 0.2. This was unfortunate, as some of the studies they examined obtained results just below that level, and a few exceeded it. In most of the programmes examined, there was only minimal contact between clients and any programme staff. What was notable, however, was the finding that within 'system diversion' programmes themselves (i.e. those run by statutory agencies) there was a correlation between the amount of such contact and recidivism reduction. Once again, the basic finding emerged that structured intervention pays off, even amongst overall results that were declared to support the view that 'nothing works'.

IMPLICATIONS FOR PRACTICE

The bulk of this chapter has been devoted to a summary of the main findings of recent research reviews and the patterns that can be seen within them concerning effective programmes of work. It is likely to be some time before this field is sufficiently developed for any detailed lessons to be drawn concerning practice. However, the findings discussed are sufficiently solid to warrant a reasonable level of confidence regarding a number of very general practice implications. These are discussed below.

First, it should be fairly evident that, where possible, if practice is to make use of the findings outlined above, it should begin to reflect an application of them in ways that would be fairly visible to an outside observer. Assessments would be articulated in terms of risk and need, and programme allocations would be made accordingly (though our present state of knowledge in this area is still fairly rudimentary, see below). The issue of client and worker style, and the matching of the two, would be taken into account where feasible. There would be more extensive use of behavioural, cognitive and cognitive–behavioural methods. Staff would be aware of the importance of programme integrity and would give thought to how it can be monitored and preserved.

Second, on the basis of the above research, it is also apparent that the provision of clear structure in programmes is an important ingredient of effectiveness. The consequent advice to practitioners must therefore be that many programmes should move towards a higher level of structure than they currently possess. Further, programme strategies once decided upon and agreed should be implemented in a consistent manner, along similar lines to those operating, for example, in a behavioural programme.

Third, evidence concerning the 'responsivity principle' highlights the vital need for staff to relate to clients in a manner that combines sensitivity and constructiveness. Though there are recurrent dilemmas in combining the roles of 'law-enforcement' and 'social work', they are not necessarily incompatible and there are tentative indications from several studies that this conjunction makes for the highest-quality supervision and the best subsequent outcomes (see Gendreau et al., 1993). An inherent prerequisite of this is, of course, that staff training and supervision are appropriate to the task.

Fourth, perhaps the single most commonly reported finding of research is that many programmes are never evaluated at all and that numerous opportunities for providing information that would be valued by practitioners, managers and researchers alike are simply lost. To help remedy this, it is self-evidently advisable that staff develop a regular practice of monitoring and evaluating programmes. Information so gained should be disseminated, applied and tested in other contexts.

IMPLICATIONS FOR PROGRAMME MANAGEMENT

The above evidence also has implications for managers of community-based offender services. The implementation of these principles will obviously have to be a gradual and evolving process, given the nature of the task, the quantity of evidence potentially available, and the organizational and political context of the work. The following are some preliminary suggestions as to how the process of acting on 'what works' principles might be advanced.

First, a primary need must be for those involved in the management of service delivery to become more familiar with the relevant research evidence. While mechanisms do exist for this, the need to remain in touch with research findings often comes as a low priority amongst many other pressures of day-to-day work. Yet it may be no exaggeration to say that there has never been a time when an awareness of research has been more important than it is at present.

Second if the 'risk' and 'criminogenic needs' principles are to be acted upon and applied expertly in practice, a major effort should be directed towards the development of reliable risk–needs assessment methods for client selection and allocation to different types of programme. This work could be commenced within individual criminal justice agencies on the initiative of management groups. It would be more advantageous, however, were it to be conducted on a wider scale, in which case it would of course be preferable if some coordinating function was created, perhaps through the establishment of a research and advisory unit, to pool and compare data.

Third, if practitioners are to engage with 'what works' principles in a systematic way, it is virtually axiomatic that this will have ramifications for managers. Foremost amongst these will be ensuring provision of necessary resources for programmes to be developed, run and evaluated. This in turn may have further repercussions: it might necessitate a lengthy period of negotiation with external (including governmental) agencies, and gradual adjustment in resource allocation. New balances of priorities might have to be discussed and associated decisions made. There would be additional implications for the nature of partnerships created between the various agencies involved in community-based work with offenders, and in the design and coordinated delivery of programmes.

Fourth, to act according to the 'responsivity principle', managers might require an enhanced knowledge of individual staff members' strengths and skills. A focus on styles of working would have implications for styles of supervision, for team management, and for staff allocation to different roles or types of work.

Fifth, departures into new types of programme, incorporating specific methods of working, would have very significant implications for the training of staff for new tasks and roles. A number of the methods that emerge as effective in recent reviews raise fundamental questions about the training of some professional groups involved directly in work with offenders. The contents of staff training, not only in terms of in-service provision but perhaps also on basic professional qualifying courses, might in due course have to be modified, even substantially revised. Such a process would clearly require extensive discussion and deliberation by managers at all levels within the prison, probation, juvenile justice and other services.

Finally, there are distinct pressures, not just from a scientific stance but also from the viewpoint of public accountability, for agencies undertaking work with offenders to become more conscious of the need to evaluate their own work. The Audit Commission report on the probation service (1989) is just one example of this. There is a responsibility, then, for the creation of a culture of empirical evaluation: for an atmosphere in which programme design, delivery and evaluation are seen as natural accompaniments to each other, and for the habit of evaluation to become firmly embedded in the thinking of managers and practitioners alike.

To take these arguments further, another suggestion has been made in recent work by Gendreau and colleagues (1994). Focusing on probation services (though applicable by analogy to other agencies also), these writers have proposed the establishment of a new generation of programmes, which they entitled 'Intensive Rehabilitation Supervision' or IRS. This innovation is designed to be responsive to four sets of pressures which the authors believe currently impinge on community offender services:

(a)   Governmental policy, perhaps backed by public opinion, demanding greater control over clients.
(b)   Evidence (including some of that reviewed above) concerning the pronounced failure of punitive measures.
(c)   Ethical and/or ideological reluctance, amongst probation and juvenile justice personnel and similar groups, concerning punishment, surveillance and allied methods.
(d)   The large quantity of evidence concerning positive outcomes and the emergence of indications as to how they are most likely to be achieved.

The answer to this given by Gendreau and co-workers (1994) is a new form of supervision that involves increased contact between clients and probation staff. However, this is not designed for surveillance purposes, but for the implementation of programme activities observing guidelines from research on effectiveness.

IMPLICATIONS FOR FUTURE RESEARCH

Although the evidence summarized earlier in this paper is very encouraging as regards the possibility of reducing reoffending, it has to be acknowledged that considerable amounts of research remain to be done (Petersilia, 1991). No field of research can remain static. To end this chapter, several important research questions still in need of answers are identified.

First, many of the studies that have been cited in this chapter require replication with different samples. Comparatively few have been conducted outside North America. The applicability of some of the methods to diverse populations, even differing simply in age, gender or cultural identity, requires examination.

Second, there are considerable gaps in research on criminogenic needs. This work is essential to provide a clearer understanding of factors influencing different forms of offence behaviour and how they can best be approached.

Third, the relative importance of different ingredients of programmes with established effectiveness requires more detailed analysis and testing. Given that existing evidence favours programmes with a number of components, this type of research may prove elusive, but it is nevertheless important. A closely related question is the link between client needs and programme contents, and associated programme design, selection and targeting issues.

Fourth, issues concerning the applicability of methods in different settings (e.g. institution versus community), and of how research findings can best be translated into practice depending on location, also need detailed exploration, and proper testing in 'real-world' conditions.

Fifth, numerous specific practical questions remain unanswered, for example concerning maximum risk levels of clients suitable for various programmes, or on relationships between addictive behaviours and offending, and how the former can be stabilized prior to participation in other programmes.

Sixth, wider practical policy questions, concerning how methods can be applied within criminal justice agencies, must be addressed if programmes are to become accepted features of practice. The relationships between some of the 'treatment' approaches described here and existing criminal sanctions also requires much elucidation, discussion and research.

Research findings of the kind reviewed here may also have further implications of a quite different order. Beyond the concerns of practitioners, managers and researchers, there is a more basic issue to be addressed. This calls into question the ends and means of criminal justice networks and sanctions, and the extent to which the continued use of counterproductive measures can be justified. Some years ago there was a widely quoted dictum, a flat and dismissive assertion that 'treatment is dead'. Given the accumulation of evidence since, the reverse case can now be made. It may not be reflected in current penological practice, but on scientific grounds at least we are in a position to say we have witnessed nothing less than the 'death of deterrence'.

NOTE

1.   While this book was in the course of being edited, an evaluation of shock incarceration ('boot camps') was published by the National Institute of Justice (MacKenzie and Souryal, 1994). Its findings show some striking similarities to those obtained by Petersilia and Turner (1993) on intensive probation. Boot camp programmes were examined in eight American states: Florida, Georgia, Illinois, Louisiana, New York, Oklahoma, South Carolina and Texas. Comparisons were made between groups allocated to shock programmes and others serving standard prison sentences; prison parolees; or probationers.

The authors' conclusion was that the impact of the programmes '... is at best negligible ... based on the totality of the evidence, boot camp programs did not reduce offender recidivism' (1994: 28, 41). The camps with the strongest, almost exclusive, emphasis on punitive elements (in Georgia) produced an increase in recidivism relative to comparison groups. Three programmes where there was weak evidence of reduced technical violation or re-offence rates (Illinois, Louisiana and New York) included a higher proportion of purposeful, non-punitive and problem-focused sessions such as counselling, alcohol and substance-abuse treatment, and education; and also contained follow-up community supervision. The results of this evaluation are complex and not firmly conclusive. Once again, however, where there is evidence of some gain it is associated with investment of time in 'treatment-related' activities.

REFERENCES

Andrews, D. A., Zinger, I., Hoge, R. D. Bonta, J., Gendreau, P. & Cullen, F. T. (1990). Does correctional treatment work? A clinically relevant and psychologically informed meta-analysis. *Criminology*, **28**, 369–404.

Antonowicz, D. & Ross, R. R. (1993). Essential components of successful rehabilitation programs for offenders. Unpublished manuscript, Department of Criminology, University of Ottawa.

Arbuthnot, J. & Gordon, D. A. (1986). Behavioral and cognitive effects of a moral reasoning development intervention for high-risk behavior-disordered adolescents. *Journal of Consulting and Clinical Psychology*, **54**, 208–216.

Audit Commission (1989). *The Probation Service: Promoting Value for Money*. London: HMSO.

Aust, A. (1987). Gaining control of compulsive shop theft. *National Association of Probation Officers Journal*, December, 145–146.

Bank, L., Patterson, G. R. & Reid, J. B. (1987). Delinquency prevention through training parents in family management. *The Behavior Analyst*, **10**, 75–82.

Barker, L. M. (1994). *Learning and Behavior: A Psychobiological Perspective*. New York: MacMillan College Publishing Company.

Bistline, J. L. & Frieden, F. P. (1984). Anger control: a case study of a stress inoculation treatment for a chronic aggressive patient. *Cognitive Therapy and Research*, **8**, 551–556.

Blackburn, R. (1980). Still not working? A look at some recent outcomes in offender rehabilitation. Paper presented to the Scottish Branch of the British Psychological Society, Conference on Deviance, University of Stirling.

Blagg, H. & Smith, D. (1989). *Crime, Penal Policy and Social Work*. Harlow: Longman.

Bond, I. K. & Hutchinson, H. C. (1960). Application of reciprocal inhibition therapy to exhibitionism. *Canadian Medical Association Journal*, **83**, 23–25.

Brody, S. (1976). *The Effectiveness of Sentencing*. Home Office Research Study No. 35. London: HMSO.

Brownell, K. D., Hayes, S. C. & Barlow, D. H. (1977). Patterns of appropriate and deviant sexual arousal: the behavioral treatment of multiple sexual deviations. *Journal of Consulting and Clinical Psychology*, **45**, 1144–1155.

Carroll, J. & Weaver, F. (1986). Shoplifters' perceptions of crime opportunities: a process-tracing study. In D. B. Cornish & R. V. G. Clarke (Eds). *The Reasoning Criminal: Rational Choice Perspectives on Offending*. New York: Springer-Verlag.

Chadwick, P. D. J. & Lowe, F. (1990). *The measurement and modification of delusional beliefs*. Research report, Department of Psychology, University of North Wales.

Chandler, M. A. (1973). Egocentrism and anti-social behaviour: the assessment and training of social perspective-taking skills. *Developmental Psychology*, **9**, 326–332.

Clare, I. C. H., Murphy, G. H., Cox, D. & Chaplin, E. H. (1992). Assessment and treatment of firesetting: a single-case investigation using a cognitive-behavioural model. *Criminal Behaviour and Mental Health*, **2**, 253–268.

Crawford, D. A. & Allen, J. V. (1979). A social skills training programme for sex offenders. In M. Cook & G. Wilson (Eds). *Love and Attraction*. Oxford: Pergamon Press.

Culbertson, F. (1957). Modification of an emotionally held attitude through role playing. *Journal of Abnormal and Social Psychology*, **54**, 230–233.

Daniel, C. J. (1987a). A stimulus satiation treatment programme with a young male firesetter. In B. J. McGurk, D. M. Thornton & M. Williams (Eds). *Applying Psychology to Imprisonment: Theory and Practice*. London: HMSO.

Daniel, C. J. (1987b). Shame aversion therapy and social skills training with an indecent exposer. In B. J. McGurk, D. M. Thornton & M. Williams (Eds). *Applying Psychology to Imprisonment: Theory and Practice*. London: HMSO.

Davies, M. (1990). Balance between court and client. *Community Care*, 25 January, 16–17.

Deffenbacher, J. L. (1988). Cognitive-relaxation and social skills treatments of anger: a year later. *Journal of Counselling Psychology*, **35**, 234–236.

Deffenbacher, J. L., Story, D. A., Stark, R. S. Hogg, J. A. & Brandon, A. D. (1987). Cognitive-relaxation and social skills interventions in the treatment of general anger. *Journal of Counselling Psychology*, **34**, 171–176.

Denicola, J. & Sandler, J. (1980). Training abusive parents in child management and self-control skills. *Behavior Therapy*, **11**, 263–270.

Doob, A. N. & Brodeur, J.-P. (1989). Rehabilitating the debate on rehabilitation. *Canadian Journal of Criminology*, **31**, 179–192.

Dwyer, S. M. & Myers, S. (1990). Sex offender treatment: A six-month to ten-year follow-up study. *Annals of Sex Research*, **3**, 305–318.

Epstein, L. H. & Peterson, C. L. (1973). Control of undesired behavior by self-imposed contingencies. *Behavior Therapy*, **4**, 91–95.

Evans, D. R. & Hearn, M. T. (1973). Anger and systematic desensitization: A follow-up. *Psychological Reports*, **32**, 569–570.

Fabiano, E. A. & Porporino, F. (1992). Rational rehabilitation. Paper presented at the conference What Works. Salford University, Manchester, UK.

Farrington, D. P., Langan, P. A. & Wikstrom, P. H. (1994). Changes in crime and punishment in America, England and Sweden between the 1980s and 1990s. *Studies on Crime and Crime Prevention, Annual Review*, **3**, 104–130. Oslo/Stockholm: Scandinavian University Press.

Feindler, E. L. & Ecton, R. B. (1986). *Adolescent Anger Control: Cognitive–Behavioral Techniques*. Oxford: Pergamon Press.

Feindler, E. L. and Fremouw, W.J. (1983). Stress inoculation training for adolescent anger problems. In D. Meichenbaum & M. E. Jaremko (Eds). *Stress Reduction and Prevention*. New York: Plenum Press.

Feindler, E. L., Marriott, S. A. & Iwata, M. (1984). Group anger control training for junior high school delinquents. *Cognitive Therapy and Research*, **8**, 299–311.

Feindler, E. L., Ecton, R. B., Kingsley, D. & Dubey, D. R. (1986). Group anger-control training for institutionalized psychiatric male adolescents. *Behavior Therapy*, **17**, 109–123.

Felson, M. (1994). *Crime and Everyday Life: Insight and Implications for Society*. Thousand Oaks: Pine Forge Press.

Fischer, J. (1973). Is casework effective? A review. *Social Work*, **18**, 5–20.

Fischer, J. (1978). Does anything work? *Journal of Social Service Research*, **3**, 213–243.

Fowler, D. & Morley, S. (1989). The cognitive–behavioural treatment of hallucinations and delusions: A preliminary study. *Behavioural Psychotherapy*, **17**, 267–282.

Foxx, R. M., McMorrow, M. J., Hernandez, M., Kyle, M., & Bittle, R. G. (1987). Teaching social skills to emotionally disturbed adolescent inpatients. *Behavioral Residential Treatment*, **2**, 77–88.

Foy, D. W., Eisler, R. M. & Pinkston, S. (1975). Modeled assertion in a case of explosive rages. *Journal of Behavior Therapy and Experimental Psychiatry*, **6**, 135–138.

Foy, D. W., Miller, P. M. Eisler, R. M. & O'Toole, D. H. (1976). Social-skills training to teach alcoholics to refuse drinks effectively. *Journal of Studies on Alcohol*, **37**, 1340–1345.

Frederiksen, L. W., Jenkins, J. O., Foy, D. W. & Eisler, R. M. (1976). Social skills training to modify abusive verbal outbursts in adults. *Journal of Applied Behavior Analysis*, **9**, 117–125.

Garland, D. (1990). *Punishment and Modern Society: A Study in Social Theory*. Oxford: Clarendon Press.

Garrett, C. J. (1985). Effects of residential treatment on adjudicated delinquents; A meta-analysis. *Journal of Research in Crime and Delinquency*, **22**, 287–308.

Gendreau, P. (1989). Programs that do not work: a brief comment on Brodeur and Doob. *Canadian Journal of Criminology*, **31**, 193–195.

Gendreau, P. & Andrews, D. A. (1991). Tertiary prevention: What the meta-analyses of the offender treatment literature tell us about 'what works'. *Canadian Journal of Criminology*, **32**, 173–184.

Gendreau, P & Ross, R. R. (1980). Effective correctional treatment: bibliotherapy for cynics. In R. R. Ross and P. Gendreau (Eds). *Effective Correctional Treatment*. Toronto: Butterworths.

Gendreau, P. & Ross, R. R. (1987). Revivification of rehabilitation: Evidence from the 1980s. *Justice Quarterly*, **4**, 349–407.

Gendreau, P., Paparozzi, M., Little, T. & Goddard, M. (1993). Does 'punishing smarter' work? An assessment of the new generation of alternative sanctions in probation. *Forum on Corrections Research*, **5**, 31–34.

Gendreau, P., Cullen, F. T. & Bonta, J. (1994). Intensive Rehabilitation Supervision: the next generation in community corrections? *Federal Probation*, **58**, 72–77.

Genevie, L., Margolies, E. & Muhlin, G. L. (1986). How effective is correctional intervention? *Social Policy*, **17**, 52–57.

Gibbs, J. C., Arnold, K. D., Ahlborn, H. H. & Cheesman, F. L. (1984). Facilitation of sociomoral reasoning in delinquents. *Journal of Consulting and Clinical Psychology*, **52**, 37–45.

Gibbs, J. P. (1986). Deterrence theory and research. In: G. B. Melton (Ed.). *The Law as a Behavioral Instrument*. (Nebraska Symposium on Motivation, 1985). Lincoln and London: Nebraska University Press.

Glass, G., McGaw, B. & Smith, M. L. (1981). *Meta-analysis in Social Research*. Beverley Hills: Sage Publications.

Goldstein, A. P. & Keller, H. (1987). *Aggressive Behavior: Assessment and Intervention*. Oxford: Pergamon Press.

Goldstein, A. P., Glick, B., Reiner, S., Zimmerman, D., Coultry, T. M. & God, D. (1986). Aggression Replacement Training: A comprehensive intervention for the acting-out delinquent. *Journal of Correctional Education*, **37**, 120–126.

Goldstein, A. P., Glick, B., Irwin, M. J., Pask-McCartney, C. & Rubama, I. (1989). *Reducing Delinquency: Intervention in the Community*. Oxford: Pergamon Press.

Goldstein, A. P., Glick, B., Carthan, W. & Blancero, D. A. (1994). *The Prosocial Gang: Implementing Aggression Replacement Training*. Thousand Oaks: Sage Publications.

Gottschalk, R., Davidson, W. S., Mayer, J. P. & Gensheimer, L. K. (1987). Behavioral approaches with juvenile offenders: A meta-analysis of long-term treatment efficacy. In E. K. Morris & C. J. Braukmann (Eds). *Behavioral Approaches to Crime and Delinquency: A Handbook of Application, Research, and Concepts*. New York: Plenum Press.

Grant, L. & Evans, A. (1994). *Principles of Behavior Analysis*. New York: Harper Collins.

Guidry, L. S. (1975). Use of a covert punishment contingency in compulsive stealing. *Journal of Behavior Therapy and Experimental Psychiatry*, **6**, 169.

Hains, A. A. (1984). A preliminary attempt to teach the use of social problem-solving skills to delinquents. *Child Study Journal*, **14**, 271–285.

Hains, A. A. & Hains, A. II. (1988). Cognitive–behavioral training of problem solving and impulse control with delinquent adolescents. *Journal of Offender Counseling, Services and Rehabilitation*, **12**, 95–113.

Harbert, T. L., Barlow, D. H., Hersen, M. & Austin, J. B. (1974). Measurement and modification of incestuous behavior: A case study. *Psychological Reports*, **34**, 79–86.

Hartman, L. M. & Cashman, F. E. (1983). Cognitive–behavioural and psychopharmacological treatment of delusional symptoms: A preliminary report. *Behavioural Psychotherapy*, **11**, 50–61.

Hay, W. M., Hay, L. R. & Nelson, R. O. (1977). The adaptation of covert modeling procedures to the treatment of chronic alcoholism and obsessive–compulsive behavior: Two case reports. *Behavior Therapy*, **8**, 70–76.

Hazaleus, S. L. & Deffenbacher, J. L. (1986). Relaxation and cognitive treatments of anger. *Journal of Consulting and Clinical Psychology*, **54**, 222–226.

Hedberg, A. G. & Campbell, L. (1974). A comparison of four behavioral treatments of alcoholism. *Journal of Behavior Therapy and Experimental Psychiatry*, **5**, 251–256.

Henderson, J. Q. (1981). A behavioral approach to stealing: A proposal for treatment based on ten cases. *Journal of Behavior Therapy and Experimental Psychiatry*, **12**, 231–236.

Hollin, C. R. (1990). *Cognitive–Behavioural Interventions with Young Offenders*. Elmsford: Pergamon Press.

Home Office (1992). *Criminal Statistics England and Wales 1991*. Cmn 2134. London: HMSO.

Home Office (1994). *Prison Statistics 1992*. Cmn 2581. London: HMSO.

Hood, R. (1989). *The Death Penalty: A World-Wide Perspective*. Oxford: Oxford University Press.

Horton, A. M. & Johnson, C. H. (1977). The treatment of homicidal obsessive ruminations by thought stopping and covert assertion. *Journal of Behavior Therapy and Experimental Psychiatry*, **8**, 339–340.

Izzo, R. L. & Ross, R. R. (1990). Meta-analysis of rehabilitation programmes for juvenile delinquents. *Criminal Justice and Behavior*, **17**, 134–142.

Kaufman, L. M. & Wagner, B. R. (1972). Barb: a systematic treatment technology for temper control disorders. *Behavior Therapy*, **3**, 84–90.

Klein, N. C., Alexander, J. F. & Parsons, B. V. (1977). Impact of family systems intervention on recidivism and sibling delinquency: A model of primary prevention and program evaluation. *Journal of Consulting and Clinical Psychology*, **45**, 469–474.

Kolko, D. J. & Milan, M. A. (1983). Reframing and paradoxical instruction to overcome 'resistance' in the treatment of delinquent youths: A multiple-baseline analysis. *Journal of Consulting and Clinical Psychology*, **51**, 655–660.

Lab, S. P. & Whitehead, J. T. (1988). An analysis of juvenile correctional treatment. *Crime and Delinquency*, **34**, 60–83.

Lambert, M. J. & Bergin, A. E. (1994). The effectiveness of psychotherapy. In A. E. Bergin & S. L. Garfield (Eds) *Handbook of Psychotherapy and Behavior Change*. New York: Wiley.

Lanyon, R. I., Primo, R. V., Terrell, F. & Wener, A. (1972). An aversion-desensitization treatment for alcoholism. *Journal of Consulting and Clinical Psychology*, **38**, 394–398.

Laws, D. R. (1980). Treatment of bisexual pedophilia by a biofeedback-assisted self-control procedure. *Behaviour Research and Therapy*, **18**, 207–211.

Laws, D. R. & O'Neil, J. A. (1981). Variations on masturbatory conditioning. *Behavioural Psychotherapy*, **9**, 111–136.

Lawson, D. M. (1983). Alcoholism. In M. Hersen (Ed.). *Outpatient Behavior Therapy: A Clinical Guide*. New York: Grune & Stratton.

Lelliott, P. & Marks, I. (1987). Management of obsessive–compulsive rituals associated with delusions, hallucinations and depression: A case report. *Behavioural Psychotherapy*, **15**, 77–87.

Light, R., Nee, C. & Ingham, H. (1993). *Car Theft: The Offender's Perspective*. Home Office Research Study No. 130. London: HMSO.

Lipsey, M. W. (1992a). Juvenile delinquency treatment: A meta-analytic inquiry into the variability of effects. In T. Cook et al. (Eds). *Meta-analysis for Explanation: A Casebook*. New York: Russell Sage Foundation.

Lipsey, M. W. (1992b). The effect of treatment on juvenile delinquents: results from meta-analysis. In F. Lösel, T. Bliesener & D. Bender (Eds). *Psychology and Law: International Perspectives*. Berlin: de Gruyter.

Lipsey, M. W. & Wilson, D. B. (1993). The efficacy of psychological, educational, and behavioral treatment; confirmation from meta-analysis. *American Psychologist*, **48**, 1181–1209.

Lipton, D., Martinson, R. & Wilks, J. (1975). *The Effectiveness of Correctional Treatment: A Survey of Treatment Evaluation Studies*. New York: Praeger.

Lochman, J. E., Burch, P. R., Curry, J. F. & Lampron, L. B. (1986). Treatment and generalization effects of cognitive–behavioral and goal-setting interventions with aggressive boys. *Journal of Consulting and Clinical Psychology*, **52**, 915–916.

Logan, C. H. (1972). Evaluation research in crime and delinquency: A reappraisal. *Journal of Criminal Law, Criminology and Police Science*, **63**, 378–387.

Lösel, F. (1993a). *Evaluating psychosocial interventions in prisons and other penal contexts*. Paper presented to the 20th Criminological Research Conference, Council of Europe. Strasbourg: Council of Europe.

Losel, F. (1993b). The effectiveness of treatment in institutional and community settings. *Criminal Behaviour and Mental Health*, **3**, 416–437.

Lösel, F. & Koferl, P. (1989). Evaluation research on correctional treatment in West Germany: A meta-analysis. In H. Wegener, F. Lösel & J. Haisch (Eds). *Criminal Behavior and the Justice System: Psychological Perspectives*. New York: Springer-Verlag.

MacDonald, G., Sheldon, B. & Gillespie, J. (1992). Contemporary studies of the effectiveness of social work. *British Journal of Social Work*, **22**, 615–643.

MacKenzie, D. L. & Souryal, C. (1994). *Multisite Evaluation of Shock Incarceration: Evaluation Report*. Washington DC: National Institute of Justice.

Marshall, W. L., Jones, R., Ward, T., Johnston, P. & Barbaree, H. E. (1992). Treatment outcome with sex offenders. *Clinical Psychology Review*, **11**, 465–485.

Martinson, R. (1974). What works?—Questions and answers about prison reform. *The Public Interest*, **10**, 22–54.

Martinson, R. (1979). New findings, new views: A note of caution regarding sentencing reform. *Hofstra Law Review*, **7**, 243–258.

Marzagao, L. R. (1972). Systematic desensitization treatment of kleptomania. *Journal of Behavior Therapy and Experimental Psychiatry*, **3**, 327–328.

Mayers, M. O. (1980). *The Hard-Core Delinquent*. Farnborough: Saxon House.

Mayhew, P., Maung, N. A. & Mirrlees-Black, C. (1993). *The 1992 British Crime Survey*. Home Office Research Study No. 132. London: HMSO.

McCullough, J. P., Huntsinger, G. M. & Nay, W. R. (1977). Self-control treatment of aggression in a 16-year-old male. *Journal of Consulting and Clinical Psychology*, **45**, 322–331.

McDougall, C., Barnett, R. M., Ashurst, B. & Willis, B. (1987a). Cognitive control of anger. In B. J. McGurk, D. M. Thornton & M. Williams (Eds). *Applying Psychology to Imprisonment: Theory and Practice*. London: HMSO.

McDougall, C., Thomas, M. & Wilson, J. (1987b). Attitude change and the violent football supporter. In B. J. McGurk, D. M. Thornton & M. Williams (Eds). *Applying Psychology to Imprisonment: Theory and Practice*. London: HMSO.

McGuire, J. (1995). Community-based reasoning and rehabilitation programs in the UK. In: R. R. Ross (Ed.). *Thinking Straight*. Ottawa: Cognitive Centre, in press.

McGuire, J. & Priestley, P. (1985). *Offending Behaviour: Skills and Stratagems for Going Straight*. London: Batsford.

McGuire, J., Broomfield, D., Robinson, C. & Rowson, B. (1995). Short-term impact of probation programs: an evaluative study. *International Journal of Offender Therapy and Comparative Criminology*, **39**, 23–42.

McIvor, G. (1990). *Sanctions for Persistent or Serious Offenders: A Review of the Literature*. Glasgow: Social Work Research Centre, University of Stirling.

Meichenbaum, D. (1977). *Cognitive–Behavior Modification: An Integrative Approach*. New York: Plenum.

Miller, P. M., Hersen, M., Eisler, R. M. & Watts, J. G. (1974). Contingent reinforcement of lowered blood/alcohol levels in an outpatient chronic alcoholic. *Behaviour Research and Therapy*, **12**, 261.

Milton, F., Patwa, V. K. & Hafner, R. J. (1978). Confrontation vs. belief modification in persistently deluded patients. *British Journal of Medical Psychology*, **51**, 127–130.

Miner, M. H., Marques, J. K., Day, D. M. & Nelson, C. (1990). Impact of relapse prevention in treating sex offenders: Preliminary findings. *Annals of Sex Research*, **3**, 165–185.

Monahan, J. & Steadman, H. J. (1994). *Violence and Mental Disorder: Developments in Risk Assessment*. London and Chicago: University of Chicago Press.

Moon, J. R. & Eisler, R. M. (1983). Anger control: An experimental comparison of three behavioral treatments. *Behavior Therapy*, **14**, 493–505.

- Morris, E. K. & Braukmann, C.J. (Eds). (1987). *Behavioral Approaches to Crime and Delinquency: A Handbook of Application, Research, and Concepts*. New York: Plenum Press.

Mulvey, E. P., Arthur, M. W. & Reppucci, N. D. (1993). The prevention and treatment of juvenile delinquency: a review of the research. *Clinical Psychology Review*, **13**, 133–167.

Nomellini, S. & Katz, R. C. (1983). Effects of anger control training on abusive parents. *Cognitive Research and Therapy*, **7**, 57–68.

Novaco, R. W. (1975). *Anger Control: The Development and Evaluation of an Experimental Treatment*. Lexington: D. C. Heath & Co.

O'Donnell, C. R. & Worell, L. (1973). Motor and cognitive relaxation in the desensitization of anger. *Behaviour Research and Therapy*, **11**, 473–481.

O'Donnell, C. R., Lydgate, T. & Fo, W. S. O. (1979). The Buddy system: Review and follow-up. *Child Behavior Therapy*, **1**, 161–169.

Palmer, T. (1975). Martinson re-visited. *Journal of Research in Crime and Delinquency*, **12**, 133–152.

Palmer, T. (1992). *The Re-Emergence of Correctional Intervention*. Newbury Park: Sage.

Perkins, D. (1987). A psychological treatment programme for sex offenders. In B. J. McGurk, D. M. Thornton & M. Williams (Eds). *Applying Psychology to Imprisonment: Theory and Practice*. London: HMSO.

Petersilia, J. (1991). The value of corrections research: learning what works. *Federal Probation*, **55**, 24–26.

Petersilia, J. & Turner, S. (1993). Intensive probation and parole. *Crime and Justice*, **17**, 281–335.

Pitts, J. (1992). The end of an era. *Howard Journal of Criminal Justice*, **31**, 133–148.

Polakow, R. L. & Doctor, R. M. (1973). Treatment of marijuana and barbiturate dependency by contingency contracting. *Journal of Behavior Therapy and Experimental Psychiatry*, **4**, 375–377.

Polakow, R. L. & Doctor, R. M. (1974). A behavioral modification program for adult drug offenders. *Journal of Research in Crime and Delinquency*, **11**, 63–69.

Polakow, R. L, & Peabody, D. (1975). Behavioral treatment of child abuse. *International Journal of Offender Therapy and Comparative Criminology*, **19**, 100–103.

Prentky, R. & Burgess, A. (1990). Rehabilitation of child molesters: A cost–benefit analysis. *American Journal of Orthopsychiatry*, **60**, 108–117.

Priestley, P., McGuire, J., Flegg, D., Hemsley, V., Welham, D. & Barnitt, R. (1984). *Social Skills in Prisons and the Community: Problem-Solving for Offenders*. London: Routledge & Kegan Paul.

Rahaim, S., Lefebvre, C. & Jenkins, J. O. (1980). The effects of social skills training on behavioral and cognitive components of anger management. *Journal of Behavior Therapy and Experimental Psychiatry*, **11**, 3–8.

Raynor, P. & Vanstone, M. (1994). *STOP (Straight Thinking on Probation)*: Third Interim Evaluation Report. Bridgend: Mid Glamorgan Probation Service.

Reid, J. B. & Patterson, G. R. (1976). The modification of aggression and stealing behavior of boys in the home setting. In E. Ribes-Inesta & A. Bandura (Eds). *Analysis of Delinquency and Aggression*. Hillsdale: Lawrence Erlbaum Associates.

Reid, W. J. & Hanrahan, P. (1981). The effectiveness of social work: recent evidence. In E. M. Goldberg & J. Connelly (Eds). *Evaluative Research in Social Care*. London: Heinemann.

Rice, M. E. & Chaplin, T. C. (1979). Social skills training for hospitalized male arsonists. *Journal of Behavior Therapy and Experimental Psychiatry*, **10**, 105–108.

Rimm, D. C., Hill, G. A., Brown, N. N. & Stuart, J. E. (1974). Group-assertive training in the treatment of expression of inappropriate anger. *Psychological Reports*, **34**, 791–798.

Robinson, D., Grossman, M. & Porporino, F. (1991). *Effectiveness of the Cognitive Skills Training program. From Pilot Project to National Implementation*. Ottawa: Correctional Services of Canada.

Rosenkoetter, L. I., Landman, S. & Mazak, S. G. (1986). The use of moral discussion as an intervention with delinquents. *Psychological Reports*, **16**, 91–94.

Ross, R. R. & Fabiano, E. A. (1990). *Reasoning and Rehabilitation. Instructor's Manual*. Ottawa: Cognitive Station.

Ross, R. R., Fabiano, E. A. & Ewles, C. D. (1988). Reasoning and rehabilitation. *International Journal of Offender Therapy and Comparative Criminology*, **32**, 29–35.

Russell, M. N. (1990). *Clinical Social Work*. Newbury Park: Sage Publications.

Sarason, I. G. (1978). A cognitive social learning approach to juvenile delinquency. In R. D. Hare & D. Schalling (Eds). *Psychopathic Behavior: Approaches to Research*. New York. Wiley.

Sheldon, B. (1994). Social work effectiveness research: implications for probation and juvenile justice services. *Howard Journal of Criminal Justice*, **33**, 218–235.

Snyder, J. J. & White, M. J. (1979). The use of cognitive self-instruction in the treatment of behaviorally disturbed adolescents. *Behavior Therapy*, **10**, 227–235.

Stumphauzer, J. S. (1976). Elimination of stealing by self-reinforcement of alternative behavior and family contracting. *Journal of Behavior Therapy and Experimental Psychiatry*, **7**, 265–268.

Sundel, S. S. & Sundel, M. (1993). *Behavior Modification in the Human Services:*

A Systematic Introduction to Concepts and Applications. Newbury Park: Sage.

Tarling, R. (1993). *Analysing Offending: Data, Models and Interpretations*. London: HMSO.

Tarrier, N., Beckett, R., Harwood, S., Baker, A., Yusupoff, L. & Ugarteburu, I. (1993). A trial of two cognitive–behavioural methods of treating drug-resistant residual psychotic symptoms in schizophrenic patients: I. Outcome. *British Journal of Psychiatry*, **162**, 524–532.

Thornton, D. M. (1987). Treatment effects on recidivism: A reappraisal of the 'nothing works' doctrine. In B. J. McGurk, D. M. Thornton & M. Williams (Eds). *Applying Psychology to Imprisonment: Theory and Practice*. London: HMSO.

Thornton, D. M., Curran, L., Grayson, D. & Holloway, V. (1984). *Tougher Regimes in Detention Centres: Report of an evaluation by the Young Offender Psychology Unit*. London: HMSO.

Van Den Haag, E. (1982). Could successful rehabilitation cut the crime rate? *Journal of Criminal Law and Criminology*, **73**, 1022–1035.

Watts, F., Powell, G. V. & Austin, C. V. (1973). The modification of abnormal beliefs. *British ournal of Medical Psychology*, **46**, 359–363.

Welch, G. J. (1985). Contingency contracting with a delinquent and his family. *Journal of Behavior Therapy and Experimental Psychiatry*, **16**, 253–259.

Whitehead, J. T. & Lab, S. P. (1989). A meta-analysis of juvenile correctional treatment. *Journal of Research in Crime and Delinquency*, **26**, 276–295.

Wickramasekera, I. (1968). The application of learning theory to the treatment of a case of sexual exhibitionism. *Psychotherapy: Theory, Research, and Practice*, **5**, 108–112.

Wolf, F. M. (1986). *Meta-analysis: Quantitative Methods for Research Synthesis*. Beverley Hills: Sage Publications.

Wooldredge, J. D. (1988). Differentiating the effects of juvenile court sentences on eliminating recidivism. *Journal of Research in Crime and Delinquency*, **25**, 264–300.

CHAPTER 2

The Psychology of Criminal Conduct and Effective Treatment

Don Andrews

Carleton University, Ottawa, Canada

My underlying theme is that there now exists a psychology of criminal conduct (PCC) that is empirically defensible and whose applications are promising for the design and delivery of effective direct service programmes. This rational empirical psychology of crime, in particular the general personality and social psychological approach to understanding the criminal conduct of individuals, provides an intellectually serious and practical base for the prediction of criminal behaviour and the modification of criminal propensity. Moreover, the general psychological approach is an open, inclusive and flexible conceptual approach to the pursuit of effective prevention and rehabilitation. These positive characteristics of the general psychology of the criminal conduct of individuals, I suggest, exist without denial of the importance of the ideals of justice and without denial of the contributions of political economy, social structure and culture to definitions of 'criminal acts' and to the processing of 'criminal actors'. In brief, this chapter is a summary and update of several recent studies and reports on principles of PCC and effective correctional treatment (as reviewed in more detail by Andrews and Bonta, 1994).

PCC is open to the full range of potential correlates of criminal conduct. These correlates are not only situational and circumstantial but biological, personal, interpersonal and familial, and they may reflect broader

What Works: Reducing Reoffending—Guidelines from Research and Practice.
Edited by J. McGuire. © 1995 John Wiley & Sons Ltd.

social arrangements in terms of structure, culture, and political economy. In contrast, mainstream sociological criminology has been preoccupied with economic and political inequality evident through analyses of age, gender, race, class and neighbourhood. Mainstream criminal justice, in contrast, relies on the very weak versions of a psychology of crime that are represented within deterrence, labelling and just desert theory. Similarly, relative to mainstream mental health perspectives, the multi-foci of a general psychology of crime extend well beyond personal strain as evident in low self-esteem, anxiety, depression or being 'mentally disordered'.

TOWARDS A HUMAN SCIENCE OF CRIME

A general personality and social psychology of criminal conduct is in the midst of a major revival (Andrews et al., 1990a; Cullen & Gendreau, 1989; Currie, 1989; Wilson and Herrnstein, 1985). Strong evidence of the predictability of criminal behaviour, for example, comes from the Loeber and Stouthamer-Loeber (1987) meta-analytic review of longitudinal studies, and strong evidence of the effectiveness of treatment comes from the meta-analytic review of Andrews and colleagues (1990b) and Lipsey (1990). PCC is gaining attention because of its ability to predict criminal activity, to influence criminal activity, and to explain criminal activity. The recent meta-analyses of the prediction and treatment literatures demonstrate a solid empirical base for the psychology of crime, an appreciation of the current limits of predictive accuracy and intervention effectiveness, and also suggest an emergence of theoretical consensus. Consider the following evidence.

Prediction: Risk/Need Factors

The largest body of well established research findings in the whole of criminology is that devoted to the prediction of the criminal conduct of individuals (Andrews, 1989). Few scholars who are actually familiar with the research literature now deny that individuals varying in their criminal past (as documented by cross-sectional studies) and their criminal future (as documented in longitudinal studies) may be differentiated at levels well above chance on a number of situational, circumstantial, personal, interpersonal, familial and structural/cultural/economic factors. A similar conclusion regarding the predictability of criminal recidivism is drawn by mental health professionals who attend to the systematic empirical literature on the validity of systematic risk/need assessments (as opposed to the validity of unstructured clinical judgement). The best established of the risk/need factors may be assigned to a major set and a minor set (see Andrews & Bonta, 1994). The major set includes:

1. Antisocial/procriminal attitudes, values, beliefs and cognitive-emotional states (that is, personal cognitive supports for crime).
2. Procriminal associates and isolation from anticriminal others (that is, interpersonal supports for crime).
3. Temperamental and personality factors conducive to criminal activity, including psychopathy, weak socialization, impulsivity, restless aggressive energy, egocentricism, below average verbal intelligence, a taste for risk, and weak problem-solving/self-regulation skills.
4. A history of antisocial behaviour evident from a young age, in a variety of settings and involving a number and variety of different acts.
5. Familial factors that include criminality and a variety of psychological problems in the family of origin and, in particular, low levels of affection, caring and cohesiveness, poor parental supervision and discipline practices, and outright neglect and abuse.
6. Low levels of personal educational, vocational or financial achievement and, in particular, an unstable employment record.

The minor set of risk/need factors most notably include the following:

7. Lower class origins as assessed by adverse neighbourhood conditions and/or parental educational/vocational/economic achievement.
8. Personal distress, whether assessed by way of the sociological constructs of anomie, strain and alienation or by way of the clinical psychological constructs of low self-esteem, anxiety, depression, worry or officially labelled 'mental disorder'.
9. A host of biological/neuropsychological indicators that have yet to be integrated in a convincing manner by way of either theory or the construction of practical risk/need assessment instruments.

Over the next few years researchers based at University of New Brunswick Saint John and Carleton University will be reporting on the findings of a meta-analysis of predictors of criminal behaviour. I thank the Corrections Branch of the Ministry Secretariat within the Solicitor General of Canada, and Paul Gendreau, Claire Goggin and Françoise Chanteloupe for access to the most recent version of this expanding databank (Andrews & Bonta, 1994). The project involves a survey of all studies of the correlates of crime published in English since 1970. The studies were uncovered through automated library searches, surveys of key review articles and by following up on reference lists of the studies in hand. At the time of writing, approximately 1000 studies have been listed, 700 studies located, and 372 studies subjected to content and meta-analysis. These 372 studies yielded over 1770 Pearson Product moment correlation coefficients, each of which reflected the covariation of some potential risk factor and criminal behaviour.

The mean correlation coefficients for each of six categories of risk/need factors derived from the general psychology of crime were as follows (with number of coefficients in parentheses):

1. Lower class origins   0.06   (97)
2. Personal distress/psychopathology   0.08   (226)
3. Personal education/vocational achievement   0.12   (129)
4. Parental/family factors   0.18   (334)
5. Temperament/misconduct/personality   0.21   (621)
6. Antisocial attitudes/associates   0.22   (168)

Intervention: Punishment, Treatment and Prevention

The number of English language reports on controlled evaluations of criminal justice and corrections is fast approaching 500 (Lipsey, 1990). This is not an insubstantial number for studies that included some type of control or comparison intervention condition and hence approximated the ideals of classical experimental designs. Moreover, considerable order is found in this literature once a distinction is made between studies of the effects on recidivism of (a) variation in criminal justice processing and (b) variation in the delivery of direct human service of the prevention and/or rehabilitative type. Within our models of crime and service delivery, variations in sanctions (diversion, alternatives, probation, custody, etc.) primarily represent setting conditions (that is, conditions under which appropriate human service may or may not be delivered).

Effects on Recidivism of Variation in Criminal Justice Processing

To my knowledge, not a single review of the controlled outcome research in criminal justice and corrections has found large or consistent effects on recidivism through variations in the type or severity of the criminal penalty or judicial disposition (Andrews et al., 1990b, c; Lipsey, 1990). Careful reading of Kirby (1954), Bailey (1966), Logan (1972), Martinson (1974), Gendreau and Ross (1979, 1987), Lab and Whitehead (1988; Whitehead & Lab, 1989) reveals that the research findings, in fact, have always favoured treatment over punishment. According to Andrews and colleagues (1990b), the average effect of an increase in the severity of the penalty was a very small increase in recidivism, plus a detectable (but not strong) tendency for custody to attenuate the positive effects of appropriate human service programmes. According to Lipsey (1990), operationalizations of deterrence theory, and the use of residential placements in particular, yielded higher recidivism rates than did community-based programming. The expanding databanks at Carleton University and the University of New Brunswick Saint John continue to reveal that variations in official punishment fail to produce reductions in criminal recidivism.

Effects on Recidivism of Variation in Prevention/Rehabilitation Service

In dramatic contrast to the effects of criminal justice punishment, it is now well established that controlled investigations of the effects of direct service on recidivism, overall, reveal a mild-to-moderate effect in the direction of reduced recidivism. At least 40% and up to 80% of the studies of correctional treatment services, as summarized in review articles published from the 1950s to the 1980s (Andrews & Bonta, 1994), revealed significant reductions in recidivism through correctional treatment services. According to both of the largest recent meta-analytic reviews (Andrews et al., 1990a; Lipsey, 1990), the average effect of correctional treatment services—across a variety of settings established by official 'dispositions' such as diversion, probation, group homes and incarceration—was at least a modest reduction in recidivism (an average correlation coefficient of 0.15 in the Carleton University study).

With consideration of the clinical appropriateness of treatment services, the average reduction in recidivism produced by psychologically appropriate treatment reached the level of 50% relative to control conditions (or an average correlation between appropriate treatment and reduced recidivism of 0.30). Once again, ongoing analyses of our expanding meta-analytic databanks continue to confirm our earlier published findings (Andrews, 1994).

Theoretical Summary

Whatever their value in studies of aggregated crime rates and in studies of the rhetoric and organization of criminal justice, the class-based theories (e.g. anomie/strain, subcultural and labelling/Marxist perspectives) and the justice models (e.g. labelling, deterrence and just deserts) have been found to be very weak when applied to the analysis of individual criminal conduct. Recent attempts to revive anomie and labelling theory and to render critical/Marxist criminology 'real' support my assessment in that the more intellectually serious modifications reflect the reintroduction of a sophisticated general personality and social psychological perspective on individual criminal conduct (anomie: see Agnew, 1992; Vold & Bernard, 1986; labelling: see Patemoster & Iovanni, 1989; intellectually serious: see Hagan, 1989).

To argue in favour of a clinical criminology and in favour of ethical, legal and decent applications of PCC does not condone economic inequality, racism, sexism and elitism. Nor does it negate the pursuit of reduced personal distress of individuals irrespective of their age, race or class, or of their officially or otherwise defined offender status. Similarly, sociological criminology and analyses of age, sex, class and race undoubtedly offer something of importance to the analysis of aggregated crime rates and the analysis of criminal law and criminal justice institutions. The recognition of clinical concerns, however, does insist that a criminology of broad value should *not* be occupied exclusively with aggregated crime rates (i.e. areal and historical variations in crime rates), with the 'state' (e.g. structured political and economic inequality that may be linked with age, class, gender and ethnicity), with the 'rule of law' (e.g. law and order), nor with seemingly endless variations on themes of official punishment (e.g., more tolerance, less tolerance, zero tolerance, less punishment, more punishment, innovative/intermediate/alternative just desert, and what I have described elsewhere as 'twist-after-crazy-twist' on official punishment).

In brief, a psychology of crime that respects diversity asks that the reality of multiple sources of variation in deviant pursuits be recognized and not be masked by single-minded appeals to structured inequality in the distribution of societal resources or by appeals to tragically sentimental views of human nature. As suggested by Andrews & Wormith (1989a), it is the underpinnings of genocide to believe that one may protect individuals through the denial and discounting of human diversity, while simultaneously exaggerating the effects of social location as indexed by age, sex, class, ethnicity and neighbourhood. The general psychology of crime, as will be documented in detail below, suggests that the causes of criminal conduct are not unlike the causes of any other socially valued human behaviour in that the causal factors are situational and circumstantial, and they are personal, interpersonal, and familial. The causes of crime are also structural/cultural and political economic, but they are not exclusively so except in so far as one is willing to defy both logic and evidence by asserting that the constants of a particular social arrangement (that is, those conditions that apply to everyone within a particular social location) are able to account for the variation in individual behaviour that is found within that particular social arrangement.

The psychology of crime is back! In summary, there is strong professional and political support building for a clinical criminology that places high value upon prevention and rehabilitation.

PRINCIPLES OF EFFECTIVE PROGRAMMING IN PREVENTION AND REHABILITATION

My thesis in regard to effective correctional treatment is a relatively straightforward extension of general personality and social psychological perspectives on the criminal conduct of individuals. The thesis, in brief, is that the planning and delivery of *effective* correctional treatment involves attention to individual differences in risk, need and responsivity and to the use of professional discretion. Stated in clinically relevant ways, the principles purport to cover three key concerns, with considerations of ethicality, legality, decency, cost-efficiency and individualized appropriateness incorporated in the fourth principle of professional discretion:

1. To whom do we offer intensive correctional treatment services? The risk principle suggests that intensive treatment service is best reserved for individuals at risk for criminal conduct.
2. What do we target if an ultimate objective is reduced recidivism? The criminogenic need principle suggests that the appropriate targets are those dynamic characteristics of higher risk individuals and their circumstances that actually are related to criminal conduct.
3. What modes and styles of treatment service do we employ if we target the criminogenic needs of those at risk for criminal conduct The responsivity principle suggests that approaches to treatment be matched with intermediate targets and the learning styles of individuals at risk.

Since publication of the above-noted thesis, however, my colleagues, students and I have been exploring extensions and refinements of the four principles of risk, need, responsivity and professional discretion. We have access to new information, including recently published studies on prediction and treatment and some insights and some misunderstandings evident in reviews of our earlier papers. Thus, certain updates are added to our statement of principles of effective rehabilitation. The following expanded set of principles remain hypotheses, but they are hypotheses with rational and empirical support sufficient to suggest that they may be used to guide evaluated policy and practice that is concerned with the reduction of criminal conduct (that is, reduction of criminal victimization in the community). The major lesson for me has been that the four principles of risk, need, responsivity and professional discretion subsumed much that was still so controversial that perhaps a more step-by-step set of principles would be valuable (see Table 2.1 for a brief summary of the expanded set of principles).

Principle 1—Understanding Criminal Conduct: General Personality and Social Psychological Perspectives on Criminal Conduct

The general personality and social psychological perspectives with superior predictive validity must foremost include the socially informed psychodynamic causal formula of Sheldon and Eleanor Glueck (1950).

They argued for a fair sampling of the multiple aspects of a complex biopyschocial problem, and followed Freud by insisting that the analysis should focus upon both personal and environmental variables. Their theory was psychodynamic at the core in that criminal acts reflected 'untamed impulses', 'self-centered desires' and 'uninhibited energy-expression'.

Their 'tentative causal formula', they suggested, was relevant to the majority of, but not all, delinquent males. The major variables for the analysis of the delinquency of males were as follows (with, from the

Table 2.1. Principles of effective prevention and correctional treatment through direct service.

1. Social psychological principle	The most promising conceptual base for prevention and rehabilitation programmes is a general personality and social psychological understanding of criminal conduct and a general social psychological perspective on programming
2. The methodological principle: Knowledge construction is preferred over knowledge destruction	Critics of psychological prediction and correctional treatment service typically discount positive findings through the application of irrational knowledge destruction techniques, while uncritically accepting negative findings. A rational empirical approach to knowledge construction is preferred to this tradition of knowledge destruction
3. Official processing/ punishment principle	Criminal sanctioning without the delivery of correctional treatment services does not work
4. Principle of residential treatment as the last resort	Community-based treatment services yield more positive effects than residential-based treatment services
5. Principle of risk assessment	Substantial differences in the prevalence and incidence of future criminal conduct are assessable through systematic surveys of the number and variety of risk/need factors present for individual cases
6. Risk principle of case classification	Intensive treatment services are best delivered to higher risk cases (because lower risk cases will do as well or better without intensive service)
7. Need principle	Treatment services best target those character-istics of higher risk individuals and their circumstances that, when changed, actually link with variation in criminal conduct
8. Principle of individualized assessment of risk/need	Systematic quantitative surveys of risk/need are best supplemented by individualized assessments that uncover the particular patterns of high-risk situations and interpretations applicable with an individual case (that is, build an understanding of *this* client's criminality)

Table 2.1. *Continued.*

9.	General responsivity principle	The most effective styles and modes of treatment service are those matched with the needs, circumstances and learning styles of high-risk individuals. Generally, the most effective styles and modes of service are structured and active ones such as social learning and cognitive–behavioural approaches, as opposed to reliance upon evocative, relationship-dependent, self-reflective, verbally interactive and insight-oriented approaches
10.	Specific responsivity considerations	Interpersonally and cognitively immature clients in particular require structured services while the more psychologically mature client may respond to more evocative styles of service; interpersonally anxious clients in particular respond poorly to highly confrontational services; other specific considerations may also be applicable for some subtypes of offenders
11.	Principle of targeting weak motivation for service	Therapeutic resistance and weak motivation for treatment do not suggest exclusion from treatment but the design of treatment contigencies that support participation and target increased motivation for service
12.	Principle of structured follow-up	Criminogenic needs are dynamic by definition and anticipation of future problems should be part of on-going programming, structured post-programme follow-ups are indicated
13.	Principle of therapeutic integrity	Treatment services that are appropriate according to risk, need and responsivity are most effective when a treatment model of some specificity is applied by well trained and well supervised therapists
14.	Principle of professional discretion	Effective therapists are those who apply the principles of risk, need, responsivity and therapeutic integrity with sensitivity to moral, ethical, legal and economic considerations as well as to the uniqueness of the individuals involved
15.	The principle of social support for the delivery of quality treatment services	Creation of settings within which the prevention and rehabilitation efforts of human service professionals are supported in active and direct ways through training, supervision and respect for the process and goals of service will yield even stronger effects of treatment than have so far been documented under less than supportive conditions
16.	Principles of implementation and programme development	Implementation and programme development also depend upon principles of effective consultation and effective organizational and societal change

perspective of intervention, the treatment settings of most relevance being home, school, neighbourhood, and peer groups):

1.   Constitution and temperament: mesomorphy (solid, closely knit, muscular), restless energy, impulsiveness, extroversion, aggressivity.
2.   Cognition: direct and concrete rather than symbolic, and less methodical in problem solving.
3.   Familial: reared in homes of little understanding, affection, stability and morality by parents who are less effective guides and protectors and less desirable sources for emulation and the construction of a consistent, well balanced, and socially normal superego during the early stages of character development.
4.   Attitudinal: hostile, defiant, resentful, suspicious, stubborn, socially assertive, adventurous, unconventional, non-submissive to authority.

The Gluecks also recognized a number of minor risk factors that, on their own or even in combination, were incapable of accounting for much of the variation in delinquency. These minor risk factors included the following: intergenerational culture conflict; poor economic circumstances and low educational and occupational levels of parents; psychopathology and personal distress (except for the personal and early behavioural indicators of psychopathy).

To my knowledge, and in contrast to the anti-Glueck rhetoric in mainstream criminology for the past 40 years (Laub & Sampson, 1991), no piece of *predictive* research conducted since the Gluecks provides a serious empirical challenge to the psychodynamic theory that the Gluecks themselves had so cautiously labelled 'tentative'. Much has happened since the 1950s in psychology, however, including the behavioural, humanistic, social learning and cognitive revolutions in general human psychology. These revolutions were important because they sharpened definitions of constructs such as 'personality' and 'attitudes' and because they offered technologies of behavioural influence that were much more powerful than orthodox psychoanalysis.

Most of the powerful examples of a general psychology of crime are linked to the basic Freudian/psychodynamic/Glueckian model. These models include, for example, all of the following: (1) the behavioural, psychodynamic and anthropological perspective of the Yale school (e.g. Dollard et al., 1939); (2) control theory (Hirschi, 1969) and now self-control theory (Gottfredson & Hirschi, 1990); integrated psychodynamic/control theory (LeBlanc et al., 1988); (3) psychosocial control theory (Mak, 1990, 1991); (4) an algebra of antisocial conduct (Megargee, 1982; Wilson & Herrnstein, 1985); (5) a general theory of youth problem behaviour (Jessor & Jessor, 1977); (6) a developmental cognitive behavioural approach (Ross & Fabiano, 1985); and (7) PIC-R (a personal, interpersonal and community-reinforcement approach: Andrews, 1982; Andrews & Bonta, 1994).

According to PIC-R and the other general theories, the immediate causes of human behaviour are to be found in the context of the person in immediate situations of action. The interaction of immediate personal and situational variables produces variation in the *most immediate* causal variables which have been described by phrases such as 'intentions', 'definitions of situations', 'personal choice', and 'shifts in the *signalled* density of rewards/costs'. These diverse phrases reflect different psychological perspectives but each perspective agrees that human conduct reflects immediate cognitions. Basic work on construct validity is required in order to understand the extent to which 'intentions', 'self-efficacy beliefs' and 'definitions of situations' are reflecting the same underlying variables. For now, variables in the most immediate set all suggest that, in particular situations, illegal conduct is judged 'OK', 'appropriate', or 'likely to pay off and I am able to perform the acts'.

The sources of variation in these most immediate causes of crime, as noted above, include the antisocial set of cognitions, associates, behavioural history and personality. The immediate situation also contributes, although empirical studies of the dimensions of the 'objective' external situation are less well represented than are studies of personal attitudes and personally perceived support for the action. I have opted for the language of temptation, facilitation, inhibition and stress in describing immediate situations.

A positive feature of this immediate PCC is the general value of the model of action. The same psychology of action applies even if the criterion behaviour shifts from the ultimate outcome of criminal behaviour to, for example, the intermediate outcomes of looking for a job, completing a homework assignment, or not drinking. According to the general personality and social psychological perspectives, the immediate situations in which people find themselves and the attitudes they bring to the situations are themselves the reflection of background personal, interpersonal and structural/cultural factors. Thus, while variation in the immediate contingencies of action accounts for variation in behaviour, these influential contingencies themselves are produced, maintained and modified by biological, personal, interpersonal and structural/cultural factors. The structural, interpersonal and personal factors may be ordered from the distal to the most immediate factors:

1. The broad context defined in terms of political economy, structure, culture and geography includes, for example, dominant values, level and distribution of wealth and power, labour market conditions, legislation and policy, convention, patriarchy and competitive individu-

alism. This level of structural/cultural variables is important in determining underlying value systems, including legislation governing definitions of crime and the processing of offenders.

2. The more immediate social context may be defined in terms of the political economy, social structure, culture and geography of the neighbourhood, the family, the community settings associated with school, work and recreation, and the formal intervention agencies of the mental health and justice systems. These more immediate structural factors set the conditions for the operation of the still more important interpersonal and personal factors.

3. The interpersonal network, defined in terms of the process and content of interpersonal interaction (e.g. family interactions, peer interactions, interactions within school). Here, the broader structure, including the personal characteristics of significant others, impacts directly on the individual.

4. The personal factors, defined in terms of personal characteristics and life circumstances (e.g. temperament, attitudes, personal behavioural history, perceived social environment). Here are found the variables that will most strongly link with the conduct of individuals, particularly when assessed in the context of the immediate situation of action.

5. The immediate situation of action, or the person in immediate situations, is the situation in which 'intentions'/'choices' are formed and acted upon.

Within a general PCC it is also useful to work from a conceptualization of the intervention process. Thus, it becomes possible to outline and order the multiple sources of variation in the outcome of direct service. This model presents a broad perspective on programme operation and evaluation that underscores the important structural and interpersonal aspects of direct service agency operations and how agency efforts may impact on individual conduct. The action in regard to influencing recidivism, however, is found to reside in the specifics of the treatment services planned and delivered, and the intermediate changes in the person and circumstances that are achieved (Andrews & Kiessling, 1980; Hoge & Andrews, 1986).

Principle 2: Knowledge Destruction Versus Knowledge Construction

The rational empiricism of the general personality and social psychological approach demands that research findings be subjected to unsparing criticism with the caveat that respect for evidence will be paramount. Thus, for example, rational empiricists do not deny well established research findings because the findings are inconsistent with a preferred theory. Rational empiricists, under these circumstances, are more likely to modify the theory. Mainstream sociological criminology, on the other hand, chose to reject the findings and maintain faith in sociological and justice theories.

The simple fact is that mainstream criminology engaged in outrageous knowledge destruction exercises aimed at both the prediction and treatment literatures. In regard to the unpredictability of individual criminal conduct, the knowledge destroyers depicted psychologists as authoritarian personalities, they denied the logical possibility of prediction, they denied the theoretical relevance of prediction, and—the biggest lie of all—they asserted that the personal, interpersonal and familial predictors were really reflections of socio-economic class of origin. In regard to the literature on treatment effectiveness, they actually endorsed official punishment (which had never been shown to work) and rejected treatment services (which had been shown to work).

Overall, unsparing criticism for purposes of knowledge construction is more valuable than criticism aimed at knowledge destruction. For example, the research evidence has always favoured the predictive validity of assessments of psychopathic personality under various methodological conditions, even though mainstream criminology denied that evidence (Andrews & Wormith, 1989a). More recently, Simourd and colleagues (unpublished, 1992) have shown that some methodological problems do inflate validity estimates but, once again, the predictive criterion validity of assessments of psychopathy survived the introduction of meta-analytic controls for a number of these threats to validity.

Similarly, methodological issues, in addition to treatment concerns, contribute to estimates of the magnitude of the effect of correctional treatment services on recidivism. The two recent meta-analyses (Andrews et al., 1990b; Lipsey, 1990) insisted that any contributions of treatment variables to reduced recidivism would be considered only if evident after controls were introduced for potential methodological problems. The contribution of some methodological variables (e.g. sample size) to the magnitude of effect size was substantial, but treatment continued to make meaningful and incremental contributions to variation in the magnitude of effect size estimates in both reviews of the literature. This pattern of results continues to this day (Andrews, 1994).

Principle 3: Official Punishment

The research evidence has never favoured a concentration on punitive sanctioning (that is, variation in the criminal penalty) as a means of reducing recidivism. From the perspective of understanding effects on recidivism, the penalty (or disposition) is primarily a setting condition, that is, a setting within which appropriate or inappropriate treatment services may be delivered.

The research findings were noted previously. In addition, the criminal justice theories of labelling, deterrence and just desert are such weakly developed theories of criminal conduct that there is no reason to expect major positive or negative effects of processing. Studies completed since our meta-analysis support our conclusion to a degree that surprises even me. There is simply no evidence that criminal sanctioning without the delivery of correctional treatment services will be rewarded by substantial reductions in criminal recidivism. Even the initially promising evidence regarding the deterrent effects of arrest on wife abusers now seems locked in a debate regarding 'the who, what, when and how' of arrest (Sherman, 1993).

Thus, the most recent literature supports the caveats included in our summary of our meta-analytic findings (Andrews et al., 1990b, c). In brief, incapacitation effects have yet to be well appreciated, distinctions among sanctions have been only weakly developed as yet, and any effects of sanctioning will require attention to offender characteristics. Now it appears too that even the direction of effects of criminal processing may reverse from shorter to longer-term follow-up (at least under some very specific but not yet well understood circumstances).

Principle 4: Custody as the Last Resort

This principle is still weakly established on empirical grounds but the indirect evidence must be considered. The meta-analysis of Andrews and coworkers (1990b), however, reported a mild but detectable tendency for the effects of inappropriate service to be particularly negative within custody settings, and for effects of clinically relevant service to be particularly positive in community settings. Lipsey also reported that treatment effects were attenuated in institutions. Lipsey's meta-analysis (1990) also found that positive outcome increased with longer duration of treatment and with meaningful programme–client contact *except*, however, when custody was involved. I now think that my colleagues and I initially underestimated the negative effect of custody. We are now much more willing to say that even the research findings on recidivism affirm a widely shared belief that custody is best viewed as the last resort. Moreover, it is particularly important that the clinical appropriateness of service be attended to in residential settings, and that linkages be made with the community (see Principle 12).

Principle 5: Risk Assessment

Risk factors refer to characteristics of people and their circumstances that are predictive of future criminal conduct. Some of the best known predictors of criminal conduct were summarized above. That list is not exhaustive but it is reasonably comprehensive and it underscores the point that there is now a knowledge base for risk assessment. I am not going to review here the fact that there now exist risk/need instruments that are both practically useful and reflect the content reviewed above (Andrews et al., 1990a).

Rather than review the research issues in risk assessment that have already been covered elsewhere, I want to focus here on several additional important and unresolved issues for immediate research. The discussion begins with attention to the empirically weakest of the risk/need factors that are still promoted by many scholars and practitioners within criminology and mental health. The discussion closes with some of the most persistent problems particular to the general personality and social psychological approach.

The construct and assessment of lower class origins.   It would seem incomprehensible, on rational empirical grounds, that the construct of lower class origins, as measured by neighbourhood characteristics or indices of parental education/occupation/income, could still be touted as a major risk factor in the domain of individual criminal conduct. But it continues to be so touted (see, for example, Hastings (1991) and Short (1991)), even in the face of counterevidence involving hundreds of specific meta-analytic tests (Loeber & Stouthamer Loeber, 1987; Tittle et al., 1978), detailed narrative reviews (Tittle & Meier, 1990), studies of neighbourhood factors that control for individual differences, a brand new search for the rela tionship conducted in nearly 500 contexts with a variety of measures of class and crime (Tittle & Meier, 1991), and the meta-analytic results reviewed above.

Because lower class origins are more of a sacred variable than an empirically explorable construct for some criminologists, some theological reframing may be valuable. Perhaps, for example, family of origin and other personal risk factors may be relabelled 'inequalities in the distribution of psychosocial resources' (cultural capital). At the same time, however, conceptually and empirically we should be prepared to distinguish lower class origins from parental problems, parenting problems, personal attitudes, gender, age, ethnicity, racism, sexism, and elitism— no matter how intertwined the issues appear sometimes to be.

Assessment of structural variables.   The empirical weakness of class of origin does not negate the value of documenting better than has been done so far the importance of political, structural and cultural variables in the analysis of individual criminal conduct. The failure of both the social and human sciences to move beyond mere assertion and to demonstrate empirically the importance of broad (and narrow) social arrangements in the analysis of individual conduct is as serious a problem for the psychology of crime as it is for the sociology of crime. Most notably, ecological studies have not explored the effects of membership composition across the full range of membership characteristics that might be used to define social structure and culture. The most important of the risk factors at the personal level obviously are not socio-economic but the personality variables and certain familial, attitudinal, interpersonal and behavioural characteristics implicated by the general personality and social psychological perspectives on crime.

Thus, for example, assessments of antisocial attitudes may be used to define structure by employing a membership composition approach (e.g. proportion of members of a group scoring high on antisocial attitudes), just as 'structural' social class is often defined as the proportion of membership in poverty or unemployed. In this way, variation in individual criminal activity may be examined as a function of both personal and social structural representations of the socio-economic, personality, attitudinal and other variables. In order to render the personal into the structural, assessment instruments must be administered to target subjects as well as to other members of the natural groups of target subjects. There are many reasons to predict that the effects of structural personality and structural attitudes, for example, will exceed those of structural socio-economic status, and that the effects of structural variables, whether based on socio-economic, personality or attitudinal variables, will be minimal relative to their personal contributions to criminal conduct. My prediction is that personal assessments of age, class, ethnicity, gender, personality, attitudes and behavioural history will correlate more strongly with individual criminal conduct than will structural and cultural assessments of those variables based on membership composition. I also predict that the personal variables suggested to be of most importance by the general personality and social psychological perspective will readily subsume the variables suggested to be of importance by the class-based anomie, subcultural and critical/Marxist theories.

The construct and assessment of 'personal strain'.   Over and over again, with only the slightest of evidence but the most powerful of rhetoric, the constructs of alienation, anomie, low self-esteem, anxiety, depression and emotional distress are linked with criminal conduct. Here too some basic work is required on construct and predictive criterion validity issues. My colleagues Allen Leschied, Bob Hoge and I are beginning to think that personal strain may be particularly important in the early developmental stages of delinquency. This is our understanding of recent conference presentations by Rolf Loeber and it is also, very tentatively, what seems to be emerging from our recent study of young offenders in Toronto.

The construct and assessment of problem solving skills, self-management skills, self-control skills and impulsivity. For many writers, from Lombroso and Freud through the Yale school and up to Gottfredson and Hirschi (1990), the essence of criminality has to do with a lack of self-control. To my knowledge, the field, after years of research and conceptualization, has not been able to reach a high consensus conceptualization of what is meant by self-control, nor does it have available a set of assessment instruments that actually demonstrate the *dominance* of self-control deficits in the analysis of criminal conduct. My prediction is that 'what people think' (antisocial attitudes) will prove more important than 'how people think'. Whatever, conceptual and empirical contributions in this domain would be warmly welcomed by all, and one contribution here may reside in consideration of situational variables (as below).

The assessment of situational variables. The theory and technology of relapse prevention will certainly inspire better and more individualized assessment of high-risk situations. Everyone concerned with this awaits the reports of Ralph Serin on the validity of his innovative survey of situational factors. In addition, the answer to the above-noted problem of understanding self-control may reside in fusing that issue with interpretations of immediate situations.

The construct and assessment of empathy and egocentricism. What is meant by 'empathy' and under what conditions does it relate to criminal conduct? How many constructs are represented within the following list: sensitivity to people, sensitivity to victims, recognition/appreciation of the feelings and intentions of others, recognition/appreciation of the suffering of others, recognizing the expectations of others, recognizing the informational requirements of others, being able to reflect feelings and paraphrase the content of others, callousness? Of the dimensions or factors that can be measured with some degree of construct validity, which ones in fact correlate with criminal conduct? If I appear confused here in that I only ask questions, it is because I *am* confused here. To me, being willing to assault and rob other human beings sounds a lot more like a problem of socialization (insensitivity to rules and regulations) than a problem of either emotional or cognitive empathy (insensitivity to the feelings and perspective of other people).

The construct and assessment of 'being whole and healthy'. Some of the friends of federally sentenced women are becoming quite vocal in their insistence that we should not waste our time researching criminogenic risk/need factors but should help people to become whole and healthy. I do not want to argue against the value of either wholeness or health, particularly when what the proponents of health have in mind is the healing of women who have histories of terrible abuse at the hands of men. When the focus is on the objective of reduced victimization of other human beings, however, perhaps advances here too may require some specification, operationalization, and testing of the predictive criterion validity of assessments of the underlying constructs of being 'whole and healthy' and of 'healing'.

The role of protective factors.   The majority of the current risk/need scales score the absence of a condition that might be considered pleasing if present (e.g. doing well in school, high IQ) as the presence of a risk factor. Some researchers, however, are suggesting that the presence of something like 'doing well in school' deserves to be scored on its own as a protection factor. Protection factors, it is suggested, contribute to the prediction of antisocial conduct not only incrementally but in interaction with risk factors. The specific suggestion is that the presence of protection (pleasing/pleasant/nice) factors will attenuate the effect of risk (displeasing/unpleasant/not nice) factors. These interactions remain to be well documented and replicated in the prediction of criminal conduct.

My intuition is that criminal conduct is a function of the number and variety of risk factors present (whether the empirically established risk factors involve the presence of socially devalued conditions, the absence of socially valued conditions, or the presence of socially neutral risk conditions). The personal, interpersonal and community-reinforcement perspective suggests that interactions among risk factors are indeed a possibility, but that this possibility has nothing to do with the niceness of the predictive factors but is related to the background density (that is, number and variety) of risk factors that are present. Thus, for example, the effect of any single risk factor (e.g. antisocial attitudes) is minimal when other risk factors (e.g. antisocial behavioural history, antisocial associates) are absent or when many other risk factors are present. On the other hand, any single risk factor such as antisocial attitudes will be a particularly strong correlate of criminal conduct when, for example, the only other risk factor present is antisocial associates.

Assessing the role of antisocial attitudes and associates.   Is the predictive role of antisocial attitudes and antisocial associates not being overestimated by virtue of the very real possibility that their assessment is confounded with the assessment of the criterion behaviour of criminal conduct? The answer is 'yes, to some, as yet unspecified, extent'. The background variables suggested by the general personality and social psychological perspectives, however, still outperform the alternatives suggested by the social location/social reaction/criminal justice perspectives.

Personality factors. The empirical evidence regarding the existence of personality-based subtypes of offenders is now overwhelming (Hare, 1980; Van Voorhis, 1988, undated). Although the general personality and social psychological perspective is capable of accommodating these subtypes, perhaps it is time that the variety of routes to frequent and serious criminality be more directly addressed in the general theory. The quest in regard to 'psychopathy' appears particularly important because of the recurring notion that the psychopath is a very special person beyond simply the number and variety of standard risk factors surveyed. We must resist, however, those personality theorists who have become so enamoured of the well documented stability of individual differences in antisocial behaviour that they flirt with denial of the possibility of change (e.g. Gottfredson and Hirschi, 1990).

Special categories of offenders. A recurring issue is whether sex offenders, violent offenders, mentally disordered offenders, spouse abusers, and white collar offenders require their own special personality and social psychology of crime. I expect not, because the behavioural, attitudinal and social support variables of the general PCC approach may be readily adapted to sample behaviour, attitudes, values, beliefs and associates supportive, in particular, of sex offences, violent offences, family violence and white collar crime.

Gender and ethnicity. Finally, issues surrounding gender and ethnicity are at long last becoming high priority ones. Are the risk factors for women or for black people different from the risk factors for white males? The answer to date would appear to be 'no, not much', but knowledge of criminal conduct generally will surely grow as the research agenda is expanded to include the theoretical constructions of those who explicitly reject the framework of variables of the current personality and social psychological approach. At this time, reconceptualizations of the broader political/social/structural scene may be expected, but so far the immediate psychology of action employed by these reconceptualizations appears very similar to the general social psychological approach. It is time to turn to treatment in a more direct way.

Principle 6: Risk and Treatment Services

The risk principle asserts much more than that there are individual differences in the probability of criminal conduct. The risk principle additionally asserts that correctional treatment service is most profitably offered and delivered to higher rather than lower risk cases. As obvious as this principle may appear ('if it ain't broke, don't fix it'), it must be acknowledged that much of the rhetoric of criminal justice theorists and of mental health professionals is in direct contrast to the risk principle (that rhetoric will not be rereviewed here). This chapter, however, concentrates on what, in my opinion, is the state of the empirical literature: empirically, the validity of the risk principle of case classification has so far proven very robust. Yet validity with the highest risk cases remains questionable because of the lack of studies of interventions with such cases that are not only intensive but also appropriate according to need and responsivity.

Evidence in support of the risk principle continues to grow and my position on the risk principle remains the same as indicated in earlier reviews: the validity of the risk principle of case classification is sufficiently strong that it warrants routine review in evaluations of correctional treatment programmes. Remember, however, that the risk principle has to do with treatment services and does not purport to predict differential outcomes of variations in the severity of the criminal sanction.

Principle 7: The Need Principle

The quality and depth of the research evidence regarding dynamic risk factors (that is, the validity of criminogenic need factors as determined by multiwave longitudinal studies) continues to suffer in comparison to the evidence regarding the simple predictive criterion validity of risk factors (as established through uniwave longitudinal and cross-sectional studies). Minimally, the establishment of criminogenic need requires evidence that reassessments of particular risk factors (or change scores) possess incremental predictive validity relative to initial assessments. Preferably, the validity of assessments of criminogenic need should be established through experimental demonstrations that deliberately induced change is associated with shifts in the chances of recidivism. It would be better still if the magnitude of the link between a deliberate intervention and recidivism is reduced by the introduction of statistical controls for treatment-induced changes on the presumed criminogenic need factor.

Table 2.2, adapted from Andrews (1989) and Andrews & Bonta (1994), lists some more promising and some less promising targets of rehabilitative service (the list reflects available data plus inferences from a general personality and social psychological perspective on criminal conduct). Overall, exploration of the predictive validities of assessments of change remains a major issue and is, perhaps, the major issue for the development of theory and practice in the psychology of crime. Andrews (1983) and Andrews et al. (1990a) provide some technical details on the still unre-

Table 2.2. Criminogenic need factors—some promising and some less promising intermediate targets for rehabilitative programming (Andrews, 1989; Andrews & Bonta, 1994).

Promising Intermediate Targets
- Changing antisocial attitudes
- Changing antisocial feelings
- Reducing antisocial peer associations
- Promoting familial affection/communication
- Promoting familial monitoring and supervision
- Promoting identification/association with anticriminal role models
- Increasing self-control, self-management and problem solving skills
- Replacing the skills of lying, stealing and aggression with more prosocial alternatives
- Reducing chemical dependencies
- Shifting the density of the personal, interpersonal and other rewards and costs for criminal and non-criminal activities in familial, academic, vocational, recreational and other behavioural settings, so that the non-criminal alternatives are favoured
- Providing the chronically psychiatrically troubled with low-pressure, sheltered, supportive living arrangements
- Changing other attributes of clients and their circumstances that, through individualized assessments of risk and need, have been linked reasonably with criminal conduct
- Ensuring that the client is able to recognize risky situations, and has a concrete and well rehearsed plan for dealing with those situations

Less Promising Intermediate Targets
- Increasing self-esteem (without simultaneous reductions in antisocial thinking, feeling and peer associations)
- Focusing on vague emotional/personal complaints that have not been linked with criminal conduct
- Increasing the cohesiveness of antisocial peer groups
- Improving neighbourhood-wide living conditions, without touching the criminogenic needs of higher risk individuals
- Showing respect for antisocial thinking on the grounds that the values of one culture are equally valid to the values of another culture
- Increasing conventional ambition in the areas of school and work without concrete assistance in realizing these ambitions
- Attempting to turn the client into a 'better person', when the standards for being a 'better person' do not link with recidivism

solved issue of how best to demonstrate and statistically summarize 'dynamic predictive criterion validity'.

Principle 8: Individualized Assessment of Risk/Need

Systematic quantitative surveys of risk/need are best supplemented by individualized assessments that uncover the particular patterns of high-risk situations applicable to an individual case (that is, building an understanding of a particular client's criminality). Risk factors may be highly individualistic and thus individualized reviews of high risk personal states, thought processes, thought content, circumstances and situations are indicated.

Principle 9: General Responsivity

I am unaware of any recent research or theorizing that would change my earlier summaries of effective styles and modes of service (Andrews, 1989). Based on the general personality and social psychology of crime, the best modes of service are *behavioural*; in particular, they employ the cognitive–behavioural and social learning techniques of modelling, graduated practice, role playing, reinforcement, extinction, resource provision, concrete verbal suggestions (symbolic modelling, giving reasons, prompting) and cognitive restructuring. Five dimensions of effective correctional supervision and counselling were identified in the 1970s that are still worthy of review:

(a)   Authority: 'firm but fair', distinguishing between rules and requests, reinforcing compliance, *not* interpersonal abuse.
(b)   Anticriminal modelling and reinforcement: demonstrating and reinforcing vivid alternatives to procriminal patterns.
(c)   Concrete problem solving (skill building and removal of obstacles) towards increased reward levels for anticriminal behaviour in settings such as home, school and work.
(d)   Advocacy and brokerage, as long as the receiving agency offers appropriate correctional service.
(e)   Relationship factors: relating in open, enthusiastic, caring ways.

On the other hand, some styles and modes of treatment have very poor track records in correction. These weakly validated approaches include programmes designed according to the principles of clinical sociology, the principles of deterrence and labelling, innovative alternative intermediate punishments, non-directive, client-centred counselling, and unstructured psychodynamic therapy.

Principle 10: Specific Responsivity Considerations

Clinical lore, personality-based classification systems and some research leads are sufficiently strong that certain specific responsivity considerations deserve separate notation. Some offenders—the more interpersonally and cognitively mature individuals—may respond to less structured, more evocative and more relationship-dependent styles of service than are represented within our general responsivity principle. I think the data are also sufficiently strong to warn against highly confrontational therapy with anxious, and in particular interpersonally anxious, individuals. The findings of Grant Harris and Marnie Rice reveal in a dramatic manner the very negative implications of offering evocative, peer-assisted and anti-behavioural programming to psychopaths. Gender, age, intelligence and ethnicity are other possible responsivity factors awaiting systematic study in the context of correctional treatment.

Principle 11: Motivation for Service as a Responsivity Factor

Weak motivation for service frequently accompanies high need status. Rather than use poor motivation as an exclusionary factor, however, increasing numbers of clinicians/reseachers are viewing resistance and poor motivation as important intermediate targets of change. In addition, it may well be that for some higher risk offenders treatment services may be best embedded within a probation order or other legal contingencies.

Principle 12: The Principle of Structured Follow-up

The relapse prevention literature has most strongly advocated the notion of building transfer training into residential programmes and the importance of relapse prevention training in all programmes. The elements of relapse prevention include all of the following: (1) The ability to monitor and to recognize and anticipate problem (risky) situations; (2) Planning and rehearsing alternative responses; (3) Practising new behaviours in increasingly difficult situations and rewarding improved competencies; (4) Booster sessions; (5) Training significant others to provide reinforcement.

Principle 13: Therapeutic Integrity

Assuming that risk, need and responsivity are considered, it is important too that the treatment be delivered with some degree of integrity (Andrews et al., 1993; Hill et al., 1991). Don Gordon, James Hill, Kevin Kurkowski and I have been working with a composite measure of therapeutic integrity that samples specificity of the treatment model, training and supervision of therapists, training of the supervisor, systematic monitoring of therapeutic process and intermediate change, printed treatment and training manuals, and the adequacy of dosage. James Hill, Bob Hoge and I have worked also with a direct single-item rating of therapeutic integrity. Our conclusion is that therapeutic integrity is a significant source of variability

in outcome, and a possibility is that integrity increases the effectiveness
of appropriate treatment but renders inappropriate treatment even more
criminogenic.

Principle 14: Professional Discretion

The principles of risk, need, responsivity, individualized assessment and
therapeutic integrity must all be applied by sensitive and psychologically
informed clinicians. Most notably, however, decision-makers must also
respond to considerations of ethicality, decency, legality and cost-efficiency
as they apply to particular cases in particular settings under particular
circumstances.

Principle 15: Social Support for Treatment Services

The upper limits of the power of correctional treatment services have not
yet been tested because we have yet to see appropriate services offered
under the conditions of agency-wide and community-wide support for the
delivery of correctional treatment services. Many of us expect, but cannot
yet empirically demonstrate, that effectiveness increases when the total
agency and community surround is supportive of treatment process, goals
and outcomes.

Principle 16: Working Towards Implementation and Development of Effective Programmes

At least two components of effective implementation and programme development are identifiable. One has to do with the appropriate use of consultants and appropriate support of programme designers. The other has
to do with general societal support for prevention and rehabilitation.

Over the years, Paul Gendreau and I, with the outstanding support of
work done by Margaret Lederman, have been exploring the conditions
under which programmes are introduced into agencies and actually survive
beyond the exit of the consultant or programme designer. Several identifiable factors are associated with the implementation and maintenance
of programmes:

1.   Initiation comes from the programme designer *and* host agency.
2.   The agency is well prepared for and supportive of programme.
3.   The agency administration and staff exhibit good morale.
4.   A senior administrator and a front-line clinician identify with and
     champion the programme.
5.   The programme designer is trained in educational/psychological area

(this factor was uncovered in meta-analyses, but the more important point is the knowledge and skill of the programme designer).

6. The programme designer has professional credibility and a history of association with workable programmes.
7. Sociopolitical and programme values of programme designer and agency are congruent.
8. The programme designer is action oriented and works with staff in setting up and maintaining programme.
9. Agency staff are intimately involved in programme.
10. The programme is cost-effective, flexible and sustainable.
11. Funding comes from the agency—watch out in particular for the highly financed, independent 'model/demonstration' programme that dies as soon as the experiment is over.

CONCLUSION

A clinical criminology that considers matching service and client characteristics in a manner consistent with a general personality and social psychological approach to understanding criminality is a very promising route to risk management and risk reduction (that is, to reduced victimization). A rational empirical orientation to knowledge, however, warns that this promising approach to effective prevention and service must continue to attend to evidence and not be seduced by morally superior visions that not only discount evidence but devalue decency and ethicality at the level of individuals. Indeed, the evidence favouring a decent and humane psychology of crime is becoming so strong and so generally accepted that we must be careful that a new psychological orthodoxy does not begin to discount or deny the contributions of either sociological or traditional psychiatric/mental health approaches. To this date, however, the empirically validated contributions of mainstream sociological criminology and mainstream mental health to effective prevention and rehabilitation have been minimal relative to the general psychological approach. Once again, a clinical criminology informed by the psychology of criminal conduct may provide the basis for exciting interdisciplinary developments in prevention and rehabilitation.

REFERENCES

Agnew, R. (1992). Foundation for a general strain theory of crime and delinquency. *Criminology*, **30**, 47–87.
Andrews, D. A. (1982). *A Personal, Interpersonal and Community-reinforcement*

Perspective on Deviant Behaviour (PIC-R). Toronto: Ontario Ministry of Correctional Services, 1982.

Andrews, D. A. (1983). The assessment of outcome in correctional samples. In M. L. Lambert, E. R. Christensen & S. S. DeJulio (Eds). *The Measurement of Psychotherapy Outcome in Research and Evaluation*. New York: Wiley.

Andrews, D. A. (1989). Recidivism is predictable and can be influenced: Using risk assessments to reduce recidivism. *Forum on Corrections Research* 1,(2), 11–18.

Andrews, D. A. (1994). Effective correctional treatment. A component of the Treatment Seminar of the National Institute of Corrections (Community Division), as presented at the NIC Academy, Longmont, CO, January 1994.

Andrews, D. A. & Bonta, J. (1994). *The Psychology of Criminal Conduct*. Cincinnati: Anderson.

Andrews. D. A. & Kiessling, J. J. (1980). Program structure and effective correctional practices: A summary of the CaVIC research. In R. R. Ross & P. Gendreau (Eds). *Effective Correctional Treatment*. Toronto: Butterworths.

Andrews, D. A., & Wormith, J. S. (1989a). Personality and crime: Knowledge destruction and construction in criminology. *Justice Quarterly*, **6**, 289–309.

Andrews, D. A. & Wormith, J. S. (1989b). Rejoinder—Personality and crime: Toward knowledge construction. *Justice Quarterly*, **6**, 325–332.

Andrews. D. A., Bonta, J. & Hoge, R. D. (1990a). Classification for effective rehabilitation: Rediscovering psychology. *Criminal Justice and Behavior*, **17**, 19–52.

Andrews, D.A., Zinger, Ivan, Hoge, R.D., Bonta, J., Gendreau, Paul, & Cullen F.T. (1990b). Does correctional treatment work? A clinically relevant and psychologically informed meta-analysis. *Criminology*, **28**, 369–404.

Andrews, D.A., Zinger, I., Hoge, R.D., Bonta, J., Gendreau, Paul, & Cullen, F.T. (1990c). A human science approach or more punishment and pessimism—rejoinder. *Criminology*, **28**, 419–429.

Andrews, D. A., Gordon, D. A., Hill, J., Kurkowski K. & Hoge, R.D. (1993). Programme integrity, methodology, and treatment characteristics: A meta-analysis of effects of family intervention with young offenders. (Submitted for publication.)

Bailey, W. C. (1966). Correctional outcome: An evaluation of 100 reports. *Journal of Criminal Law, Criminology and Police Science*, **57**, 153–160.

Barlow, H. D. (1986). *Introduction to Criminology*. Boston: Little, Brown and Company.

Cullen, F. T. & Gendreau, P. (1989). The effectiveness of correctional rehabilitation. In L. Goodstein & D. L. MacKenzie (Eds). *The American Prison: Issues in Research Policy*. New York: Plenum.

Currie, E. (1989). Confronting crime: Looking toward the twenty-first century. *Justice Quarterly*, **6**, 5–25.

Dollard, J., Doob, L., Miller, N., Mowrer, O. & Sears, R. (1939). *Frustration and Aggression*. New Haven: Yale.

Gendreau, P. & Ross, R. R. (1979). Effectiveness of correctional treatment: Bibliotherapy for cynics. *Crime and Delinquency*, **25**, 463–489.

Gendreau, P. & Ross, R. R. (1987). Revivification of rehabilitation: Evidence from the 1980s. *Justice Quarterly*, **4**, 349–408.

Glueck, S. & Glueck, E. T. (1950). *Unravelling Juvenile Delinquency*. Cambridge: Harvard University Press.

Gottfredson, M. R. (1979). Treatment destruction techniques. *Journal of Research in Crime and Delinquency*, **16**, 39–54.

Gottfredson, M. R. & Hirschi, T. (1990). *A General Theory of Crime*. Stanford: Stanford University Press.

Hagan, J. (1989). *Structural Criminology*. New Brunswick: Rutgers University Press.

Hare, R.D. (1980). A research scale for the assessment of psychopathy in criminal populations. *Personality and Individual Differences*, **1**, 111–119.

Hastings, R. (1991). Corrections with class. *Forum on Corrections Research*, **3**, 36.

Hill, J., Andrews, D. A. & Hoge, R. D. (1991). Meta-analysis of treatment programs for young offenders: The effect of clinically relevant treatment on recidivism, with controls for various methodological variables. *Canadian Journal of Program Evaluation*, **6**(1), 97–109.

Hirschi, T. (1969). *Causes of Delinquency*. Berkeley: University of California Press.

Hoge, R. D. & Andrews, D. A. (1986). A model for conceptualizing interventions in social service agencies. *Canadian Psychology*, **27**, 332–341.

Jessor, R. & Jessor, S. L. (1977). *Problem Behavior and Psychosocial Development: A Longitudinal Study of Youth*. New York: Academic Press.

Kirby, B. C. (1954). Measuring effects of treatment of criminals and delinquents. *Sociology and Social Research*, **38**, 368–374.

Lab, S. P. & Whitehead, J. T. (1988). An analysis of juvenile correctional treatment. *Crime and Delinquency*, **34**, 60–85.

Laub, J. H. & Sampson, R. J. (1991). The Sutherland–Glueck debate: On the sociology of criminological knowledge. *American Journal of Sociology*, **96**, 1402–11410.

LeBlanc, M., Ouimet, M. & Tremblay, R. E. (1988). An integrative control theory of delinquent behavior: A validation 1976–1985. *Psychiatry*, **51**, 164–176.

Lipsey, M. W. (1990). Juvenile delinquency treatment: A meta-analytic inquiry into the variability of effects. Paper prepared for the Research Synthesis Committee of the Russell Sage Foundation (unpublished).

Loeber, R. & Stouthamer-Loeber, M. (1987). Prediction. In H. C. Quay (Ed.). *Handbook of Juvenile Delinquency*. New York: John Wiley, pp. 325–382.

Logan, C. H. (1972). Evaluation research in crime and delinquency: A reappraisal. *Journal of Criminal Law, Criminology and Police Science*, **63**, 378–387.

Mak, A. S. (1990). Testing a psychological control theory of delinquency. *Criminal Justice and Behavior*, **17**, 215–230.

Mak, A. S. (1991). Psychosocial control characteristics of delinquents and nondelinquents. *Criminal Justice and Behavior*, **18**, 287–303.

Megargee, E. I. (1982). Psychological determinants and correlates of criminal violence. In M. E. Wolfgang & N. A. Weinder (Eds). *Criminal Violence*. Beverly Hills: Sage.

Paternoster, R. & Iovanni, L. A. (1989). The labeling perspective and delinquency: An elaboration of the theory and assessment of the evidence. *Justice Quarterly*, **6**, 359–394.

Ross, R. R. & Fabiano, E. A. (1985). *Time to Think: A Cognitive Model of Delinquency Prevention and Offender Rehabilitation*. Johnson City, TN: Institute of Social Sciences and Arts.

Sherman, L. W. (1993). Defiance, deterrence, and irrelevance: A theory of the criminal sanction. *Journal of Research in Crime and Delinquency*, **30**, 445–473.

Short, J. F. Jr. (1991). Poverty, ethnicity, and crime: Change and continuity in U.S. cities. *Journal of Research in Crime and Delinquency*, **28**, 501–518.

Simourd, L., Andrews, D. A. & Hoge, R. D. (1992). Gender differences in the corre-
    lates of juvenile delinquency. Unpublished paper, Carleton University.
Tittle, C. R. & Meier, R. F. (1990). Specifying the SES/delinquency relationship.
    Criminology, **28**, 271–299.
Tittle, C. R. & Meier, R. F. (1991). Specifying the SES/delinquency relationship
    by social characteristics of contexts. *Journal of Research in Crime and Delin-
    quency*, **28**, 430–455.
Tittle, C. R., Villimez, W. J. & Smith, D. A. (1978). The myth of social class and
    criminality: An empirical assessment of the empirical evidence. *American Soci-
    ological Review*, **43**, 643–656.
Van Voorhis, P. (1988). A cross-classification of five offender typologies: Issues
    of construct and predictive validity. *Criminal Justice and Behavior*, **15**, 109–124.
Van Voorhis, P. (undated). *Psychological Classification of the Adult Male Prison
    Inmate*. Final report, Department of Criminal Justice, University of Cincin-
    nati, OH.
Vold, G. B. & Bernard, T. J. (1986). *Theoretical Criminology*. (3rd edn) New York:
    Oxford University Press.
Whitehead, J. T. & Lab, S. P. (1989). A meta-analysis of juvenile correctional treat-
    ment. *Journal of Research on Crime and Delinquency*, **26**, 276–295.
Wilson, J. Q. & Herrnstein, R. J. (1985). *Crime and Human Nature*. New York:
    Simon & Schuster.

CHAPTER 3

What do We Learn from 400 Research Studies on the Effectiveness of Treatment with Juvenile Delinquents?

Mark W. Lipsey

Vanderbilt University, Nashville, Tennessee, USA

The translation of research into practice and policy is plagued with many difficulties. For instance, research is often seen by practitioners and policymakers as irrelevant to current concerns or, if relevant, ambiguous and inconsistent. I want to begin this chapter on delinquency treatment by pointing out, in a simplified way, one reason why it is difficult for even sophisticated reviewers to assess the practical importance of a research study or a body of such studies.

The prototypical study of delinquency treatment effectiveness examines change in delinquency levels for a treated group in comparison to an untreated (or differently treated) control group and attempts to determine if there is any difference attributable to treatment, that is, a treatment effect. Figures 3.1 and 3.2 illustrate the results of such pre–post treatment–control comparisons for a collection of studies using fabricated, but realistic, data. These figures demonstrate a discernible, but not blatantly obvious, 10% reduction in delinquency for the juveniles in the treatment groups.

The uniform 10% treatment effect is made somewhat difficult to detect in this set of studies by the scatter or dispersion in the points representing

What Works: Reducing Reoffending—Guidelines from Research and Practice.
Edited by J. McGuire. © 1995 John Wiley & Sons Ltd.

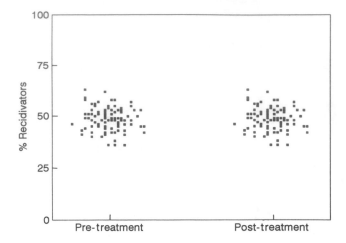

Figure 3.1. Pre- and post-treatment study results with low variability and no treatment effect.

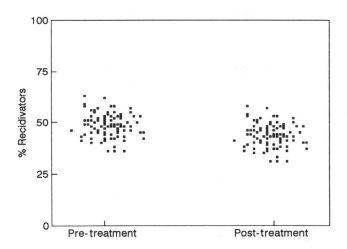

Figure 3.2. Pre- and post-treatment study results with low variability and a 10% treatment effect.

the measured delinquency levels of the juveniles represented in each study. Such dispersion or extraneous variance is inherent in data on outcome. It stems from differences among the juveniles in their individual delinquency patterns, unreliable measurement (reflecting the chance component in, say, police apprehension of offenders), sampling error and other such sources.

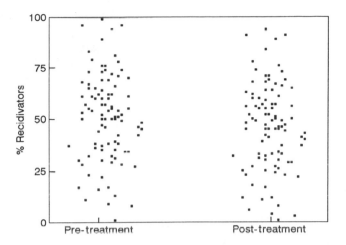

Figure 3.3. Pre- and post-treatment study results with high variability and a 10% treatment effect.

In delinquency treatment research, any single study typically deals with data reflecting many chance factors and showing wide dispersion. The result over a body of studies is more like that shown in Figure 3.3 than that in Figure 3.2. Under such circumstances it is quite difficult to discern either visually or statistically whether a treatment effect is present (though, indeed, the data in Figure 3.3 represent the same 10% mean change as those in Figure 3.2). Moreover, the chance factors can be so large as to overwhelm any treatment effect and make it appear zero or even negative.

Typical research review practices examine the results of each study individually and appraise those results according to whether they reached acceptable levels of statistical significance. With this approach it is quite possible to find apparently inconsistent results among studies and high proportions of null results (not statistically significant) when reviewing a body of research *even under conditions of uniformly effective treatment*. These circumstances explain in large part why we might find few individual studies with definite, unambiguous treatment effects in delinquency treatment research and why we might find varying and inconsistent results in even careful and comprehensive research reviews.

META-ANALYSIS

In recent years a new technique for integrating research studies with quantitative outcome information has been developed and widely applied (Glass et al., 1981; Hunter & Schmidt, 1990; Rosenthal, 1991). This technique is known as 'meta-analysis' and its essence is the aggregation of the statistical results of a number of studies into a single database that allows the results to be analysed collectively rather than individually. In this aggregation process the idiosyncracies and extraneous variance in each individual study tend to average out or be statistically controllable and hence diminish in influence. Overall treatment effects, if present, thus become more evident. Meta-analysis has the advantage, therefore, of revealing broad patterns of findings in a body of research with much more clarity and consistency than traditional research review techniques. The corresponding disadvantage is that it is limited to examination of issues that are so widely represented in the literature that they can be systematically coded for sufficient numbers of studies to make quantitative synthesis possible. Meta-analysis thus can provide a broad overview of a research literature, but it cannot address many of the fine points that appear in specific individual studies.

In the remaining sections of this chapter I will present summary results from a large-scale meta-analysis of research on the effectiveness of treatment for juvenile delinquency.

EFFECTS OF TREATMENT FOR DELINQUENCY

The results reported here derive from a meta-analysis of nearly 400 control or comparison group studies of the effectiveness of treatment for delinquency. These studies include all eligible published and unpublished research from English-speaking countries since 1950 that could be identified and retrieved after sustained search. They represent over 40 000 individual juveniles, aged 12–21, and every treatment found in the eligible research literature that was targeted on delinquency reduction. Additional details can be found in Lipsey (1992).

What follows is a relatively non-technical overview of the main findings of this meta-analysis on two fundamental issues. The first of these is the question of net or average treatment effects over the entire body of research. The second issue to be considered is the question of differential effects—treatment approaches and circumstances associated with larger and smaller effects.

Net Effects

Against the background of the 'nothing works' conclusions of a previous generation of research reviews (e.g. Lipton et al., 1975; Martinson, 1974), it is of considerable interest to use the findings of meta-analysis to address the broad question of whether, in general, delinquency treatment is effective. We interpret this question as one of whether, across all credible studies of treatment, the average effects are positive and of a non-trivial order of magnitude.

Delinquency Effects

The most common delinquency outcome measure found in this body of research is recidivism indexed by whether or not a juvenile had a record of police contact or arrest subsequent to treatment. Where this was unavailable, alternate delinquency measures were recorded in the meta-analysis and statistically translated into terms compatible with the recidivism index.

Over a period averaging about 6 months subsequent to treatment, untreated (or 'treatment as usual') control groups averaged about 50% recidivism Figure 3 4 shows that the average for treated juveniles was about 45%. A five percentage point reduction from a 50% baseline yields a 10% overall average reduction in recidivism. While not an overwhelming effect that can be announced as a 'cure' for delinquency, a net 10% average reduction cannot be called trivial—it is, for example, within the range of effects viewed as significant in medical treatment and other such domains.

Considerable probing of this overall average effect has been conducted to ensure that it is robust and does not reflect some obvious artifact. The details are not appropriate here but it should be noted that this finding is statistically significant and that the same order of magnitude of overall

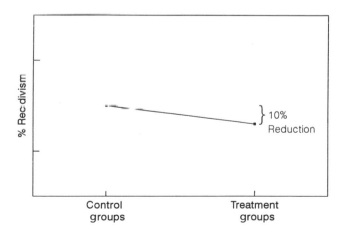

Figure 3.4. Average effect of treatment on delinquency ($n = 397$ studies).

effect is found when we examine only the subgroup of studies that meet
the highest standards of methodological quality, when we make statistical corrections for influences of different research procedures, and when
we examine results on differently defined delinquency outcome variables.

Other Effects

Many of the studies included in this meta-analysis measured outcomes
on other variables in addition to delinquency. Because of the great diversity of such variables, what is reported here are findings on broad aggre-
gations of variables representing similar domains. In particular, each
non-delinquency outcome variable was categorized as to whether it represented a psychological outcome (e.g. attitudes, self-esteem, MMPI or other
clinical scales), interpersonal adjustment (e.g. peer or family relationships,
interpersonal skills), school participation (e.g. attendance, drop-out), academic performance (e.g. grades, achievement tests), or vocational performance (e.g. job status, wages). Since variables within each of these
categories were combined for purposes of the following summaries, the
results should be interpreted only in terms of global effects of treatment
on a broad domain and do not imply that every specific variable included
in that domain necessarily showed the same pattern of results.

Figures 3.5 to 3.9 show the findings of the meta-analysis in each of these
broad outcome domains. To simplify presentation of the statistical results,
these figures report a translation of effects into 'success rates'. The overall
median level of the measures of interest in each category is arbitrarily

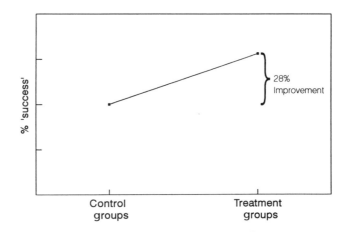

Figure 3.5. Average effect of treatment on psychological measures ($n = 86$ studies).

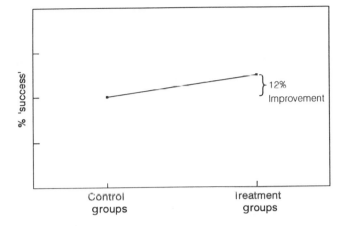

Figure 3.6. Average effect of treatment on interpersonal adjustment ($n = 58$ studies).

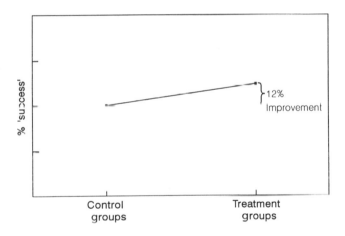

Figure 3.7. Average effect of treatment on school participation ($n = 93$ studies).

set as the success threshold. Using this cut-off, the respective proportions of the control and treatment groups that reach this success criterion are determined. The percentage improvement shown on these figures, in turn represents the relative improvement of the treatment group relative to the control group on the respective success rates.

As Figures 3.5 to 3.9 indicate, positive treatment effects were found in all of these various outcome domains, ranging from 10% improvement

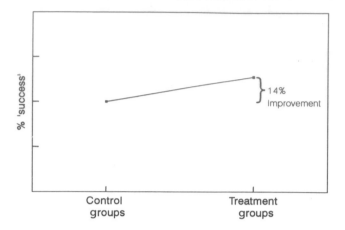

Figure 3.8. Average effect of treatment on academic performance (n = 42 studies).

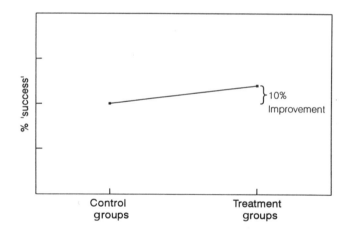

Figure 3.9. Average effect of treatment on vocational accomplishment (n = 44 studies).

to nearly 30% improvement. These results, therefore, reinforce those found on delinquency outcome. Treatment appears to have widespread positive effects of at least modest magnitude.

Relationships Among Outcomes

Since, as noted above, many studies reported effects on one or more variables in addition to delinquency, it was possible for the meta-analysis to examine the covariation among the various outcomes. The question we ask here is whether the greater or lesser changes in delinquency shown by treatment groups in these studies are accompanied by greater or lesser changes in the other outcome variables.

Table 3.1 presents the correlations across studies for the delinquency effect size and effect sizes in the other outcome domains. The most surprising finding was that effects in the broad domain of psychological change were not strongly correlated with delinquency effects. Thus it appears that when a treated group of juveniles reduces its delinquency, there is not necessarily an accompanying broad change in psychological variables. The widespread presumption that psychological change mediates changes in delinquent behaviour, therefore, does not seem to be borne out by the meta-analytic results. It remains possible, of course, that certain particular psychological changes at a level more specific than the broad aggregate category used here do accompany change in delinquent behaviour.

By contrast, we find that school participation outcomes and, to a lesser extent, vocational and interpersonal outcomes do tend to covary with delinquency effects. Since these variables, like delinquency, largely represent overt behaviour, it may be that these results indicate broad interrelated behavioural change that is somewhat independent of change in the other psychological domains.

Conclusion on Net Effects

Summarized over the body of available research, there are clear positive net treatment effects on delinquency and the other outcome domains that have been widely examined. The ambiguities and inconsistencies that have plagued traditional reviews and attempts to interpret individual studies do not appear to be as problematic in this meta-analysis. The advanced research synthesis techniques used here, therefore, indicate that, in general, delinquency treatment 'works'. The statistical noise levels

Table 3.1. Across-study correlations between effect sizes on delinquency outcome and effect sizes on other outcomes.

Outcome category	Weighted correlation with delinquency effect size (N)	
Psychological measures	0.12 (80)	n.s.
Interpersonal adjustment	0.25 (54)	$p<0.01$
School participation	0.57 (84)	$p<0..01$
Academic performance	0.09 (40)	n.s.
Vocational accomplishment	0.30 (40)	$p<0.05$

n.s., not significant.

resulting from various sources of extraneous variance in typical delinquency research have impeded proper interpretation of the literature and obscured the detection of the modest but non-trivial effects revealed by meta-analysis.

Differential Effects

Reported above are the positive average effects of delinquency treatment. No individual treatment, however, necessarily produces average effects. We must consider how much variability exists around that average. If the results of all studies were tightly clustered around the average, ranging, say, from 9% to 11% improvement in delinquency levels, it would matter very little which particular treatment or approach we chose. If, on the other hand, there was great variability, ranging, say, from negative effects through quite large positive effects, we would need to know just which treatment circumstances were involved before knowing what sort of delinquency effect to expect.

The results from the meta-analysis showed great variability across studies—three or four times as much as would have been expected if all studies reflected the same underlying treatment effect. This makes it a matter of considerable interest to examine differential treatment effects and, especially, to attempt to identify the factors associated with larger or smaller effects.

Possible sources of variation among studies that might influence the size of effects found are methodological and procedural differences. If we found, for example, that studies involving one type of treatment yielded larger effects than studies using another type of treatment, we would need to be sure that there were not also major differences in the methods used by the studies in the various groups. If so, the differences in effect might only reflect differences in method, not differential treatment effects. In what follows, all discussions of differential or comparative effects are based on statistical procedures that adjust away, so much as possible, the differences among studies in method and procedure. We then answer the question of whether, when study results are statistically adjusted to represent comparable methodology, we find differential effects for different treatments, clients and the like.

To summarize the overall findings of this approach, two sets of factors do seem to differentiate circumstances yielding larger effects on delinquency from those yielding smaller effects. In particular, the characteristics of the juveniles treated have some modest relationship with the size of effect found and the characteristics of the treatment and treatment circumstances have major influences.

Client Characteristics

Such juvenile characteristics as age, ethnicity and prior arrest history are related to treatment effects. The general pattern of this relationship is that juveniles of higher risk or severity (e.g. older, more prior history) show larger delinquency reductions from treatment than those of lower risk. In part, this may be due to the obvious fact that low-risk cases have little room for improvement since, by definition, their delinquent involvement is rather slight to begin with. It is most important to recognize, however, that this relationship is very modest. In general, treatment seems to have much the same overall average effects whatever the characteristics of the treated juveniles.

Treatment Characteristics

By contrast, factors related to the nature and circumstances of the treatment delivered have very strong relationships to the magnitude of effects produced. The major influences come from three factors which, in order of importance, are: the modality or specific type of treatment, the degree of researcher involvement in the design and implementation of treatment, and the amount of treatment delivered. Each of these will be reviewed in turn.

Treatment type. Treatment type or modality was first divided according to whether the treatment was an adjunct to supervision in the juvenile justice system (probation, institutionalization, parole) and then further categorized by the specific type of treatment involved. In interpreting the results it is important to keep in mind that the research literature available to meta-analysis does not provide fine-grained reporting of the treatment procedures under study. Most typical are simple labels or brief, general descriptions. Thus when meta-analysis coders attempt to construct treatment variables, they inevitably end up with rather broad, fuzzy categories.

Under these circumstances, it is best not to single out any one, or even a few, treatment types that yield larger effects and assume that those specific approaches are superior. It is proposed instead to rank order the coded categories of treatment types from those associated with the largest average effect sizes to those with the smallest. We will then look for some overarching patterns or themes that characterize the better and worse approaches.

Figures 3.10 and 3.11 present the results of this procedure for treatments under juvenile justice system auspices and those not under such auspices. As a group, treatment under justice system auspices was associated with slightly smaller delinquency effects than that under other sponsorship, but the difference was small. The more striking features of Figures 3.10 and 3.11 are, first, how much difference there is from best to worst treatment type and, second, how similar the overall ranking is between the two charts.

If, as suggested, we look broadly at the pattern of results in these two figures rather than trying to pick out the 'magic bullet' treatment that is best, a relatively clear continuum can be discerned. At the high end of both charts are treatments that have a more concrete, behavioural/or skills-oriented character. At the lower end of the continuum are treatments that are more oriented to psychological processes, e.g. the several forms of counselling. The middle ground is held by various enhancements to juvenile justice supervision (e.g. early release, reduced caseloads, restitution) and general casework or advocacy approaches.

The inherent fuzziness of these coded categories makes futile any discussion of whether behaviour modification, or whatever your particular pet treatment might be, is universally superior to, say, family counselling. It does seem clear, however, that it is much better to target behaviour for change, and approach it in a relatively structured, concrete fashion, than to target psychological process for change and approach it using variations on traditional counselling and casework techniques. The good showing of multimodal treatment combinations, however, suggests that there may be advantage in combining different approaches.

It is worth recalling the earlier finding that, across studies, effects on delinquency were not associated with corresponding effects on the broad category of psychological outcome variables. In conjunction with the pattern shown in Figures 3.10 and 3.11, a case can be made that behavioural and psychological variables reflect only partially overlapping systems that are not tightly coupled. If you desire behaviour change, then treatment dealing directly with overt behaviour seems best advised. Treatment targeted on psychological processes may well produce psychological change but that, in turn, may not result in behaviour change.

Some particular attention should be given to the few treatment categories associated with negative effects. Most notable are the deterrence approaches such as shock incarceration. Despite their popularity, the available studies indicate that they actually result in delinquency increases rather than decreases. Unfortunately, there are distressingly few studies in this category, making any conclusions provisional. The studies we do have, however, raise grave doubts about the effectiveness of these forms of treatment.

We might note in passing the apparently good performance of employment-related treatment with juveniles under justice system supervision (Figure 3.10) and its poor performance in programmes

Treatment modality

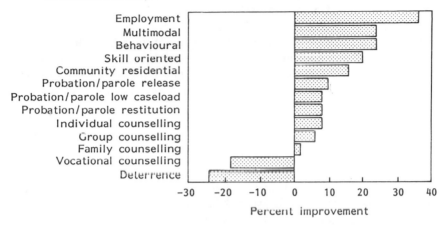

Figure 3.10. Percentage improvement over control group by modality—juvenile justice treatments.

Treatment modality

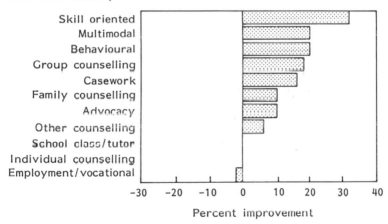

Figure 3.11. Percentage improvement over control group by modality—non-juvenile justice treatments.

mounted by other sponsors (Figure 3.11). This is another category in which there are too few studies for definitive conclusions. It may be that juveniles who are under supervision or institutionalized take quite a different attitude toward employment-related programmes from those outside the system. Alternatively, there may simply be some statistical fluke appearing here. Resolution of this issue will have to await further study and analysis.

Researcher involvement.   Second to treatment modality, the treatment characteristic most associated with positive delinquency outcome involved a small set of study factors reflecting the extent of the researcher's involvement in treatment design and implementation. A cynical view might attribute this to some biasing or 'wish fulfilling' influence researchers have on the outcome of studies they control. I see another interpretation as more plausible, however. When a researcher is closely involved in treatment design and/or implementation, there is likely to be a high level of treatment integrity. That is, treatment is likely to be closely monitored and supervised to ensure that it is delivered consistently and as intended to all clients. This interpretation is bolstered by another finding of the meta-analysis, namely that smaller research studies generally yield larger effects. A small study or, correspondingly, treatment to a limited number of clients at one time, is likely to be associated with a higher level of monitoring and integrity than larger-scale operations.

Treatment dosage.   The third important factor associated with differential treatment effects is amount of treatment delivered. Here we aggregated a variety of indicators that give different representations of service amount and simply dichotomized at the median to distinguish treatments with above and below average dosage. Looked at in terms of the individual dimensions within the aggregate, low dosage refers to treatment of 26 weeks or less duration, less than two client contacts per week, and/or less than 100 total contact hours. Conversely, high dosage refers to more than 26 weeks duration, two or more contacts per week, and/or more than 100 hours total contact.

Treatment factors in combination.   Figure 3.12 depicts the pattern of differential delinquency effects found as a function of treatment type, researcher involvement and dosage. As can be seen, the most favourable combinations are associated with delinquency reductions of the order of 25%—a rather substantial effect of meaningful practical significance. At the other end of the continuum, the least favourable combinations yield delinquency effects of the order of 1% reductions—a trivial result.

Also indicated in Figure 3.12 is the relative importance of the various factors. One of the 'best' treatments, closely monitored, for instance, has effects that are nearly as strong in lower dosages as in higher dosages. This reflects the larger role of treatment type in determining effects than

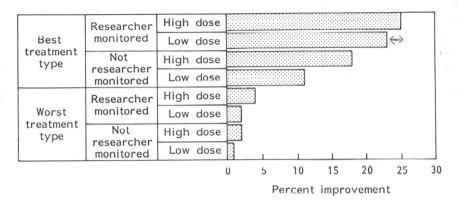

Best treatment type	Researcher monitored	High dose	
		Low dose	
	Not researcher monitored	High dose	
		Low dose	
Worst treatment type	Researcher monitored	High dose	
		Low dose	
	Not researcher monitored	High dose	
		Low dose	

Percent improvement

Figure 3.12. Delinquency change from a 50% recidivism control group baseline for various combinations of treatment conditions.

that of sheer amount of treatment. More generally, the significance of Figure 3.12 is the demonstration that there are sizeable differential effects possible in delinquency treatment. Sponsors who make good selections of treatment and deliver it well in reasonable amounts can attain results that are four or five (or more) times better than less appropriate selections would yield. Programme personnel, therefore, cannot merely trust to the overall average positive effect discussed earlier to ensure that they attain good effects, but must attempt to optimize their approach.

CONCLUSIONS

The large body of research on the effectiveness of delinquency treatment, when systematically assessed with advanced statistical techniques, shows positive average treatment effects of modest but not trivial magnitude. This positive result, however, does not appear uniformly over all treatments, juveniles and circumstances. There is wide variation ranging from circumstances in which treatment actually seems to increase delinquency to those in which the reductions are quite substantial.

The best general practical advice for treatment sponsors that can be derived from the results of this meta-analysis is as follows:

1. Focus treatment around behavioural, training or skills issues appropriate to the clientele using concrete, structured approaches as much as possible. Assemble treatment in appropriate multimodal packages, possibly including psychologically oriented treatment elements in the package.

2. Monitor, supervise and implement the treatment well. Have a treat-
    ment plan and maintain fidelity to that plan in the service delivery
    so that the intended treatment is actually delivered to each intended
    client.
3. Provide a sufficient amount of service, preferably 100 or more total
    contact hours, delivered at two or more contacts per week over a period
    of 26 weeks or more.

Note, however, that the above advice is general and broadbrush, as is appropriate from a meta-analytic base which aggregates over a wide range of
studies. All treatment development and delivery must be carefully tailored
in its details to the pertinent clientele and circumstances. Undoubtably
there are circumstances where the above advice is not applicable. Since
the broad guidelines derived from meta-analysis have the advantage of
a substantial empirical base, however, they warrant serious consideration.

One final conclusion cannot be overemphasized. It is no longer constructive for researchers, practitioners and policymakers to argue about whether
delinquency treatment and related rehabilitative approaches 'work' as
if that were a question that could be answered with a simple 'yes' or 'no'.
As a generality, treatment clearly works. We must get on with the busi-
ness of developing and identifying the treatment models that will be most
effective and providing them to the juveniles that they will benefit.

REFERENCES

Glass, G. V., McGaw, B. & Smith, M. L. (1981). *Meta-analysis in Social Research*.
    Newbury Park: Sage.
Hunter, J. E. & Schmidt, F. L. (1990). *Methods of Meta-analysis: Correcting Error
    and Bias in Research Findings*. Newbury Park: Sage.
Lipsey, M. W. (1992). Juvenile delinquency treatment: A meta-analytic inquiry
    into the variability of effects. In T. D. Cook, H. Cooper, D. S. Cordray, H. Hart-
    mann, L. V. Hedges, R. J. Light, T. A. Louis & F. Mosteller, (Eds.). *Meta-analysis
    for Explanation: A Casebook*. New York: Russell Sage Foundation, pp. 83–127.
Lipton, D., Martinson, R. & Wilks, J. (1975). *The Effectiveness of Correctional
    Treatment: A Survey of Treatment Evaluation Studies*. New York: Praeger.
Martinson, R. (1974). What works? Questions and answers about prison reform.
    Public Interest, **10**, 22–54.
Rosenthal, R. (1991). *Meta-analytic Procedures for Social Research* (Revised
    edition). Newbury Park: Sage.

CHAPTER 4

The Efficacy of Correctional Treatment: A Review and Synthesis of Meta-evaluations

Friedrich Lösel

University of Erlangen–Nuremberg, Germany

In 1974, Martinson published probably the most frequently cited paper on the treatment of offenders. Personally, I am not sure that the text has actually been read as often as it has been cited. In fact, the heading 'nothing works', which received so much attention, is presented only in the form of a question. In his preprint of selected findings from the study of Lipton and colleagues (1975), Martinson states: 'This is not to say that we found no instances of success or partial success; it is only to say that these instances have been isolated, producing no clear pattern to indicate the efficacy of any particular method of treatment' (Martinson, 1974: p. 49). According to his evaluation, the available studies were generally very poorly controlled in methodological terms, contained effects of external variables, were insufficiently grounded in theory, assessed very different and frequently too short follow-up periods, did not take enough system effects into account and were not replicated frequently enough.

This critical evaluation of the state of research was in line with various reviews published in the 1960s and 1970s (e.g. Bailey, 1966; Brody, 1976; Greenberg, 1977; Lipton et al., 1975; Logan 1972; Martin et al., 1981; Sechrest et al., 1979; Wright & Dixon, 1977). None the less, other authors came to the conclusion that some measures of offender rehabilitation do work (e.g. Blackburn, 1980; Gendreau & Ross, 1979; Hood, 1967; Palmer,

What Works: Reducing Reoffending—Guidelines from Research and Practice.
Edited by J. McGuire. © 1995 John Wiley & Sons Ltd.

1975; Quay, 1977; Romig, 1978). Even Martinson published a more opti-
mistic analysis in 1979. However, in crime policy the concept of rehabilitation declined (Allen, 1981). The spirit of the times moved on to other
concepts, such as just-deserts punishment, retribution or deterrence.

Since the end of the 1980s, the discussion on offender treatment has
revived (e.g. Gendreau & Andrews, 1990; Gendreau & Ross, 1987; Palmer,
1992; Lipsey, 1988; Lösel, 1992; Thornton, 1987). This revival has been
largely due to recent meta-analyses (see Table 4.1). The goal of meta-
analysis is to provide a highly systematic, representative and objective
integration of research findings by using statistical methods (for a comprehensive overview see Cooper & Hedges, 1994). There are several advantages of meta-analysis on treatment evaluation. First, individual studies
with mostly small samples can be integrated, thus permitting a more reliable estimation of effects based on a large number of cases. Second,
computing effect samples instead of mere statistical significance leads to
a better judgement of the practical significance of an intervention. Third,
statements on differential indication are possible, for example, to say which
types of treatment show which effects in which contexts and on which
persons (moderator analyses).

As a number of meta-analyses on offender treatment are now available, it should be possible to draw clearer, more differentiated and more
widely acceptable conclusions on treatment efficacy. However, points of
view still remain just as controversial as they were 20 years ago. For
example, according to Andrews and co-workers (1990b), we now have
convincing proof of the effectiveness of clinically relevant and psychologically informed treatment programmes. McGuire and Priestley (1992:
p. 171) talk about the ill-founded belief that 'nothing works' when referring to recent findings. And Palmer (1992: p. 76) concludes that the positive outcome of adequate studies leaves little doubt that many programmes
work. In contrast, Lab and Whitehead (1990: p. 405) view the findings
of Andrews and colleagues as the 'latest stop on the search for the secular
grail'. Ortmann (1994) considers that the statement 'nothing works' essentially still holds. And Logan and colleagues (1991: p. 25) argue that no
conclusions can be drawn until those meta-analyses 'have been subjected
to critical and painstakingly thorough evaluation by independent experts
who do not share the missionary zeal of "believers" in rehabilitation'.

There can be no doubt that the differences in the interpretation of the
available data are related to basic attitudes and values regarding crime
policy (see Lösel, in press). However, they are also due to intrinsic problems within meta-analysis. The individual research syntheses address
different issues, and they each integrate different samples of primary
studies. They turn specific spotlights onto the field of treatment evaluation that do not necessarily have to lead to a unified perspective. Despite

efforts to be systematic and objective, meta-analyses contain more or less subjective categorizations and decisions on the choice of methods. Although these can be tested, we are still basically confronted with the same problems of objectivity, reliability and validity that we find in primary studies (see Bullock & Svyantek, 1985; Lösel, 1991; Matt & Cook, 1994). Inconsistencies between various meta-analyses of the same issue indicate that principles of replication and critical multiplism (Cook, 1985) also apply to research synthesis.

Against this background, the present paper systematically compares, integrates and evaluates findings from various meta-analyses on offender treatment. As the material is very heterogeneous and comprehensive, I shall restrict myself to the following aspects: general effects, types of treatment, setting and organizational characteristics, outcome measures and design quality.

SELECTED META-ANALYSES

Table 4.1 summarizes some characteristics of 13 meta-analyses on offender treatment. Many of the results of these research syntheses are not independent of each other because of overlapping samples in the primary studies. For example, Andrews and colleagues (1990b) have explicitly integrated the primary studies of Whitehead and Lab (1989) into their analysis. Gottschalk and colleagues have evaluated overlapping subsamples from their study pool in various papers (Gottschalk et al., 1987a; 1987b). These overlap in turn with the studies analysed by Garrett (1985), Whitehead and Lab (1989), and Andrews and co-workers (1990b). As Lipsey (1992a, 1992b) has performed the 'biggest' meta-analysis to date, containing over 400 studies, his selection can be assumed to provide almost complete coverage of the study samples in all earlier meta-analyses of *juvenile* delinquency. This total is supplemented by the studies on adult offenders of Andrews and colleagues (1990b) and Antonowicz and Ross (1994) as well as the non-English studies from the meta-analyses by Lösel and co-workers (1987) and Redondo (1994). Thus, the meta-analyses cover a total of more than 500 evaluation studies.

The number of evaluations particularly addressing offender treatment has reached a size that is in the range of the more comprehensive meta-analyses of general psychotherapy (e.g. Grawe et al., 1994; Smith et al., 1980). At first glance, this is impressive and allows us to anticipate more conclusive statements compared with the 1970s. However, at the same time, various constraints have to be taken into account. The majority of the studies assessed come from North America or Anglo-American countries. Studies from other countries have been integrated into most

Table 4.1. Selected meta-analyses of correctional treatment evaluations.

	Andrews et al. (1990b)	Antonowicz & Ross (1994)
Description of studies	Correctional treatment of juvenile and adult offenders	Rehabilitation programmes for juvenile and adult offenders
No. of comparisons (studies)	154 (80)	44
Publication mode	Journal, book	Journal, book
Time period		
Designs	Rand., non-rand.	Rand., non-rand.
Outcome measure	Recidivism	Recidivism
Mean effect size (ES = r)	0.10	—
Treatment type as moderator	Largest ES for appropriate treatments (according to risk, need, responsivity principles); smaller ES for unspecified treatments; negative ES for inappropriate treatments and criminal sanctions	Successful (vs. unsuccessful) programmes more often included a sound conceptual model, the need and responsivity principle, multi-faceted programmes, role playing/modelling, social cognitive skills training
Setting type as moderator	Larger ES for community vs. institutional settings (in the case of appropriate treatment)	No significant differences between community and institutional settings
Outcome measure as moderator	—	—
Design quality as moderator	No difference between weaker and stronger designs	—

Garrett (1985)	Gensheimer et al. (1986)	Gottschalk et al. (1987a)
Treatment of juvenile delinquents in residential settings	Diversion programmes for juvenile delinquents	Community-based interventions with juvenile offenders
121 (111)	51 (44)	101 (90)
Journal, book, unpubl. 1960–1983	Journal, book, unpubl.	Journal, book, unpubl.
Rand., non-rand., pre-post	Rand., non-rand., pre–post	Rand., non-rand., pre–post
Recidivism, delinquent behaviour, others	Recidivism, delinquent behaviour, others	Recidivism, delinquent behaviour, others
0.18	0.09	0.12
No consistent differences between psychodynamic, behavioural, life skills and other programmes; tendency for larger ES of cognitive–behavioural approaches	—	Larger percentage of positive effects in behavioural, educational/vocational and group psychotherapy programmes vs casework, including psychotherapy and non-specific programmes
—	—	—
Smaller ES in recidivism vs various adjustment measures	Tendency for smaller ES in recidivism vs various attitude measures	Smaller ES in recidivism vs various attitude measures
Larger ES in less rigorous vs more rigorous designs	Positive correlation between investigator's influence in the treatment and ES; trend toward smaller ES in pre–post vs CG designs	Tendency for a positive correlation between random group assignment and ES; tendency for higher ES in pre–post vs CG designs

Table 4.1. *Contiued*

	Gottschalk et al. (1987b)	Izzo & Ross (1990)
Description of studies	Behavioural programmes for juvenile offenders	Treatment programmes for juvenile delinquents
No. of comparisons (studies)	30 (25)	46
Publication mode	Journal, book, unpubl.	Journal
Time period		
Designs	Rand., non-rand., pre—post	Rand., non-rand.
Outcome measure	Recidivism, delinquent behaviour, others	Recidivism
Mean effect size (ES = r)	0.20	—
Treatment type as moderator	—	Larger ES for programmes with a cognitive component vs non-cognitive programmes
Setting type as moderator	—	Larger ES in community vs institutional settings
Outcome measure as moderator	Smaller ES in recidivism vs programme and social behaviour	—
Design quality as moderator	Smaller ES in pre—post vs CG designs	—

Kaufmann (1985) (in Lipsey, 1988)	Lipsey (1992a) Lipsey (1992b)	Lösel, et al. (1987), Lösel & Köferl (1989), Lösel (in press)
Preventive treatments for preadjudicated juvenile delinquents	Treatment programmes for juvenile offenders	Treatment of adult offenders in social-therapeutic prisons
20	443	18 (8)
Journal, book, unpubl.	Journal, book, unpubl.	Journal, book
Rand.	Rand., non-rand.	Rand., non-rand.
Recidivism, delinquent behaviour	Recidivism, delinquent behaviour, others	Recidivism, delinquent behaviour, others
0.12	0.05/0.08	0.11
Larger ES for contingency contracting vs counselling, casework, etc.	Larger ES for behavioural skill-oriented and multimodal programmes vs other treatment approaches	No significant overall differences in ES between the studies
—	Smaller ES in custodial institutions, public facilities and the juvenile	---
One extremely large ES for self-reported delinquency	Lower ES in recidivism, other delinquency measures, school participation, etc. vs psychological measures; lower ES in measures with weak reliability, and long spans of time covered	No significant differences in ES for recidivism vs personality measures
—	No relationship between randomization and ES; mixed results for non-oquivalence of CG; larger ES in studies with low attrition and no treatment CG	Negative correlation between construct validity and ES; similar tendency for descriptive validity; no relationship of ES with statistical, internal, and external validity

Table 4.1. *Contiued*

	Mayer et al. (1986)	Redondo (1994)
Description of studies	Social learning treatment within juvenile justice	Treatment programmes for juvenile delinquents and adult offenders
No. of comparisons (studies)	39 (34)	57
Publication mode	Journal, book, unpubl.	Journal, book
Time period	1967–1983	1982–1993
Designs	Rand., non-rand., pre–post	Rand., non-rand., pre–post
Outcome measure	Recidivism, delinquent behaviour, others	Recidivism, delinquent behaviour, others
Mean effect size (ES = r)	0.36	0.15
Treatment type as moderator	Only one significant correlation relation between ES and specific treatment characteristics (token economies)	Larger ES for behavioural and cognitive–behavioural programmes vs other therapeutic and educational approaches, punishment and retributions
Setting type as moderator	—	No significant differences between community and prison settings; tendency for larger ES in juvenile prisons
Outcome measure as moderator	Smaller ES in recidivism vs behavioural measures	Smaller ES in recidivism vs follow-up measures like psychological or work adjustment and social skills
Design quality as moderator	Larger ES in pre–post vs CG designs; no significant correlation between randomization and ES	Larger ES in studies with low vs high methodological quality; tendency for larger ES in pre–post vs CG designs

Whitehead & Lab (1989)

Treatment of juvenile
offenders

50

Journal, book
1975 1984
Rand., non-rand.

Recidivism

0.13

Tendency for larger ES in
system diversion vs non-
system diversion,
community corrections,
and institutional
programmes; no
difference between
behavioural and non-
behavioural treatments

Larger ES for community
vs institutional settings

—

Tendency for smaller ES
in randomized designs

meta-analyses only if they have been published in the English language. But, in Europe alone, Redondo and his colleagues have documented a total of 250 evaluations, of which a sample of 57 studies has currently been meta-analysed (Redondo, 1994). The concentration of treatment evaluations on North America is in line with the international dominance of North American psychology and criminology. However, this situation should not be neglected in the discussion on offender treatment. As the penal system varies greatly across cultures, the question of generalizability still has to be tested empirically. There is also a second limitation: approximately 80% of the primary studies assessed in previous analyses refer to *juvenile* delinquency. Despite the fact that social rehabilitation and relapse prevention among relatively persistent and severe offenders is the classical topic of offender rehabilitation, only one single meta-analysis (Lösel et al., 1987; Lösel & Köferl, 1989) exclusively addresses the treatment of adult offenders in prison settings.

I cannot discuss here the problems involved in concepts such as 'rehabilitation', 'treatment,' and so forth (see Palmer, 1992). However, Table 4.1 illustrates the heterogeneity of the research in this field. For example, the comprehensive meta-analysis on juvenile delinquency treatment of Lipsey (1992a) contains not only studies on adjudicated offenders (as in, for example Garrett, 1985) but also studies on more informally defined juvenile delinquents, antisocial children, and children at risk. This raises the threat that results will be generalized inappropriately. However, the very broad concept of treatment does not necessarily have to be negative: on the one hand, similarities in the content of problem behaviour and not just formal criteria of the justice system are used to define the field. On the other hand, this also increases the number of studies, thus permitting differentiated analyses. None the less, the heterogeneity of the research summarized under the heading 'offender treatment' should receive more attention in the scientific and crime policy discussion. If, for example, studies on early intervention in families of at-risk children or children with antisocial behaviour are also included, the borders between treatment and prevention become fuzzier (e.g. Eysenck & Gudjonsson, 1989; Lösel, 1987) than pleas for the latter approach would suggest (e.g. Farrington, 1992; McCord & Tremblay, 1992).

The meta-analyses also do not just deal with content features of programmes (e.g. psychoanalytical or behavioural therapy) but also formal categories (e.g. diversion, probation/parole) that can each be organized in very different ways. Sometimes even pure criminal sanctions (Andrews et al., 1990b) or measures of deterrence (Lipsey, 1992a) are included. Such interventions can be subsumed under a very broad concept of treatment (e.g. Meltzoff & Kornreich, 1970) when punishment, deterrence, and the like are conceived as basic principles of behaviour modification (e.g. Brennan & Mednick, 1994). Hence, offender treatment should not be simply equated with a 'soft' or 'liberal' approach to criminal policy.

The more heterogeneous the studies included, the more it is necessary to perform highly differentiated assessments in the meta-analyses in order to avoid mixing up apples and pears. It is precisely such empirical differentiations that are the strength of meta-analysis compared to the traditional qualitative reviews. However, for differential assessments, the number of relevant primary studies is often so small that it is questionable how far the findings are replicable. General effects based on a larger number of studies are probably more reliable.

GENERAL EFFECT

As Table 4.1 shows, all meta-analyses on offender treatment have a positive mean effect size. This also holds for those studies that have not computed an overall effect and generally tend to support the nothing-works hypothesis (e.g. Whitehead & Lab, 1989). Because of the large number of studies, this effect is highly significant. If one sets aside the two meta-analyses addressing specific treatment modalities, mean effect sizes are also fairly consistent. They vary between 0.05/0.08 (dependent on weighting of sample sizes; Lipsey, 1992a) and 0.18 (Garrett, 1985). An exact estimation of the mean general effect is not possible because the sets of primary studies overlap in the various meta-analyses.

When evaluating the 'true effect', the following should be taken into account: the mean effect in Garrett (1985) drops to 0.12 when only methodologically more rigorous studies are considered. Lipsey (1992a) has made the most conservative weighting of individual effects according to sample size and taken into account the highest number of studies. His analysis probably also has no publication bias, because he included unpublished research reports and doctoral dissertations. This is important, because various findings suggest that selective decisions by authors and editors tend to overestimate effects (see Lipsey & Wilson, 1993; Rosenthal, 1991). The mean effect in Lipsey (1992a) probably sets the lower limit for an estimated general effect. Other analyses that have included unpublished studies or have carried out a total assessment for their topics (Garrett, 1985; Gensheimer et al., 1986; Lösel et al., 1987) produce somewhat higher values. The same holds for those meta-analyses that have included studies on the treatment of adult offenders or originate in Europe (Andrews et al., 1990b; Lösel et al., 1987; Redondo, 1994). Thus, the mean effect of all assessed studies probably has a size of about 0.10.

Although this positive effect counters the thesis that nothing works, it is still only small. It is markedly lower than the mean effect sizes found in more general meta-analyses of psychotherapy for adults (e.g. Shapiro & Shapiro, 1983; Smith et al., 1980). These are two to three times as high. Similarly, meta-analyses on psychotherapy or more specified forms of behaviour modification and social competence training in children and adolescents have larger effect sizes (e.g. Baer & Nietzel, 1991; Beelmann et al., 1994; Casey & Berman, 1985; Durlak et al., 1991; Weisz et al., 1987). The mean effect in offender treatment is also rather low in comparison with various psychological, social and educational interventions in other fields (Lipsey & Wilson, 1993). This confirms, on the one hand, that anti-social disorders belong to those behaviour problems that are particularly difficult to treat (e.g. Corrigan, 1991; Kazdin, 1987; Lösel et al., 1987). On the other hand, it could also be an indication that there may be unfavourable conditions within the criminal justice system such as insti-tutionalization or motivational deficits that counteract positive behav-iour modifications (see below). Nevertheless, there are inconsistencies in the comparative findings. For example, the meta-analyses on psycho-therapy and social competence training in youngsters do not show substan-tial differences between internalizing problems (anxiety, depression, etc.) and externalizing problems (aggression, delinquency, etc.). However, in these analyses as well, effect sizes are smaller when follow-up studies are performed (e.g. Beelmann et al., 1994). As recidivism is relatively frequently used as an outcome measure in evaluations of offender treat-ment, this may indicate a methodological reason for different results. In addition, meta-analyses of general psychotherapy frequently contain analogue studies of relatively undisturbed clients carried out in psychoso-cially more favourable conditions.

Only a small mean effect in offender rehabilitation is plausible also because the impact of treatment is overlaid by other, possibly stronger, influences. For example, alongside gender, age is a variable that corre-lates most strongly with crime (e.g. Farrington et al., 1986). This applies not only to the frequency of offending (e.g. Blumstein et al., 1988) but also to recidivism. For example, almost 77% of German 15–20-year-olds are reincarcerated within 5 years of their first prison sentence. Among 20–25-year-olds, these recidivism rates sink to approximately 50%, and among 25–30-year-olds, to approximately 35% (Generalbundesanwalt, 1990). Hence, general developmental processes and the impact of 'natural' protective factors (e.g. Lösel & Bliesener, 1994; Rutter, 1990) may overlay the interventions of the criminal justice system. Their impact can unfold only in relation to this. These phenomena support the need for a stronger combination of developmental–longitudinal and experimental–intervention designs (see Loeber & Farrington, 1994).

It is also necessary to consider that the potential effect size is constrained by the fact that treatment is generally not compared with 'nothing'. For example, the control groups in studies of social therapy in Germany come from normal prisons. These also carry out rehabilitation measures that are, in some respects, very similar to those in social therapy institutions (e.g. work, education). As a result, a low effect size may well be partially due to control group conditions being relatively favourable. The lower the relapse rate in the control groups, the smaller is the effect of any additional treatment.

From a methodological perspective, it has to be taken into account that the independent variable (treatment) and frequently also the dependent variable (recidivism) are only dichotomized. There are also deficits in the reliability of treatment and outcome. Both reduce statistical power (Cohen, 1988; Lösel & Wittmann, 1989). For these reasons, a high effect size cannot be anticipated from the very beginning in many studies.

However, a treatment effect that is only small does not have to be meaningless for practice (Prentice & Miller, 1992). As Rosenthal (1991) or Lipsey and Wilson (1993) have shown, a number of medical interventions have only small effects. They are nevertheless practically significant, because better alternatives are not yet available. Even from the perspective of cost-effectiveness, an offender treatment programme with a small effect size can be worthwhile. For example, Prentky and Burgess (1992) have shown that a programme for child molesters leads to approximately 15 percentage points less recidivism than normal incarceration. This enables substantial savings in costs. On the basis of an effect size of 0.10, I have performed a cost–utility analysis for German social-therapeutic prisons compared with regular prisons. This indicates that a monetary saving can be anticipated when the observed delay of recidivism (e.g. Dünkel & Geng, 1993; Egg, 1990) means that offenders from social therapeutic prisons receive one prison sentence less across their lifespan.

MODE OF TREATMENT

Two of the meta-analyses presented in Table 4.1 address the specific content of programmes, namely, behavioural treatment and social learning (Gottschalk et al., 1987b; Mayer et al., 1986). Mean effect sizes are relatively high in both. This trend is also confirmed in differential analyses of several other studies (e.g. Andrews et al., 1990b; Izzo & Ross, 1990; Lipsey, 1992a). It is mostly cognitive–behavioural, skill-oriented and multimodal programmes that yield the best effects. Less structured approaches such as casework or individual and group counselling are repeatedly less successful.

Two meta-analyses show no differential effect of treatment type. In Lösel (1994), this is probably due to the fact that a very complex bundle of measures are being evaluated in a social therapeutic prison, whereas the institutional, organizational and educational features are very homogeneous. Therefore, more specific effects of one treatment type do not stand out clearly. The fact that Whitehead and Lab (1989), regarded only an effect size of 0.20 as a positive treatment outcome is relevant. This probably made their internal comparisons less sensitive. In addition, they used mostly formal categories as classifications. In a further comparison, 44% of the 'behavioural programmes' show effects of over 0.20. However, this positive finding is clouded by equally frequent negative effect sizes. Without weighting according to sample size, I computed a mean effect of 0.12 for the behavioural programmes in Whitehead and Lab (1989). This is about the same size as the overall mean.

In the large meta-analysis of Lipsey (1992a, 1992b), the effect sizes for skill-oriented, behavioural, and multimodal programmes are similarly large both inside and outside the juvenile justice system (0.10 to 0.16). This effect is higher than the general effect. In the study by Andrews and colleagues (1990b), the differential effects are much higher in absolute terms. They categorized their primary studies according to theoretically derived principles of 'appropriate treatment' (Andrews et al., 1990a): (a) risk principle: higher levels of service are reserved for higher risk cases; (b) need principle: the targets of services are matched with criminogenic needs of offenders; and (c) responsivity principle: styles and modes of service are matched to the learning styles and abilities of offenders. Treatment measures that met these three principles (and these were, above all, behavioural programmes) were clearly more successful (mean $\phi = 0.32$) than unspecified (0.10) and inappropriate (-0.07) services or pure criminal sanctions (-0.08). The unspecified measures have the same magnitude as the general effect size estimated above. In inappropriate measures and pure criminal sanctions, controls even did better than the treatment group. This last finding agrees with Lipsey (1992a), who also reported a negative effect size for measures of deterrence.

The meta-analyses of Andrews and colleagues (1990b), Lipsey (1992a, 1992b), and others indicate that some programmes do work relatively well in offender rehabilitation, while others are possibly contra-indicative. This is one of the most important messages for practice: within the treatment approach, one can do something right as well as something wrong. The problem of appropriate versus inappropriate or even damaging measures is similar to the situation in early intervention (McCord, 1978). Such a differentiation is also found in meta-analyses on general psychotherapy. Here as well, a more detailed inspection reveals that although there is a positive main effect, this does not mean—as sometimes claimed—that everybody has won a prize. For a number of disorders, cognitive–

behavioural measures show relatively high effects (e.g. Glass & Kliegl 1983; Grawe et al., 1994).

Some of the larger effects in offender treatment may be due to weaker designs or softer effect criteria. For example, Garrett (1985) reports that findings in the comparison between behavioural and psychodynamic treatment differ depending on which outcome measures are used. However, several meta-analyses have used regression analysis or analysis of variance to control for such effects without the moderator effect of treatment disappearing (e.g. Andrews et al., 1990b; Izzo & Ross, 1990; Lipsey, 1992a).

Cognitive behavioural approaches in offender treatment are also supported by practical experience (e.g. Goldstein et al., 1989; Hollin, 1990). None the less, it is necessary to warn against overambitious hopes for a royal path of successful intervention. The available differential findings are only partially consistent and they contain various problems. It is not clear how far blindness toward the effect sizes was really present in the classification of treatments in the primary studies. In particular, the responsivity principle in the study by Andrews and colleagues (1990b) contains problems of circularity: If treatments are classified according to their adequate matching to the learning styles and abilities of offenders, this raises the risk that categorization is latently performed according to the observed effects that should actually be predicted. Some examples in Andrews et al. (1990b) suggest this danger (see Lab & Whitehead, 1990; Logan et al., 1991). Even findings on the cognitive–behavioural programme of Ross and Fabiano (1985), which can be viewed as a relatively successful, appropriate treatment, caution against too much optimism. For example, McGuire (1994) reports from Great Britain an effect size of approximately 0.15. This agrees with the relatively successful programmes in Lipsey (1992a).

As Table 4.1 shows, the differential effects of appropriate cognitive–behavioural, skill-oriented or multimodal and similar programmes are also not fully consistent in detail. For example, in their well controlled studies, Antonowicz and Ross (1994) have found that successful programmes are characterized more frequently by a sound conceptual model that took account of the need principle and the responsivity principle and contained role-playing/modelling, social–cognitive skills training, or a multifaceted treatment. However, no differences could be found for the risk principle and more specific features of cognitive–behavioural programmes (e.g. token economies, contingency contracting, social perspective taking). Mayer and colleagues (1986) have reported similar findings. Up to now, there are too few controlled evaluation studies available to furnish more detailed analyses of successful programme features (Antonowicz & Ross, 1994).

SETTING AND ORGANIZATIONAL CHARACTERISTICS

Table 4.1 shows that the setting of the treatment is a significant moderator in many meta-analyses. Mostly, treatment in community settings yields higher effect sizes than treatment in institutional/residential settings. This finding is plausible at first glance: learning processes and behavioural modifications that occur in institutions are often difficult to generalize to the later life context. In contrast, community-oriented programmes have lower transfer problems. Particularly in custodial treatment, we have to anticipate those negative effects that are described under headings such as prisonization, institutionalization and so forth. Some authors consider that the unfavourable effects of prisons and similar closed institutions are generally so strong that successful rehabilitation becomes impossible (e.g. Bondeson, 1989; Ortmann, 1994).

This is not the place to discuss claims that custody and rehabilitation are in principle incompatible. There is no clear empirical proof of this. Some meta-analyses yield no difference in effectiveness between institutional and community treatment, including meta-analyses of studies that are particularly sound methodologically (e.g. Antonowicz & Ross, 1994). This had already been found by Blackburn (1980). Of course, in meta-analyses with a moderator effect of setting, differences between the clients also have to be taken into account. Most primary studies did not directly compare institutional and ambulatory measures. Well controlled comparisons of imprisonment versus community interventions are rare and still contain several plausible interpretations of outcome differences (e.g. Petersilia & Turner, 1986). Normally, in studies on institutional-custodial treatment, offenders are more persistently antisocial, disordered or dangerous. They have not entered ambulatory programmes for precisely these reasons. Although confounds with other variables are partially controlled by multivariate analyses (e.g. Andrews et al., 1990b; Izzo & Ross, 1990; Lipsey, 1992a), such controls have particularly concentrated on methodological features and characteristics of the content of treatment. Characteristics of the clients are not so well reflected in the meta-analyses, which probably has something to do with the very heterogeneous structure of offences, particularly among the young. When third variables are controlled for, the moderator effect of the setting is not very strong (e.g. Lipsey, 1992a). In addition, it is necessary to anticipate interactions between setting and type of treatment. For example, Andrews and co-workers (1990b) found that the setting moderated the effect size only in appropriate programmes. Inappropriate services, however, are equally ineffective in either institutional or community settings.

Although 'alternatives to custody' have gained in importance in recent years, we cannot overlook the fact that they have not led to any real reduction in the prison population in many countries (e.g. Junger-Tas, 1993). Even if the aim is to avoid prison sentences and similar stationary measures as far as possible, institutional measures remain important for such reasons as just punishment, proportionality, and security of the public. This particularly applies to the small group of chronic offenders who are responsible for the majority of classical crime (see, for example, Farrington, 1987; Tracy et al., 1990), and are correspondingly the most important target group of treatment. Although the effectiveness of psychosocial interventions may be impaired under custodial conditions, they are not necessarily ineffective (e.g. Garrido & Redondo, 1993; Thornton & Hogue, 1993; Wexler et al., 1990). They also may contribute to reducing negative effects of institutionalization (Zamble & Porporino, 1990). For example, even Martinson (1979) reported that treatment had particularly beneficial effects when given in prison and when compared with standard youth confinement in 'group home' settings.

Actually, the alternative 'community versus institution' is too undifferentiated. Interventions in both settings can vary very broadly (e.g. Gendreau et al., 1994; Mair, 1990). For example, in the community, they can range from diversion with no further intervention to intensive control through electronic monitoring; in institutional settings, from open halfway houses to high security prisons. There are more or less fuzzy borders between the two areas, as in, for example, community residential centres.

As in the contents of treatment, we require differentiated analyses of the impact of specific setting characteristics. As the review of Bonta and Gendreau (1990) has shown, the negative effects of prison life are not as general as is sometimes claimed. Incarceration and prisonization effects depend on numerous moderators. For example, Moos (1975) has already shown that the quality of the organizational climate can differ greatly between penal justice institutions. Cooke (1992) has reported that institutional climate is relevant for the behaviour of violent offenders. The importance of institutional and educational climate is also shown in schools and halfway houses. According to Rutter and co-workers (1979), in comparable populations of students, schools that exhibit particular features of climate in the school organization, in lessons, and in teaching behaviour (e.g. prosocial atmosphere, structured teaching, dosed responsibilities, etc.) have fewer problems with delinquency. In a longitudinal study of residential homes, Lösel (1994) has found that resilient adolescents experienced a more positive socioemotional climate and a more strongly norm-oriented and structured educational climate than deviants.

Alongside the institutional and educational climate, a number of other variables can have a moderating impact on negative effects of the institution. These include the offender's history of prior adjustment problems and antisocial behaviour, the duration of residence, the age of the inmates, the activation of coping mechanisms, offender personality, objective and subjective crowding, the stability of group relations, the extent of control and repression, features of the subculture, the degree of isolation from external reality, the ecological design, and so forth (e.g. Bonta & Gendreau, 1990, 1992; Canter et al., 1980; Farrington & Nuttall, 1980; Hürlimann, 1993; Law et al., 1993; Porporino & Baylis, 1993; Ruback & Innes, 1988; Toch & Grant, 1989; Wormith, 1984). Characteristics of the staff, such as their motivation, attitudes, role definitions, experience, training, supervision, team spirit or relationship to the offender, probably also play a significant role in successful correctional programmes (e.g. Andrews et al., 1990b; Averbeck & Lösel, 1994; Cooke, 1989; Dionne et al., 1994; Finckenauer, 1984; Lösel et al., 1988; Ross & Lightfoot, 1985). However, evaluations of offender treatment and their meta-analyses have still paid insufficient attention to such variables (see Antonowicz & Ross, 1994).

OUTCOME MEASURE

Meta-analyses on the efficacy of psychotherapy have shown repeatedly that results also depend on the type of outcome measure applied (see Glass & Kliegl, 1983; Shapiro, 1985). Studies using 'softer' outcome criteria such as client reports or therapists' ratings yield higher effect sizes than studies with 'harder' criteria such as biographical data, everyday behaviour or objective test data. Meta-analyses on offender treatment exhibit a similar tendency. This also agrees with the findings from qualitative reviews (e.g. Basta & Davidson, 1988; Feldman, 1989). In several meta-analyses that have included studies with different outcome measures, recidivism shows relatively low effects (see Table 4.1). On measures of institutional adjustment, psychological adjustment, attitudes or other psychological criteria, effect sizes are mostly higher.

Differences are clear in some meta-analyses, whereas in others they are less clear. For example, Garrett (1985) has found that various adjustment measures (apart from vocational ones) had a much higher effect than recidivism. If the recidivism criterion only is taken into account, the overall effect size drops from 0.18 to 0.13 (and in more rigorously controlled studies, as low as 0.05). In contrast, Lipsey (1992b) has reported that the effect sizes for interpersonal adjustment, school participation, academic performance and vocational accomplishment were of a similar size to those for delinquency. Only for psychological outcome measures (attitudes and personality), were effects more than twice as high.

Such differences are probably not just due to the study samples. Different coding procedures also play a role. Lipsey's 'primary delinquency measure' (1992a) has a relatively broad definition. Alongside arrest, police contact, probation/parole or court contact, it also includes to a lesser extent unofficial delinquency and other indicators of antisocial behaviour. The follow-up periods for the delinquency measures could also be critical. According to Lipsey (1992a), they are rarely longer than one year, but they correlate negatively with effect size. However, the different findings on outcome measures cannot be traced back to follow-up periods alone. For example, Redondo (1994) has reported larger effect sizes on measures of adjustment and social behaviour when they are assessed a long time after treatment. Lösel and Köferl (1989) have found no significant differences in the effect size between recidivism and personality measures, although the former were assessed after much longer periods following treatment.

Alongside the follow-up period, other aspects of the outcome measure have to be considered. For example, Lipsey (1992a) has reported that a larger number of delinquency outcome measures as well as their methodological weakness were associated with smaller effect sizes. In Lösel and Köferl (1989), the fact that studies with personality measures generally used a greater number of instruments whose reliability and validity varied with respect to criminal behaviour probably also had an impact. Blackburn (1980) has already pointed out that various outcome measures relate insufficiently to delinquent behaviour. On the one hand, there is a risk that treatment outcome is related to changes in broad personality characteristics that are too unspecific. For example, Hanson et al. (1993) report that long-term recidivism of child molesters is not significantly associated with personality inventories like the MMPI. On the other hand, measures of adjustment, skills or attitudes can be too restricted to specific contents of the treatment (for example, cognitive or behavioural test situations; Baer & Nietzel, 1991; Beelmann et al., 1994). To some degree, the latter approach may be meaningful, because a fair evaluation must take account of the principle of symmetry between treatment and outcome (see Lösel & Wittmann, 1989; Wittmann, 1985): The success of a very specific intervention (primary factor level) should not be tested with very broad outcome measures (secondary factor level) and vice versa. However, if the aim is an impact on delinquent behaviour in the community, attitudes, ratings of institutional adjustment or problem-solving in hypothetical situations are not sufficient indicators. From this perspective, the particularly positive effects reported for multimodal and cognitive–behavioural programmes seem plausible. These explicitly address various facets of the problem and simultaneously direct offenders toward a modification in thinking *and* behaviour.

The meta-analyses suggest that more attention should be paid to the question of adequate outcome measurement. Criteria must have a theoretical basis not only in relation to each other but also in relation to the treatment. For example, it is sometimes debated whether institutional adjustment is only superficial or whether it permits a prediction of later behaviour. Empirical data tend to support the latter point of view (e.g. Bonta & Motiuk, 1992; Law et al., 1993; Monahan, 1989). Lipsey's meta-analysis (1992) provides another example: while the effect sizes in psychological measures and academic performance have no notable correlations with those in delinquency, they correlate clearly with school participation. This criterion relates, in turn, with the others. Direct and indirect connections to delinquent behaviour can be derived from such patterns. These should agree with theoretically based longitudinal findings on delinquency, for example, the developmental sequence of stacking problem behaviours in hyperactive/inattentive youngsters (Loeber, 1990). The more an outcome variable is proximal to treatment, the larger the effect that can be anticipated. With each further step in the causal chain, there is a diminishing effect size (Lipsey, 1992b).

Official recidivism is the last link in this chain and reveals serious methodological problems, such as the large rates of undetected crime and the selection process applied by agencies of social control. Although these and other problems indicate that official recidivism is not a highly reliable and sensitive outcome measure (e.g. Kury, 1986; Lösel et al., 1987; Waldo & Griswold, 1979), it continues to be of central importance for practical work (see Palmer, 1992). However, more attention should be paid to the usefulness of delinquency criteria. For example, Lipsey (1992a) has determined that the reliability, validity and sensitivity of the measures used were not demonstrated in more than 90% of the studies. Whereas developmental psychopathology considers a multi-setting–multi-informant approach to be essential for diagnosis (see Achenbach et al., 1987), offender treatment evaluation frequently limits itself to individual and rather imprecise data. Self-reports or reports from others could supplement official measures. However, such instruments are mostly only suitable for less serious offences. Recidivism also has to be differentiated appropriately. If it is not graded according to severity, it can be a very insensitive measure, particularly in adolescence with its high base rates in delinquency. More studies with longer follow-up periods are needed. In the treatment of severe adult criminals, for example, reliable statements on further development are only possible after a period of 4 years (see, for example, Dünkel & Geng, 1993; Egg, 1990). Here as well, theoretically meaningful graduations are necessary. For example, very long time periods may well show that there was an effect during the first few years, but that this faded away over time due to a lack of suitable relapse prevention.

Although the type of outcome measure remains an insufficiently explained source of the variance in effect sizes, its influences are not so confounded that other moderators can be viewed as artifacts. Particularly in recidivism measures, effect sizes are remarkably consistent. In addition, there have also been moderator effects of treatment type in meta-analyses that have integrated only studies using recidivism as an outcome measure (e.g. Andrews et al., 1990b; Antonowicz & Ross, 1994; Izzo & Ross, 1990).

DESIGN QUALITY

Discussing the quality of research design at last does not mean that it is the least important. On the contrary, as in Lipsey's meta-analysis (1992a), one should study step by step the amount of variance explained by (a) sampling error, (b) measurement error, (c) methodological study characteristics and (d) content-related study characteristics (see Hunter & Schmidt, 1990). However, most meta-analyses on offender treatment have not placed the various moderators in any hierarchy. In those cases in which regression analyses or analyses of covariance have been used to test the separate moderator effects of methodological and content-related study characteristics, differing weights have been found for the two areas. For example, Andrews and colleagues (1990b) have reported a strong relationship of 0.72 (beta) between type of treatment and effect size, whereas the partial correlation between design quality and effect size was insignificantly low at −0.07. In Lipsey (1992a), the variable cluster labelled 'method' explained 25% of the effect size variance, whereas the variable cluster labelled 'treatment' explained 22%. This means that both were responsible for approximately half of the explained variance that could not be attributed to sampling error (27%) and measurement error (15%). In contrast, Redondo (1994) has found that methodological variables explained 61% of the effect size variance, and treatment variables, only an additional 7%.

Thus a general statement on whether content or methodological characteristics is more significant for the differences in effect sizes is not possible. The results of meta-analyses depend, on the one hand, on how homogeneous/heterogeneous the integrated primary studies are in content or methodological terms. For example, Andrews and colleagues (1990b) only integrated studies with recidivism as an outcome measure, whereas other meta-analyses have used a great variety of effect criteria. On the other hand, the level of differentiation in the category scheme used for the evaluation is probably also very important. While Andrews and co-workers (1990b), for example, limited themselves to a simple classification of the quality of the research design (weaker vs. stronger), Lipsey (1992a, 1992b) analysed a number of methodological variables that he aggregated into clusters like sample, equivalence between treatment and control groups, attrition and so forth.

Meta-analyses do not clearly reveal whether the quality of design has improved since the criticisms in the 1970s. For example, Andrews and colleagues (1990b) have reported that studies before the 1980s show (non-significantly) weaker design quality than those from the 1980s. However, this trend inverts in Whitehead and Lab (1989): older studies (1975–1979) more frequently used random assignment than more recent studies (1980–1984). It basically holds that meta-analyses contain a positive selection with regard to design quality, because certain minimum methodological standards are demanded. These are mostly control-group designs, more rarely, also pre–post designs. Lipsey's (1992a) large meta-analysis excluded pre-test–post-test studies with no control groups. The same applied to post-test-only comparisons between non-random groups with no information on group equivalence. According to Lipsey (1992a: p. 102), approximately one-half of the 443 studies had a randomized design (elsewhere, he mentions 295 studies (p. 96). When matching procedures were used, most experimental and control groups seemed to be comparable. However, Lipsey also reports that the majority of studies showed serious deficits in some aspects of design quality (e.g. in statistical power, psychometric quality of outcome measures, blinding in data collection).

As Table 4.1 shows, relationships between design quality and effect size are not consistent. Sometimes they are only low or even non-existent. In summary, the various meta-analyses suggest that stronger designs generate lower effect sizes than weaker designs. In particular, control-group designs have lower effects than pre-test–post-test designs without control groups (e.g. Garrett, 1985; Gottschalk et al., 1987b; Redondo, 1994). The difference in methodological quality is also large here, because pre–post designs without control groups contain so many threats to validity that Cook and Campbell (1979) regard them as tending to be uninterpretable.

Findings on randomization in control group designs are less clear. The true experiment with randomized assignment to treatment and control group is certainly the best way to achieve equivalence between subjects. However, this classical criterion of internal validity is not reflected clearly in effect sizes. The meta-analyses report zero correlations, weakly positive ones and weakly negative ones. This could be because randomization of assignment is not a sufficiently valid indicator of group equivalence. Some treatment studies contain a high and non-random dropout rate that causes the original experimental design to collapse (see Lösel et al., 1987). This would automatically invalidate the methodological advantages compared with quasi-experimental designs without fully equivalent control groups. Despite this, Lipsey (1992a) has shown that his 78 studies with random assignment and no appreciable attrition from experimental groups showed a slightly higher effect size than all studies combined.

These findings illustrate the problem of all-too-sweeping classifications into weak versus strong designs. As the discussion within evaluation research has shown, a study that is valid in every way is an illusion (e.g. Cronbach et al., 1980). In our own meta-analysis, we evaluated methodological quality with a very differentiated scheme (Lösel & Köferl, 1989). Drawing on Cook and Campbell (1979), this involved (a) statistical validity (seven items; e.g., statistical power, fishing for significance); (b) internal validity (13 items; e.g. maturation, attrition); (c) construct validity (10 items; e.g. mono-operation bias, experimenter expectancy); (d) external validity (four items, e.g. interactions between selection and treatment or setting and treatment); and a specially developed category (e) descriptive validity (five items; e.g. description of treatment, statistical information). The validity patterns in the individual studies showed that studies that were strong in one field could be weak in another. In all, the threats to construct and descriptive validity were greater than the threats in items that were related to internal validity in strict terms. Only construct validity had a significant negative correlation with the effect sizes; that is, less generalizable studies had higher effect sizes.

Lipsey's results (1992a) results also suggest such a differentiated view of design quality. Sample size, equivalence of groups, attrition, control group treatment, reliability and validity of outcome measures, and information on statistical results each form one cluster that correlates separately with effect size. Although random versus non-random assignment was not a significant moderator in Lipsey, most other categories confirmed the trend that more valid studies generate lower effect sizes. As the design characteristics in Lipsey's meta-analysis (1992a) were separated out with regression analysis, their effects do not impair the moderator results of treatment. This is also confirmed by Antonowicz and Ross (1994), who only selected methodologically relatively valid studies but none the less observed differential effects of treatment type.

Although the meta-analytic results on design quality do not suggest that the results on content presented above are only methodological artifacts, they in no way indicate a methodologically satisfactory state of research. The confirmation of numerous relationships with effect size raises the question regarding the nature of the most methodologically sound and corrected estimations of effects (e.g. Rubin, 1992; Sanchez-Meca, 1994). This requires, on the one hand, improved studies that control as many threats to validity as possible. The above-mentioned combination of developmental–longitudinal and experimental-intervention studies seems promising here (see Loeber & Farrington, 1994). On the other hand, there is a need for approaches that permit a weighting of the existing threats to validity in terms of their relevance to the outcome (see Bliesener, 1994; Lösel et al., 1987). Individual methodological deficits can have not only a strong or weak but also a positive or negative effect on the outcome of treatment.

CONCLUSION

This review of some findings from meta-analyses shows that the pattern of results on offender treatment efficacy has not been fully clarified since Martinson (1974). None the less, it is clearer than it was 20 years ago. All meta-analyses confirm a positive overall effect. At approximately 10 percentage points difference between treatment and control groups, this is only small but not without practical significance. Heterogeneous and partially less consistent are the findings on differential effects. However, here as well, there are some systematic trends: theoretically well founded, cognitive–behavioural and multimodal types of treatment seem most likely to be effective, and these effects are substantially higher than the general effect. There are also indications that some modes of treatment are less appropriate for offenders and can even have negative effects.

However, we should not expect too much of relatively successful, 'appropriate' treatment modes. In methodologically strong designs with recidivism outcome measures, long follow-up periods, and unfavourable institutional conditions, we have to anticipate lower effects. These moderator effects are still not fully consistent in the meta-analyses. It can also be seen that the categories of analysis are in some ways too undifferentiated. Back at the level of primary studies, better grounded approaches would be desirable, for example, regarding the causal chains of outcome measures or regarding the impact of organizational variables. For other relevant characteristics, there also are not enough studies with clear empirical indicators. For example, treatment integrity is an important precondition for the success of adequate programmes (see Hollin, 1993; Lösel & Wittmann, 1989; Quay, 1987; Rezmovic, 1984), but primary studies still show a lack of process evaluations, so that the actual implementation of a concept remains unclear. Sometimes, indirect information can be derived from findings on the intensity or dosage of treatment, revealing that programmes of long duration or with high contact frequency have a slightly better effect (e.g. Gensheimer et al., 1986; Gottschalk et al., 1987a; Lipsey, 1992a). We do not know enough about other indirect indicators such as staff motivation or competence (e.g. Antonowicz & Ross, 1994).

We also have insufficient knowledge of the differential effects of offender characteristics (Lösel, 1993). In the meta-analyses, we mostly find only categories such as age, gender, kind of offences, or high versus low risk. It is therefore not surprising that offender characteristics explain only

1% of the effect size in Lipsey (1992a). A well grounded adjustment of treatment according to the needs of offenders must assess theoretically relevant characteristics that are predictive of differential treatment responses (e.g. Bornstein et al., 1981; Eysenck & Tudjonsson, 1989; Gendreau & Ross, 1987; Quay, 1987). For example, psychopathy seems to be an impor tant moderator of intervention effects (Hart et al., 1988; Rice et al., 1992). Whereas the early concepts of differential treatment (see Sparks, 1968) were mainly based on personality typologies, offender assessment now includes a more dynamic assessment of personal and social factors that are relevant for the individual risk of reoffending (developmental behaviour characteristics, lifestyle, offence situation, related cognitions and feelings, features of the future environment etc.; e.g. Andrews et al., 1990b; Blackburn, 1992; Bonta & Motiuk, 1992; Bonta et al., 1992; Monahan, 1981). According to Palmer (1992), a successful programme has to take into account individual skill/capacity deficits, external pressures/disadvantages, and internal difficulties. There are promising examples of differentiated treatment programmes for juvenile delinquents (e.g. Guerra & Slaby, 1990; LeBlanc, 1990) or for sex offenders (e.g. Laws, 1989; Lockhart et al., 1989). Overall, however, there is a lack of replication studies on clearly structured and documented programmes for carefully assessed subgroups of offenders in specific contexts.

If the meta-analyses show some systematic patterns despite the extremely heterogeneous data material and the wide range of methods, this should not be viewed as a definitive reply to the question 'What works?'. It is more the case that these form a guide for a new generation of studies on theoretically well founded offender treatment and its evaluation. I consider that it will be worthwhile to continue along this path, even though I honestly do not think that I possess the 'missionary zeal of "believers" in rehabilitation" deplored by Logan et al. (1991: p. 25).

REFERENCES

Achenbach, T. M., McConaughy, S. H. & Howell, C.T. (1987). Child/adolescent behavioural and emotional problems: Implications of cross-informant correlations for situational specificity. *Psychological Bulletin*, **101**, 213–232.

Allen, F. A. (1981). *The Decline of the Rehabilitative Ideal: Penal Policy and Social Purpose*. New Haven: Yale University Press.

Andrews, D. A., Bonta, J. & Hoge, R. D. (1990a). Classification for effective rehabilitation. *Criminal Justice and Behavior*, **17**, 19–51.

Andrews, D. A., Zinger, I., Hoge, R. D., Bonta, J., Gendreau, P. & Cullen, F. T. (1990b). Does correctional treatment work? A clinically relevant and psychologically informed meta-analysis. *Criminology*, **28**, 369–404.

Antonowicz, D. & Ross, R. R. (1994). Essential components of successful rehabilitation programs for offenders. *International Journal of Offender Therapy and Comparative Criminology*, **38**, 97–104.

Averbeck, M. & Lösel, F. (1994). Subjektive Theorien über Jugendkriminalität [Subjective theories on juvenile delinquency]. In M. Steller, K.-P. Dahle & M. Basque (Eds.). Pfaffenweiler: Centaurus, *Straftäterbehandlung* (pp. 213–226).

Baer, R. A. & Nietzel, M. T. (1991). Cognitive and behavioral treatment of impulsivity in children: A meta-analytic review of the outcome literature. *Journal of Clinical Child Psychology*, **20**, 400–412.

Bailey, W. C. (1966). Correctional outcome: An evaluation of 100 reports. *Journal of Criminal Law, Criminology and Police Science*, **57**, 153–160.

Basta, J. M. & Davidson II, W. S. (1988). Treatment of juvenile offenders: Study outcomes since 1980. *Behavioral Sciences and the Law*, **6**, 353–384.

Beelmann, A., Pfingsten, U. & Lösel, F. (1994). The effects of training social competence in children: A meta-analysis of recent evaluation studies. *Journal of Clinical Child Psychology*, **23**, 260–271.

Blackburn, R. (1980). *Still not working? A look at recent outcomes in offender rehabilitation*. Paper presented at the Scottish Branch of the British Psychological Society Conference on Deviance, Sterling, UK, February 1980.

Blackburn, R. (1992). *The Psychology of Criminal Conduct*. Chichester: Wiley.

Bliesener, T. (1994). Der Einfluß der Forschungsqualitat auf das *Forschungsergebnis: Zur Evaluation der Validierung biographischer Daten in der Eignungsdiagnostik*. [The relationship between methodological vigour and effect size.] Habilitationsschrift, Universität Erlangen-Nürnberg.

Blumstein A., Cohen, J. & Farrington, D. P. (1988). Criminal career research: Its value for criminology. *Criminology*, **26**, 1–35.

Bondeson, U. V. (1989). *Prisoners in Prison Societies*. New Brunswick: Transaction Books.

Bonta, J. & Gendreau, P. (1990). Reexamining the cruel and unusual punishment of prison life. *Law and Human Behavior*, **14**, 347–372.

Bonta, J. & Gendreau, P. (1992). Coping with prison. In P. Suedfeld & P. E. Tetlock (Eds.). *Psychology and Social Policy*. New York: Hemisphere, pp. 343–354).

Bonta, J. & Motiuk, L. L. (1992). Inmate classification. *Journal of Criminal Justice*, **20**, 343–353.

Bonta, J., Andrews, D. A. & Motiuk, L. L. (1993). Dynamic risk assessment and effective treatment. *Paper presented at the Annual Meeting of the American Society of Criminology*, Phoenix, USA.

Bornstein, P. H., Hamilton, S. B. & McFall, M. E. (1981). Modification of adult aggression: A critical review of theory, research, and practice. *Progress in Behavior Modification*, **12**, 299–350.

Brennan, P. A. & Mednick, S. A. (1994). Evidence for the adaption of a learning theory approach to criminal deterrence: A preliminary study. In E. Weitekamp & H.-J. Kerner (Eds.). *Cross-National Longitudinal Research on Human Development and Criminal Behavior*. Dordrecht, NL: Kluwer, pp. 371–379.

Brody, S. R. (1976). *The Effectiveness of Sentencing*. London: HMSO.

Bullock, J. R. & Svyantek, D. J. (1985). Analyzing meta-analysis: Potential problems, an unsuccessful replication, and evaluation criteria. *Journal of Applied Psychology*, **70**, 108–115.

Canter, D., Ambrose, I., Brown, J., Comber, M. & Hirsch, A. (1980). *Prison Design and Use. Final report*. Guildford, UK: Department of Psychology, University of Surrey.

Casey, R. J. & Berman, J. S. (1985). The outcome of psychotherapy with children. *Psychological Bulletin*, **98**, 388–400.

Cohen, J. (1988). *Statistical Power Analysis for the Behavioral Sciences*, 2nd edn. New York: Academic Press.

Cook, T. D. (1985). Post-positivist critical multiplism. In L. Shotland & M. M. Mark (Eds.). *Social Sciences and Social Policy*, Beverly Hills: Sage, pp. 21–62.

Cook, T. D. & Campbell, D. T. (1979). *Quasi-experimentation: Design and Analysis Issues for Field Settings*. Chicago: Rand-McNally.

Cooke, D. J. (1989). Containing violent prisoners. *British Journal of Criminology*, **29**, 129–143.

Cooke, D. J. (1992). Violence in prisons: a Scottish perspective. *Forum on Corrections Research*, 4, 23–30.

Cooper, H. M. & Hedges, L. V. (Eds). (1994). *The Handbook of Research Synthesis*. New York: Russell Sage Foundation.

Corrigan, P. W. (1991). Social skills training in adult psychiatric populations: A meta-analysis. *Journal of Behavior Therapy and Experimental Psychiatry*, **22**, 203–210.

Cronbach, L. J., Ambron, S. R., Dornbusch, S. M., Hess, R. D., Hornik, R. C., Philips, D. C., Walker, D. F. & Weiner, S. S. (1980). *Toward Reform of Program Evaluation*. San Francisco: Jossey Bass.

Dionne, J., LeBlanc, M., Gregoire, J. C., Proulx, J. & Trudeau LeBlanc, P. (1994). Staff training. The corner stone of a differential approach project with delinquent adolescents. *Research and Evaluation in Group Care*, in press.

Dünkel, F. & Geng, B. (1993). Zur Rückfälligkeit von Karrierctätern nach unterschiedlichen Strafvollzugs- und Entlassungsformen [Recidivism of career criminals after different forms of imprisonment and release]. In G. Kaiser & H. Kury (Eds). *Kriminologische Forschung in den 90er Jahren*. Freiburg i. Br.: Max-Planck-Institut für ausländisches und internationales Strafrecht, pp. 193–257.

Durlak, J. A., Fuhrman, T. & Lampman, C. (1991). Effectiveness of cognitive–behavior therapy for maladapting children: A meta-analysis. *Psychological Bulletin*, **110**, 204–214.

Egg, R. (1990). Sozialtherapeutische Behandlung und Rückfälligkeit im längerfristigen Vergleich [Social-therapeutic treatment and recidivism in long-term comparison]. *Monatsschrift für Kriminologie und Strafrechtsreform*, **73**, 358–368.

Eysenck, H. J. & Gudjonsson, G. (1989). *The Causes and Cures of Criminality*. New York: Plenum Press.

Farrington, D. P. (1987). Early precursors of frequent offending. In J. Q. Wilson & G. C. Loury (Eds). *From Children to Citizens: Families, Schools, and Delinquency Prevention*. New York: Springer, pp. 27–50.

Farrington, D. P. (1992). Psychological contributions to the explanation, prevention, and treatment of offending. In F. Lösel, D. Bender & T. Bliesener (Eds). *Psychology and Law. International Perspectives*. Berlin, New York: de Gruyter, pp. 35–51.

Farrington, D. P. & Nuttall, C. P. (1980). Prison size, overcrowding, prison violence, and recidivism. *Journal of Criminal Justice*, **8**, 221–231.

Farrington, D. P., Ohlin, L. E. & Wilson, J. Q. (1986). *Understanding and Controlling Crime*. New York: Springer.

Feldman, P. (1989). Applying psychology to the reduction of juvenile offending and offences: Methods and results. *Issues in Criminological and Legal Psychology*, **14**, 3–32.

Finckenauer, J. O. (1984). *Juvenile Delinquency and Corrections: The Gap between Theory and Practice*. New York: Academic Press.

Garrido, V. & Redondo, S. (1993). The institutionalisation of young offenders. *Criminal Behaviour and Mental Health*, **3**, 336–348.

Garrett, P. (1985). Effects of residential treatment of adjudicated delinquents: A meta-analysis. *Journal of Research in Crime and Delinquency*, **22**, 287–308.

Gendreau, P. & Andrews, D. A. (1990). Tertiary prevention: What the meta-analyses of the offender treatment literature tell us about 'What works'. *Canadian Journal of Criminology*, **32**, 173–184.

Gendreau, P. & Ross, R. R. (1979). Effective correctional treatment: Bibliotherapy for cynics. *Crime and Delinquency*, **25**, 463–489.

Gendreau, P. & Ross, R. R. (1987). Revivication of rehabilitation: Evidence from the 1980s. *Justice Quarterly*, **4**, 349–407.

Gendreau, P., Cullen, F. T. & Bonta, J. (1994). Intensive rehabilitation supervision: The next generation in community corrections? *Federal Probation*, **58**, 72–78.

Generalbundesanwalt beim Bundesgerichtshof (1990). *Rückfallstatistik 1990 [Recidivism Statistics 1990]*. Berlin: Bundeszentralregister.

Gensheimer, L. K., Mayer, J. P., Gottschalk, R. & Davidson II, W. S. (1986). Diverting youth from the juvenile justice system: A meta-analysis of intervention efficacy. In S. J. Apter & A. Goldstein (Eds). *Youth Violence: Programs and Prospects*. Elmsford: Pergamon Press, pp. 39–57.

Glass, G. V. & Kliegl, R. M. (1983). An apology for research integration in the study of psychotherapy. *Journal of Consulting and Clinical Psychology*, **51**, 28–41.

Goldstein, A. P., Glick, B., Irwin, M. J., Pask-McCartney, C. & Rubama, I. (1989). *Reducing Delinquency: Intervention in the Community*. Oxford: Pergamon Press.

Gottschalk, R., Davidson II, W. S., Gensheimer, L. K. & Mayer, J. P. (1987a). Community-based interventions. In H. C. Quay (Ed). *Handbook of Juvenile Delinquency*. New York: Wiley, pp. 266–289.

Gottschalk, R., Davidson II, W. S., Mayer, J. & Gensheimer, L. K. (1987b). Behavioral approaches with juvenile offenders. A meta-analysis of long-term treatment efficacy. In E. K. Morris & C. J. Braukmann (Eds). *Behavioral Approaches to Crime and Delinquency*. New York: Plenum Press, pp. 399–423.

Grawe, K., Donati, R. & Bernauer, F. (1994). *Psychotherapie im Wandel: Von der Konfession zur Profession. [Psychotherapy in Change: From Confession to Profession]*. Göttingen: Hogrefe.

Greenberg, P. F. (1977). The correctional effects of corrections: A survey of evaluations. In D. F. Greenberg (Ed). *Corrections and Punishment*. Beverly Hills: Sage, pp. 111–148.

Guerra, N. G. & Slaby, R. G. (1990). Cognitive mediators of aggression in adolescent offenders: II. Intervention. *Developmental Psychology*, **26**, 269–277.

Hanson, R. K., Steffy, R. A. & Gauthier, R. (1993). Long-term recidivism of child molestors. *Journal of Clinical and Consulting Psychology*, **61**, 646–652.

Hart, S. D., Kropp, P. R. & Hare, R. D. (1988). Performance of male psychopaths following conditional release from prison. *Journal of Consulting and Clinical Psychology*, **56**, 227–232.

Hollin, C. R. (1990). *Cognitive–Behavioral Interventions with Young Offenders.* Elmsford: Pergamon Press.

Hollin, C. R. (1993). Advances in the psychological treatment of delinquent behaviour. *Criminal Behaviour and Mental Health*, **3**, 142–157.

Hood, R. (1967). Research on the effectiveness of punishments and treatments. In European Committee on Crime Problems (Ed.). *Collected Studies in Criminological Research*, Vol. I. Strasbourg: Council of Europe, pp. 73–113.

Hunter, J. E. & Schmidt, F. L. (1990). *Methods of Meta-analysis.* New Park: Sage.

Hürlimann, M. (1993). *Führer und Einflußfaktoren in der Subkultur des Strafvouzlzugs. [Leaders and Influences in the Prison Subculture].* Pfaffenweiler: Centaurus.

Izzo, R. L. & Ross, R. R. (1990). Meta-analysis of rehabilitation programs for juvenile delinquents. A brief report. *Criminal Justice and Behavior*, **17**, 134–142.

Junger-Tas, J. (1993). *Alternatives to Prison: Myth and Reality.* Working paper. First NISCALE Workshop on Criminality and Law Enforcement, The Hague, The Netherlands.

Kaufman, P. (1985). Meta-analysis of juvenile delinquency prevention programs. Unpublished Master's Thesis. Claremont Graduate School. [Results reported in Lipsey, 1988].

Kazdin, A. (1987). Treatment of antisocial behavior in children: Current status and future directions. *Psychological Bulletin*, **102**, 187–203.

Kury, H. (1986). *Die Behandlung Straffälliger, [The Treatment of Offenders].* Vol. 1. Berlin: Duncker & Humblot.

Lab, S. P. & Whitehead, J. T. (1990). From 'nothing works' to 'the appropriate works': The latest stop on the search for the secular grail. *Criminology*, **28**, 405–417.

Law, M. A., Gendreau, P. & Goggin, C. E. (1993). *Predicting Prison Misconducts.* Unpublished manuscript. Saint John, NB: University of New Brunswick.

Laws, D. R. (Ed.). (1989). *Relapse Prevention with Sex Offenders.* New York: Guilford Press.

LeBlanc, M. (1990). L'intervenant auprès des jeunes délinquents, omnipraticien ou spécialiste. *Revue Canadienne de Psychoéducation*, **19**, 85–100.

Lipsey, M. W. (1988). Juvenile delinquency intervention. In H. S. Bloom, D. S. Cordray & R. Light (Eds). *Lessons from Selected Program and Policy Areas. New Directions for Program Evaluation, No. 37.* San Francisco: Jossey Bass, pp. 63–84.

Lipsey, M. W. (1992a). Juvenile delinquency treatment: A meta-analytic inquiry into variability of effects. In T. D. Cook, H. Cooper, D. S. Cordray, H. Hartmann, L. V. Hedges, R. L. Light, T.A. Louis & F. Mosteller (Eds). *Meta-analysis for Explanation.* New York: Russell Sage Foundation, pp. 83–127.

Lipsey, M. W. (1992b). The effect of treatment on juvenile delinquents: Results from meta-analysis. In F. Lösel, D. Bender & T. Bliesener (Eds). *Psychology and Law: International Perspectives.* Berlin, New York: de Gruyter, pp. 131–143.

Lipsey, M. W. & Wilson, D. B. (1993). The efficacy of psychological, educational, and behavioral treatment. *American Psychologist*, **48**, 1181–1209.

Lipton, D., Martinson, R. & Wilks, J. (1975). *The Effectiveness of Correctional Treatment.* New York: Praeger.

Lockhart, L. L., Saunders, B. E. & Cleveland, P. (1989). Adult male sex offenders: An overview of treatment techniques. In J. S. Wodarski & D. L. Whitaker (Eds). *Treatment of Sex Offenders in Social Work and Mental Health Settings.* New York: The Haworth Press, pp. 1–32.

Loeber, R. (1990). Disruptive and antisocial behavior in childhood and adolescence: Development and risk factors. In K. Hurrelmann & F. Lösel (Eds). *Health Hazards in Adolescence*. Berlin, New York: de Gruyter, pp. 223–257.

Loeber, R. & Farrington, D. P. (1994). Problems and solutions in longitudinal and experimental treatment studies of child psychopathology and delinquency. *Journal of Consulting and Clinical Psychology*, **62**, 887–900.

Logan, C. (1972). Evaluation research in crime and delinquency: A reappraisal. *Journal of Criminal Law, Criminology and Police Science*, **63**, 378–387.

Logan, C. H., Gaes, G. G., Harer, M., Innes, C. A., Karacki, L. & Saylor, W. G. (1991). *Can Meta-analysis Save Correctional Rehabilitation?* Washington, DC: Federal Bureau of Prison.

Lösel, F. (1987). Psychological crime prevention: Concepts, evaluations and perspectives. In K. Hurrelmann, F.-X. Kaufmann & F. Lösel (Eds). *Social Intervention: Potential and Constraints*. Berlin, New York: de Gruyter, pp. 289–313.

Lösel, F. (1991). Meta-analysis and social prevention: Evaluation and a study on the family-hypothesis in developmental psychopathology. In G. Albrecht & H.-U. Otto (Eds). *Social Prevention and the Social Sciences*. Berlin, New York: de Gruyter, pp. 305–332.

Lösel, F. (1992). Sprechen Evaluationsergebnisse von Meta-Analysen für einen frischen Wind in der Straftäterbehandlung? *[Meta-analysis as a 'fresh breeze' in offender treatment?]* In M. Killias (Ed.), *Rückfall und Bewährung/Récidive et Réhabilitation*. Chur, Switzerland: Rüegger, pp. 335–353.

Lösel, F. (1993). The effectiveness of treatment in institutional and community settings. *Criminal Behaviour and Mental Health*, **3**, 416–437.

Lösel, F. (1994). Protective effects of social resources in adolescents at high risk for antisocial behavior. In E. G. M. Weitekamp & H.-J. Kerner (Eds). *Cross-national Longitudinal Research on Human Development and Criminal Behavior*. Dordrecht, The Netherlands: Kluwer, pp. 281–301.

Lösel, F. (in press). Increasing consensus in the evaluation of offender rehabilitation? Lessons from research syntheses. *Psychology, Crime and Law*, **2**, in press.

Lösel, F. & Bliesener T. (1994). Some high-risk adolescents do not develop conduct problems: A study on protective factors. *International Journal of Behavioral Development*, **17**, 753–777.

Lösel, F. & Köferl, P. (1989). Evaluation research on correctional treatment in West Germany: A meta-analysis. In H. Wegener, F. Lösel & J. Haisch (Eds). *Criminal Behavior and the Justice System: Psychological Perspectives*. New York: Springer, pp. 334–355.

Lösel F. & Wittmann, W. W. (1989). The relationship of treatment integrity and intensity to outcome criteria. In R. F. Conner & M. Hendricks (Eds). *International Innovations in Evaluation Methodology. New Directions for Program Evaluation, No. 42*. San Francisco: Jossey-Bass, pp. 97–108.

Lösel, F., Bliesener, T. & Molitor, A. (1988). Social psychology in the criminal justice system: A study on role perceptions and stereotypes of prison personnel. In P. J. van Koppen, D. J. Hessing & G. van den Heuvel (Eds). *Lawyers on Psychology and Psychologists on Law*. Amsterdam: Swets & Zeitlinger, pp. 167–184.

Lösel, F., Köferl, P. & Weber, F. (1987). *Meta-Evaluation der Sozialtherapie [Meta-evaluation of Social Therapy]*. Stuttgart: Enke.

Mair, G. (1990). *Evaluating the Effects of Diversion Strategies on the Attitudes and Practices of Agents of the Criminal Justice System*. Report for the 19th Criminological Research Conference: New Social Strategies and the Criminal Justice System. Strasbourg: Council of Europe.

Martin, S. E., Sechrest, L. B. & Redner, R. (1981). *New Directions in the Rehabilitation of Criminal Offenders*. Washington, DC: National Academy Press.

Martinson, R. (1974). What works? Questions and answers about prison reform. *The Public Interest*, **10**, 22–54.

Martinson, R. (1979). New findings, new views: A note of caution regarding sentencing reform. *Hofstra Law Review*, **7**, 242–258.

Matt, G. E. & Cook, T. (1994). Threats to the validity of research syntheses. In H. Cooper & L. V. Hedges (Eds). *The Handbook of Research Synthesis*. New York: Russell Sage Foundation, pp. 503–520.

Mayer, J. P., Gensheimer L. K., Davidson II, W. S. & Gottschalk, R. (1986). Social learning treatment within juvenile justice: A meta-analysis of impact in the natural environment. In S. J. Apter & A. Goldstein (Eds). *Youth Violence: Programs and Prospects*. Elmsford: Pergamon Press, pp. 24–38.

McCord, J. (1978). A thirty-year follow-up of treatment effects. *American Psychologist*, **33**, 284–289.

McCord, J. & Tremblay, R. (Eds). (1992). *Preventing Antisocial Behavior: Interventions from Birth through Adolescence*. New York: Guilford Press.

McGuire, J. (1994). Evaluation of correctional treatment in the United Kingdom. Paper presented at the 4th European Conference on Law and Psychology, Barcelona.

McGuire, J. & Priestley, P. (1992). Some things do work: Psychological interventions with offenders and the effectiveness debate. In F. Lösel, D. Bender & T. Bliesener (Eds). *Psychology and Law: International Perspectives*. Berlin, New York: de Gruyter, pp. 163–174.

Meltzoff, J. & Kornreich, M. (1970). *Research in Psychotherapy*. Chicago: Atherton

Monahan, J. (1981). *Predicting Violent Behavior: An Assessment of Clinical Techniques*. Beverly Hills: Sage.

Monahan, J. (1989). Prediction of criminal behavior: Recent developments in research and policy in the United States. In H. Wegener, F. Lösel & J. Haisch (Eds). *Criminal Behavior and the Justice System: Psychological Perspectives*. New York: Springer, pp. 40–52.

Moos, R. (1975). *Evaluating Correctional and Community Settings*. New York: Wiley.

Ortmann, R. (1994). Zur Evaluation der Sozialtherapie. Ergebnisse einer experimentellen Längsschnittstudie zu Justizvollzugsanstalten des Landes Nordrhein-Westfalen. [On the evaluation of social therapy. Results of an experimental study in prisons of Northrhine-Westphalia]. *Zeitschrift für die gesamte Strafrechtswissenschaft*, **106**, 782–821.

Palmer, T. (1975). Martinson revisited. *Journal of Research in Crime and Delinquency*, **12**, 133–152.

Palmer, T. (1992). *The Re-emergence of Correctional Intervention*. Newbury Park: Sage.

Petersilia, J. & Turner, S. with J. Peterson (1986). *Prison versus Probation in California*. Santa Monica: Rand Corporation.

Porporino, F. J. & Baylis, E. (1993). Designing a progressive penology: the evolution of Canadian federal corrections. *Criminal Behaviour and Mental Health*, **3**, 268–289.

Prentice, D. A. & Miller, D. T. (1992). When small effects are impressive. *Psychological Bulletin*, **112**, 160–164.

Prentky, R. & Burgess, A. W. (1992). Rehabilitation of child molesters: A cost–benefit analysis. In A. W. Burgess (Ed). *Child Trauma I: Issues and Research*. New York: Garland, pp. 417–442.

Quay, H. C. (1977). The three faces of evaluation: What can be expected to work? *Criminal Justice and Behavior*, **4**, 341–354.

Quay, H. C. (1987). Patterns of delinquent behavior. In H. C. Quay (Ed). *Handbook of Juvenile Delinquency*. New York: Wiley, pp. 118–138.

Redondo, S. (1994). El tratamiento de la delinquencia en Europa: Un estudio meta-analitico. [Delinquency treatment in Europe: A meta-analysis]. Tesis Doctoral. Barcelona: Universidad de Barcelona.

Rezmovic, E. L. (1984). Assessing treatment implementation amid the slings and arrows of reality. *Evaluation Review*, **2**, 187–204.

Rice, M. E., Harris, G. T. & Cormier, C. A. (1992). An evaluation of a maximum security therapeutic community for psychopaths and other mentally disordered offenders. *Law and Human Behaviour*, **16**, 39–41.

Romig, A. D. (1978). *Justice for our Children. An Examination of Juvenile Delinquent Rehabilitation Programs*. Lexington, MA: Lexington Books.

Rosenthal, R. (1991). *Meta-analytic Procedures for Social Research*, 2nd edn. Newbury Park: Sage.

Ross, R. R. & Fabiano, E. A. (1985). *Time to Think: A Cognitive Model of Delinquency Prevention and Offender Rehabilitation*. Johnson City: Institute of Social Sciences and Arts.

Ross, R. R. & Lightfoot, L. O. (1985). *Treatment of the Alcohol-abusing Offender*. Springfield: Thomas.

Ruback, R. B. & Innes, C. A. (1988). The relevance and irrelevance of psychological research: The example of prison crowding. *American Psychologist*, **43**, 683–693.

Rubin, D. B. (1992). Meta-analysis: Literature-synthesis or effect-size surface estimation. *Journal of Educational Statistics*, **17**, 363–374.

Rutter, M. (1990). Psychosocial resilience and protective mechanisms. In J. Rolf, A. Masten, D. Cicchetti, K. Nuechterlein & S. Weintraub (Eds). *Risk and Protective Factors in the Development of Psychopathology*. New York: Cambridge University Press, pp. 181–214.

Rutter, M., Maughan, B., Mortimore, P. & Ouston, J. (1979). *Fifteen Thousand Hours. Secondary Schools and Their Effects on Children*. London: Open Books.

Sanchez-Meca, J. (1994). Methodological issues in the meta-evaluation of correctional treatment. Paper presented at the 23rd Congress of Applied Psychology, Madrid.

Sechrest, L. B., White, S. O. & Brown, E. D. (1979). *The Rehabilitation of Criminal Offenders: Problems and Prospects*. Washington, DC: National Academy of Sciences.

Shapiro, D. A. (1985). Recent applications of meta-analysis in clinical research. *Clinical Psychology Review*, **5**, 13–34.

Shapiro, D. A. & Shapiro, D. (1983). Meta-analysis of comparative therapy outcome studies: A replication and refinement. *Psychological Bulletin*, **92**, 581–604.

Smith, M. L., Glass, G. V. & Miller, T. I. (1980). *The Benefits of Psychotherapy*. Baltimore: Johns Hopkins University Press.

Sparks, R. F. (1968). Types of treatment for types of offenders. In European Committee on Crime Problems (Ed.). *Collected Studies in Criminological Research*. Vol. 3. Strasbourg: Council of Europe, pp. 129–169.

Thornton, D. M. (1987). Treatment effects on recidivism: A reappraisal of the 'nothing works' doctrine. In B. J. McGurk, D. M. Thornton & M. Williams (Eds). *Applying Psychology to Imprisonment*. London: HMSO, pp. 181–189.

Thornton, D. & Hogue, T. (1993). The large-scale provision of programmes for imprisoned sex offenders: issues, dilemmas and progress. *Criminal Behaviour and Mental Health*, **3**, 371–380.

Toch, H. & Grant, D. (1989). Noncoping and maladaptation in confinement. In L. Goodstein & D. L. MacKenzie (Eds). *The American Prison: Issues in Research and Policy*. New York: Plenum Press.

Tracy, P. E., Wolfgang, M. E. & Figlio, R. M. (1990). *Delinquency Careers in Two Birth Cohorts*. New York: Plenum Press.

Waldo, G. & Griswold, D. (1979). Issues in the measurement of recidivism. In L. B. Sechrest, S. O. White & E. D. Brown (Eds). *The Rehabilitation of Criminal Offenders: Problems and Prospects*. Washington, DC: National Academy of Sciences, pp. 225–250.

Weisz, J. R., Weiss, B., Alicke, M. D. & Klotz, M. L. (1987). Effectiveness of psychotherapy with children and adolescents: A meta-analysis for clinicians. *Journal of Consulting and Clinical Psychology*, **55**, 542–549.

Wexler, H. K., Falkin, G. P. & Lipton, D. S. (1990). Outcome evaluation of a prison therapeutic community for substance abuse treatment. *Criminal Justice and Behavior*, **17**, 71–92.

Whitehead, J. T. & Lab, S. P. (1989). A meta-analysis of juvenile correctional treatment. *Journal of Research in Crime and Delinquency*, **26**, 276–295.

Wittmann, W. W. (1985). *Evaluationsforschung [Evaluation Research]*. Berlin: Springer.

Wormith, J. S. (1984). The controversy over the effects of long-term imprisonment. *Canadian Journal of Criminology*, **26**, 423–437.

Wright, E. W. & Dixon, M. C. (1977). Community prevention and treatment of juvenile delinquency. A review of evaluations. *Journal of Research in Crime and Delinquency*, **14**, 35–67.

Zamble, E. & Porporino, F. J. (1990). Coping, imprisonment, and rehabilitation: Some data and their implications. *Criminal Justice and Behavior*, **17**, 53–70.

PART II

Practical Applications and Current Developments

CHAPTER 5

The STOP Programme: Reasoning and Rehabilitation in a British Setting

Christine Knott

Greater Manchester Probation Service, Manchester, UK

This chapter deals with the programme 'Straight Thinking on Probation' (STOP), which was established by the Mid Glamorgan Probation Service in 1991. I will describe how an average-sized probation service area set about introducing and delivering a new kind of programme employing methods of cognitive training. This entailed concentrated work on the part not only of those directly involved in leading the programme, but also of all staff of the organization, who were to some extent affected by it. The chapter focuses in turn on the content of the programme, on some early research results, and on management issues raised by a departure of this kind.

The county of Mid Glamorgan, in south Wales, has a population which is predominantly spread across six towns of roughly equal size in the once relatively prosperous Welsh coalfield. There is no single pre-eminent centre of population, hence a centralized form of provision was not the best option for any new form of service. As can be seen from Table 5.1, socio economic data concerning the area show it to be very poor, one of the poorest in the United Kingdom. It has a high crime rate and a sense of there being very little hope for the economic future of local people.

Mid Glamorgan was allocated one of the four original 'Day Training Centres' established by the Home Office in 1973 (Mair, 1988) (from 1982

What Works: Reducing Reoffending—Guidelines from Research and Practice.
Edited by J. McGuire. © 1995 John Wiley & Sons Ltd.

Table 5.1. Socio-economic data for Mid Glamorgan.

Comparing the 66 counties of Britain, it has been found that Mid Glamorgan has the:

- *Third lowest* proportion of men aged 16 to 64 economically active and in employment
- *Lowest* proportion of men aged 50 to 64 economically active and in employment
- *Second lowest* proportion of single, widowed or divorced women economically active and in employment
- *Second lowest* proportion of households in social classes 1 and 2
- *Highest* proportion of households lacking an inside toilet
- *Highest* proportion of residents permanently sick
- *Second highest* standardized mortality rate
- *Fifth highest* perinatal mortality rate
- *Second highest* rate of youth unemployment
- *Fourth highest* proportion of households lacking a bath and shower
- *Sixth highest* rate of unemployment overall

known as Day Centres), designed to accept high-tariff offenders at risk of custodial sentences and provide a community-based alternative with a structured programme. It was located in the town of Pontypridd, which, although the best location that could have been chosen, was by no means equally accessible to all potential clients. During the late 1980s, the number of referrals to the Centre varied considerably, only increasing when it was under threat of closure. It was clear to all involved that such a pattern could not be sustained. At the same time, the Mid Glamorgan service was engaged in the national debate about quality of probation work. The service had been managed 'by objectives' for some years and while it was agreed that we were working with the right people, there was less clarity over whether we were doing the right things with them. With very high-risk offenders on probation, there was a correspondingly high risk of breakdown through further offending; for the latter Mid Glamorgan had the highest rate in England and Wales in 1991. While there were detectable reasons for this, management groups nevertheless felt there should be a new initiative to tackle the problem.

THE 'REASONING AND REHABILITATION' PROGRAMME AND STOP

Like staff groups in many other places, in Mid Glamorgan we had difficulty agreeing on what was 'good supervision'. Everyone appeared to know what this meant, but everyone had a different view. To try to resolve the problem we decided to look at research: perhaps good supervision was what research showed had 'worked'. Our attention was drawn to the work of Robert Ross, Elizabeth Fabiano and their colleagues in probation services in Ontario.

This work suggested that for many persistent offenders, a central problem that is linked to their offending behaviour is their lack of, or failure to apply, a number of problem-solving skills (Ross & Fabiano, 1985). Such skills include the ability to identify when they have a problem, to think of alternative courses of action, to plan the steps towards solution of a problem, to anticipate consequences and to consider the effects of their actions upon others.

To provide offenders with these skills Ross and colleagues (1989) devel oped a training course entitled *Reasoning and Rehabilitation* (R&R). This consists of 35 two-hour sessions, which are designed to teach not only the above 'cognitive' skills but also a range of social and self-control skills, negotiation, creative thinking and critical reasoning. The programme was initially evaluated by Ross and co-workers (1988) in a probation-based experiment in Pickering, Ontario, with encouraging results at a 9-month follow-up. While the reoffence rate for clients on ordinary probation supervision was 69.5%, that for the group on the cognitive programme was only 18.1%. An analysis of effective programmes suggested that the inclusion of a cognitive component greatly increased the likelihood of a favourable outcome (Izzo & Ross, 1990). The R&R course was subsequently more extensively developed in other penal settings in Canada (Robinson et al., 1991), and has since been piloted in a number of other places (De Maret, 1991; Fogg, 1992; Garrido & Redondo, 1993; Garrido & Sanchis, 1991; Ross & Ross, 1995, Weaver and Bensted, 1992).

Following enquiries about the nature of the programme, we obtained the R&R training manual and identified potential resources for enabling us to implement the programme locally. After consultations with staff groups and the Probation Committee (which oversees the work of the service), a decision was made to proceed with the programme in each one of our six field teams. Experience gained from the Day Centre enabled a range of policies, selection criteria and other administrative matters to be finalized fairly quickly. Our 1991 3-year plan contained the statement:

> We reject the notion that 'nothing works' in respect of assisting offenders to change their behaviour and thereby reduce offending. Research demonstrates that some well planned and well delivered programmes of super vision aimed at reducing reoffending work for some offenders, some of the time. We therefore re-affirm our commitment to the reform and rehabilitation of offenders as the central philosophical ideal of the Mid Glamorgan Probation Service. (Mid Glamorgan Probation Service, 1991).

Alongside these decisions another was made: to conduct a full evaluation of the work. Given the investment of time and money, this was of considerable importance. For evaluation research Dr Peter Raynor was appointed as consultant and an existing Senior Probation Officer post was converted to a partial research role. Several working groups were created to identify needs relevant to various aspects of the programme: for example, its target client group, 'marketing' to courts and sentencers; and monitoring of programme integrity. Between February and July 1991, 44 main-grade probation officers (about two-thirds of the staff available) received training of 4 or 5 days' duration from James McGuire and Philip Priestley, who were familiar with the principles and content of the R&R programme. Training was also provided for management staff. James McGuire remained as a consultant to the organization, meeting with team representatives on a monthly basis during the first year of programme implementation.

In April 1991 the first STOP Orders, as we had decided to entitle them, began to be made by courts. The first STOP group programme was run in Merthyr Tydfil commencing in June 1991. Since then over 150 such Orders have been made, all field probation teams have completed at least two group programmes, and some have run many more. Additional resources were put into teams in the expectation that demand would increase following the advent of the Criminal Justice Act (1991) in October 1992. Under the guidance of Robert Ross, the R&R programme was adapted slightly for women offenders and a 'Women only' group was successfully piloted.

RESEARCH DESIGN AND DATA COLLECTION

A number of evaluation reports have now been published concerning the STOP programme (Lucas et al. 1992; Raynor & Vanstone, 1994). For the purpose of the evaluation, a target of the first 130 Orders was set (anticipating a shortfall of approximately 30%). Several of comparison samples were identified: these were (a) Standard Probation Orders; (b) Probation with a Day Centre requirement; (c) Community Service Orders; (d) Immediate Custody of up to 12 months; and (e) Suspended prison sentences.

Table 5.2 lists the numbers of offenders in the experimental group and in available comparison samples. The 'Risk of Conviction' (ROC) scores are based on calculations from the Cambridgeshire Risk of Reconviction Scale (Merrington, 1990). In Mid Glamorgan 55+ was seen as the cut-off score for the STOP target group of high-risk offenders. Table 5.3 depicts the profile of offenders in the various groups in terms of some basic criminological indicators. As can be seen, the STOP group are heavily convicted and a very high proportion have previously served a prison sentence.

For the first 14 groups ($n = 106$ clients, an average group size of 7.5),

Table 5.2. Sample sizes for STOP evaluation research.

Sentence or type of order	Sample size
STOP	130
Standard probation	100
(High risk of custody 55+)	
Probation with Day Centre requirement	100
Community Service	100
(High risk of custody 55+)	
Immediate custody	150
(Up to 12 months; 50% of sample to be under 21 years)	
Suspended prison sentence	150
Total	730

Table 5.3. Mean ages and criminological indicators for client samples.

Group	Mean age (years	Mean no. of previous convictions (n)	Previous custodial history (%)
STOP group	22.9	9.0	76
Other probation	22.7	5.3	41
Community service	23.6	5.3	38
Immediate custody (adults 12 months or less)	29.0	7.9	54
Young offender institution	18.5	4.7	40
Suspended imprisonment	30.1	6.2	43

the mean breakdown rate was 28%. This compared favourably with the then existing breakdown rate of 48% for the Day Centre programme. The proportions completing the programme or not doing so for various reasons were as follows. A total of 69 of this group completed the programme (72% of the sample), one of whom breached probation for other reasons. Of the 27 clients who failed to complete (28% of the sample), 12 were subject to Breach of Probation, nine committed further offences, and six were both 'breached' and committed further offences.

In addition to collecting statistical data of this kind, the research manager also interviewed all members of the experimental group when they had completed a programme. Their views were sought on a number of points. For example, they were asked whether the STOP group had made them think differently. Of the first 63 clients on whom data is available, a total of 57 (90.5%) said 'yes', and six (9.5%) said 'no'. They were also asked whether they found attendance on the programme helpful. The distribution of responses to this was: 'yes' = 56 (89%); 'no' = six (9.5%); 'don't know' = one (1.5%). They were also asked questions in open-ended format concerning their views of the programme. The following are some of the comments obtained concerning what they believed they had gained.

> Nothing at all. A fucking waste of taxpayers' money.
>
> There weren't any.
>
> It's made me look back on things and slow down a bit.
>
> It's made me stop and think. It showed me to keep emotions under control and accept other people's opinions.
>
> It's made me look at things differently; helped me to think clearly about things.
>
> Before I used to act on impulse. Now I have more tendency to sit and think problems through.
>
> If I am in a row, rather than rush in I think of the consequences—what can happen to me, my family and others. I think of every option there is before I get into anything . . . it's changed my whole outlook on life. I think positive, I look on the bright side.
>
> I thought it was another one of those things—bullshit. But I learned so much that if you had said I would learn as much I would have said you were insane.
>
> I've been in jail all my life and that's not the answer to it. I don't know whether this is, but it's closer to an answer than anything I've come across.

Generally speaking, though there are criticisms, some of them vituperative, the overall flavour of the comments has been positive and many individual benefits have been reported.

RECONVICTION DATA

In the third interim evaluation report on the project (Raynor & Vanstone, 1994), 12-month reconviction rates and other data have been provided. To facilitate comparisons between the different sentence categories, the researchers compared the actual reconviction rates with predicted rates calculated from the National Risk of Reconviction Predictor instrument developed by John Copas for the Home Office (Copas, 1994). Reconviction data were obtained from the National Identification Bureau, which includes standard list offences only.

As approaching one-third of all those sentenced to STOP did not start or did not complete the programme (not all for reasons of further offending), it is important in the evaluation to distinguish those who did and did not complete the programme. We were in any case willing to accept that our assessment and targeting skills might need refining, particularly in the early stages of an experiment. In Table 5.4 the figures for those who completed the programme have been separated out and are placed in the bottom row.

However, it should be noted that a proportion of reconvictions in any offender sample followed over time will actually be for offences committed prior to the current sentence. This is more likely to occur in a community sentence than in a custodial sentence group. The researchers therefore checked this data and introduced a correction factor to eliminate 'false positives'. The adjusted results are shown in Table 5.5.

These figures show encouraging findings for all community sentences, viewed in the context of trying to 'beat' the predictor rate. As in Table 5.4, only the YOI custodial group shows as high a predicted rate as the STOP sample and in both custodial groups, obtained reconviction rates are worse than prediction.

A strong message here is that if we can improve our assessment and targeting methods together with our skills in 'holding' offenders in a group, we might be able to secure still better results. Associated with this we envisaged another possibility: that even if we were unable to reduce reof-

Table 5.4. Predicted and actual reconviction rates within 12 months.

Group	Predicted (%)	Actual (%)
Probation with STOP	49	49
Standard probation orders	46	44
Community service	40	35
Immediate imprisonment	40	45
Young offender institution	48	56
STOP completions	47	39

Table 5.5. Predicted and actual 12-month reconviction and reincarceration rates adjusted to eliminate 'false positives'.

Group	Predicted (%)	Actual (%)	Immediate custody on reconviction (%)
Probation with STOP	49	44	37
Standard probation orders	41	40	27
Community service	36	35	34
Immediate imprisonment	39	44	24
Young offender institution	47	54	26
STOP completions	42	35	0

Table 5.6. Proportions of those reconvicted for different types of offence.

Offence category	STOP programme non-completions (%)	STOP programme completions (%)
Violence (including robbery)	26	13
Burglary	19	13
Theft (including car theft and handling)	39	30
Drug offences	6	17
Criminal damage	0	17
Other less serious offences	10	14

fending, we might at least slow down the rate of reoffending, or reduce its level of seriousness and the consequent risk to the public. One way to judge this is in terms of the proportion of reoffences which result in a new sentence of imprisonment. As Table 5.5 also shows, there were encouraging trends in this outcome for those who completed STOP: none of this group who were reconvicted received a custodial sentence.

At present we can only speculate on the precise reasons for this result. However, Table 5.6 supplies one indication, in that reconvictions of STOP completers tended to be for less serious types of offence.

The results of Tables 5.5 and 5.6, though less marked than those of Ross and colleagues (1988), parallel them in a number of ways. The R&R group has the lowest rate of reconviction of all the groups studied and is the only one to show a meaningful reduction. Compared with prediction, the reoffence rate of the STOP completions group has been reduced by 16%, not dissimilar to the reductions found in a number of the meta-analyses quoted elsewhere in this volume. The findings of Ross and co-workers (1988) concerning reincarceration were 30% for the standard probation group and 0% for the cognitive group. Remarkably, in the present study the same result has emerged. Note, however, that the participants in the STOP programme were more heavily convicted than those included in the Pickering experiment (respective means of 9.0 and 6.9 previous convictions).

ASPECTS OF PROGRAMME MANAGEMENT

All the above seems to present a very positive picture, certainly results with which staff in Mid Glamorgan are delighted. None of this, however, was due simply to luck. It required hard work, commitment and careful planning by staff—managers and practitioners alike. There were times when the STOP programme appeared to dominate all our other work, and some take the view that the effort involved and the associated sacrifices have been too great. A way had to be found to encompass a diversity of views and still continue with the work.

A major point to be emphasized is that it is not enough that results obtained to date have been encouraging: even with the best and most effective programmes available, if they are not managed into existence and sustained thereafter, their chances of achieving any success are low, and of continuing long enough to be evaluated are fairly minimal. To achieve this requires a good working partnership between managers and practitioners and a clear recognition from each of the respective roles and contributions of the other. Programme implementation therefore is not merely a matter of good ideas; these must be put into practice and nurtured or they simply disappear.

Research summarized elsewhere in this volume has underlined our state of knowledge to date concerning the ingredients of effective programmes. The 'risk', 'criminogenic needs' and 'responsivity' principles have been described, together with the importance of 'programme integrity'. Focusing especially on the last of these, I want to consider some aspects of it in the context of Mid Glamorgan.

Programme Integrity

For many staff in probation services this has come as a completely new concept. Most of us received our social work education in an environment where it was assumed that 'nothing works'. It did not matter what a programme contained; the important factor the worker had to offer offenders was his or her own personality and experience. Thus, for example, Day Centre staff changed their programme regularly, always with the intention of improving it. One of our first discussions concerning R&R involved staff identifying sessions they believed they could improve and ways in which they could improve them. This was not conceit or arrogance, but because that was the style that had always been adopted. In establishing STOP, programme integrity and the avoidance of 'tinkering' became key issues for us, to the extent that a working party was set up, papers produced, instructions given on which aspects to monitor, and sessions videotaped and scrutinized by the research manager and external consultant. Where 'fidelity' fell below agreed standards, Senior Probation Officers were alerted for discussion as part of their supervisory work. Initial responses to the concept of programme integrity were to view it as a straitjacket, leaving session leaders too frightened to alter a single word or piece of material in the manual. This was natural to begin with, but staff had to feel re-empowered to distinguish between adapting a programme to the cultural context of Welsh valley offenders and trying to 'improve' major aspects of the content.

This issue caused particular difficulties for middle managers (Senior Probation Officers). While it was part of their role to supervise STOP staff and ensure programme integrity, how could they do so without experience of running the programme? Consultant and training sessions were organized to focus on this point. The middle management role was an uneasy one as this group had not been provided with the R&R training, in order to enable them to concentrate on their role as programme managers. At a later stage, one of this group was assigned the task of sampling session videotapes, providing feedback and initiating further skills training where necessary.

Resources

The question of resources in general, and of staff-to-client ratios in particular, is one where it is unlikely that managers and practitioners will ever agree. This is not just to be cynical, but working with offenders can always absorb more time and encourage a belief that you can always do something better. Quality can certainly be improved with more resources, but it can also be subject to a law of diminishing returns. In Mid Glamorgan, by reallocating resources it proved possible to fund an extra member of staff for every field probation team in order to run STOP groups. In the original work of Ross and his associates, groups were typically run by one leader only. This contrasts with the initial situation in Mid Glamorgan where groups were run by two staff acting as co-leaders, with a third outside watching the sessions through video to give direct feedback and postsessional review comments. Our group sizes were larger than in Canada and given the new role, this investment of staffing was initially accepted. However, this was not a model that could be retained in the longer term. Had management allowed this form of 'extravagance with quality' to continue, the STOP programme would have ceased to exist after its first experimental year. The level of staffing thus had to be reduced to one group leader only per session.

Programme Monitoring

The monitoring of programmes, or of any component of working, is not one of the more popular tasks in probation services, but it is an essential one if any programme is to be properly targeted, evaluated and its integrity maintained. In the context of increasing workloads and declining resources, managers demonstrate their priorities not by what they say should happen, but by what they monitor to ensure it will happen. This role is best accomplished by those with no direct role in practice; this is more likely to guarantee consistency and the maintenance of programme discipline. For those directly involved in a programme there can be a 'drift' which can lead to distortions in monitoring processes. So once again, the need for monitoring is a further instance where a strong working partnership is obligatory between management and practitioner. Without such monitoring and evaluation, probation programmes, or any other community based interventions for offenders, fall prey to the criticism that they cannot be 'shown to work' and should be curtailed or even abandoned. Probation services have neglected this issue for too long: the need to monitor and evaluate should now, more than ever, become an integral part of our organizational culture.

REFERENCES

Copas, J. B. (1994). On using crime statistics for prediction, In M. Walker (Ed.), *Statistics of Crime*. Oxford: Oxford University Press.

De Maret, W. F. N. (1991). Time to think: social/cognitive skills programming in transition in New Mexico. *Journal of Correctional Education*, **42**, 107–110.

Fogg, V. (1992). Implementation of a cognitive skills development program. *Perspectives: American Probation and Parole Association*, Winter, 24–26.

Garrido, V. & Redondo, S. (1993). The institutionalisation of young offenders. *Criminal Behaviour and Mental Health*, **3**, 336–348.

Garrido, V. & Sanchis, J. R. (1991). The cognitive model in the treatment of Spanish offenders: theory and practice. *Journal of Correctional Education*, **42**, 111–118.

Izzo, R. L. & Ross, R. R. (1990). Meta-analysis of rehabilitation programs for juvenile delinquents. *Criminal Justice and Behaviour*, **17**, 134–142.

Lucas, J., Raynor, P. & Vanstone, M. (1992). *Straight Thinking on Probation: 1 year on*. Bridgend: Mid Glamorgan Probation Service.

Mair, G. (1988). *Probation Day Centres*. Home Office Research Study No. 100. London: HMSO.

Merrington, S. (1990). *Cambridgeshire Risk of Reconviction Scale: 1990 Progress Report*. Cambridge: Cambridgeshire Probation Service.

Mid Glamorgan Probation Service (1991). *Organisational Principles and Values. Probation Service Three-year Corporate Plan*. Bridgend: Mid Glamorgan Probation Service.

Raynor, P. & Vanstone, M. (1994). *Straight Thinking on Probation: Third Interim Report*. Bridgend: Mid Glamorgan Probation Service.

Robinson, D., Grossman, M. & Porporino, F. (1991). *Effectiveness of the Cognitive Skills Training Program: From Pilot Project to National Implementation*. Ottawa: Correctional Services of Canada.

Ross, R. R. & Fabiano, E. A. (1985). *Time to Think: A Cognitive Model of Delinquency Prevention and Offender Rehabilitation*. Ottawa: Instituie of Social Sciences and Arts.

Ross, R. R. & Ross, B. (Eds). (1995). *Thinking Straight*. Ottawa: Cognitive Centre.

Ross, R. R., Fabiano, E. A. & Ewles, C. D. (1988). Reasoning and rehabilitation. *International Journal of Offender Therapy and Comparative Criminology*, **32**, 29–35.

Ross, R. R., Fabiano, E. A. & Ross, B. (1989). *Reasoning and Rehabilitation: A Handbook for Teaching Cognitive Skills*. Ottawa: The Cognitive Centre.

Weaver, C. & Bensted, J. (1992). Thinking for a change. *Probation Journal*, **39**, 196–200.

CHAPTER 6

Creating a Culture of Change: A Case Study of a Car Crime Project in Belfast

Tim Chapman

Probation Board for Northern Ireland, Belfast, UK

This chapter describes Turas, an innovative community-based project designed to reduce the theft of cars for 'joyriding' in West Belfast. The importance is emphasized, in planning and implementing programmes, of an awareness of the social and cultural conditions in which young offenders live.

In comparison with crimes of violence and sexual assault, property offences in general and car crime in particular have received comparatively little attention from researchers. Given increasing public concern over joyriding, a number of studies have been carried out in recent years to investigate those factors that contribute to it. This work has been done in several parts of the United Kingdom. Although only a small number of studies have appeared, they can be categorized into two principal groups: (a) studies of young offenders involved in car crime, with a specific focus on their motivations for offending; (b) evaluations of specially developed 'motor projects' that have been established for working with those with convictions for autocrime.

Although numbers of car thefts have risen in recent years, the rate of increase has remained more or less proportionate to the number of vehicles on the road. Theft from cars has risen much more steeply. Webb and Laycock (1992) have subdivided car thefts into three main types: (a) theft

What Works: Reducing Reoffending—Guidelines from Research and Practice.
Edited by J. McGuire. © 1995 John Wiley & Sons Ltd.

for personal use, which includes joyriding and taking cars to make a journey home; (b) professional theft for financial gain; and (c) insurance fraud. The first accounted for 65% of car thefts in 1990.

Some studies of offender motivations have had the principal aim of collecting information that might be useful in situational crime prevention. Thus individuals are asked which models of car they prefer, how they gain entry and what types of security measures are most likely to deter them and so protect cars. Information has also been collected on the most likely times of day or week, and most favoured locations, for car theft (Gow & Peggrem, 1991; McCullough et al., 1990; McGillivray, 1993; Webb & Laycock, 1992). Interview evidence and police statistics have been combined to provide systematic evidence on patterning of offences.

By far the largest proportion of joyriders, in the region of 80%, are in the 13–17 years age range. At the time of the offence most (again more than 80%) are accompanied. In a survey conducted by Greater Manchester Probation Service (1992), 60% of the sample had a first conviction for car thefts at the age of 15 or earlier. At the peak age of offending (typically found to be 15 years), individuals may steal two or three cars per week. Most studies have detected a 'car crime career' which begins with vehicle taking as a form of excitement in which whole groups participate. Initial motivations are typically described as deriving from boredom and escaping from it, the 'buzz' or excitement, and peer pressure, though money may be important to some extent. The symbolic importance of cars and their general cultural significance are also almost certainly a factor (McCaghy et al., 1977). Findings are inconsistent on the degree to which offences are impulsive or planned in advance but the majority of studies suggest the latter. Individuals later progress to theft that is more likely to be undertaken for financial gain and may be organized. This career path has been described in some detail by Light and colleagues (1993) and by Spencer (1992). The numbers of young people continuing to offend gradually decreases at each stage along the continuum.

The findings of most previous work are in agreement on one further point. Most young people interviewed appeared not to think of the risks of being caught prior to committing offences; there was little evidence that they were 'deterred' by the thought of punishment (Light et al., 1993; McGillivray, 1993; Spencer, 1992).

Partly in recognition of this but also with the broader aim of responding more appropriately to the problem, many probation services and juvenile justice agencies have developed motor vehicle or 'responsible driving' projects. These often consist of an alternative activity (e.g. go-kart or 'banger' racing) coupled with some form of structured programme. For example, the '175 Project' based in Newport, Gwent, described by Gow and Peggrem (1991) contains four elements: go-kart racing; visits to a hospital to meet accident victims; discussions with the police; and counselling on offending behaviour. However, few programmes of this kind have been evaluated systematically. McGillivray (1993) cites figures from the National Association of Motor Projects, to the effect that while 80% of those sent to prison for car theft reoffended within two years, 70% of those who remained on a motor project for three months did not reoffend within the same time period. Spencer (1992), who examined vehicle theft on a single housing estate in Sunderland, found a decline in recorded vehicle crime in the period following the commencement of a number of community-based initiatives. The latter included the introduction of Community Youth Workers, diversionary programming, and allocation of a full-time police officer to a crime education role in the local secondary school.

Turning to work with young adult offenders, Davies (1993) provides statistics on those who completed motor projects run by West Midlands Probation Service. Their two-year reconviction rate of 54% compares favourably with that for those who did not complete their courses (100%), and with typical probation day centre reconviction rates of 63% quoted by Mair and Nee (1992). Only 27% of those completing projects were convicted of another motoring offence within two years while the comparable figure for non-completers was 61%.

All the research published so far is in agreement concerning the social backgrounds of those who 'joyride'. Light and colleagues (1993) summarize the ' . . . grim but familiar backdrop against which much young offending occurs: high truancy rates, low educational attainment, high unemployment, lack of leisure facilities and so on' (Light et al., 1993: 70). Any programme that is intended to meet the needs of this group must take careful account of these factors.

THE SUBVERSIVE NATURE OF 'WHAT WORKS' EVIDENCE

The government is clearly aware that the way it has chosen to manage the economy has social consequences. As unemployment increases and public expenditure is constrained, more and more people are excluded from playing an active role in mainstream society. The maintenance of the so-called 'underclass' is considered by many to be an inevitable feature of modern social conditions, and government social and criminal justice policies make no serious attempt to change this situation.

Governmental strategy is based upon blaming and stigmatizing offenders and then containing them so that they do not interfere with those who are benefiting from the economy. They are corralled within certain 'problem' estates, and those who cannot be so controlled within their beleaguered communities are detained in institutions. This is a profoundly pessimistic philosophy based on the assumption that 'nothing works'. Thus there has emerged the notion that there are inevitable or acceptable levels of unemployment, of poverty, of homelessness, of crime, and of imprisonment. I consider this to be also partly a product of the 'culture of management' that has become so powerful during the past decade.

In reaction to this culture, a corresponding culture of resistance has developed amongst its victims. Residents of run-down estates, women, black people and other oppressed minorities, including the elderly, experience a sense of crisis and develop strategies of resistance in order to survive. Both of these cultures militate against positive change and hope.

In this context the idea that some forms of working are effective is deeply subversive. It contradicts the process of demonization of offenders, which characterizes them as unable or unwilling to change. Instead it suggests that, however persistent or serious an individual's offending may be, he or she retains the potential to limit antisocial or self-destructive behaviour that can allow him or her to strive for a better life. I see this idea as attempting to restore hope through practical and realistic programmes; this is what is meant by 'creating a culture of change'.

Joyriders in West Belfast are prime targets for this process of 'demonization'. Their offending is prolific and persistent and very destructive and dangerous. It is also highly visible and as such appears defiant of, rather than deviant from, social norms. Most crime tends to be secretive and hidden. As a group these young people tend to justify and celebrate their offending and show little or no remorse or sense of responsibility.

Consequently, the government's reaction to car crimes has been predictable. It has urged manufacturers to be more security conscious. It has increased the severity of sentencing for aggravated car crimes. It has mounted an advertising campaign portraying joyriders as hyenas. This reaction typifies the manage, contain and scapegoat policy. I do not believe that anyone, including the government, believes that it will be effective.

The public are being cheated by this appearance of doing something. As long as they see nothing effective being done they will continue to demand retribution and punishment. The only way to change this is to develop practical programmes that have an impact on offending.

CREATING A CULTURE OF CHANGE

Creating the circumstances for change is much more difficult than managing or resisting a problem. It requires a clear, integrated and effectively managed programme comprising:

- A clear focus on what is to be changed
- A clear understanding of the obstacles to change
- A clear commitment to change (rather than merely management or containment)
- A clear programme of change that can be effectively delivered.

The Turas project does not pretend to have all these requirements neatly worked out. However, it is actively addressing them.

Targeting

The aim of Turas is to reduce car crime. With this in mind it has attempted to target all the serious joyriders in those estates in West Belfast that suffer most from joyriding. It has not done so through court orders or even through voluntary referrals from statutory and voluntary agencies. Both these processes reflect the vagaries and prejudices of the criminal justice system and its organizational priorities. As such they lend themselves to the 'management model' of the system. They do not accurately reflect the reality of the volume and nature of offending in a community nor directly respond to what is happening at any given time. Consequently they reinforce the alienation the community feel towards the state's attempts to protect it.

The project targets only the most serious joyriders, as we believe that an impact on them will have a greater immediate effect. This is based upon research that suggests that a small percentage of offenders are responsible for a large percentage of offending. This is certainly true of joyriding in that there are known 'local heroes' who steal the bulk of the cars, bring them into the estates, act as role models and even teach others to steal and drive. On our current target list there are 52 serious joyriders, seven of whom are young women, ranging in age from 15 to 23.

Social Obstacles to Change

West Belfast has suffered from a combination of sectarian discrimination over many years and the marginalization of the Northern Ireland economy throughout successive recessions. This has resulted in widespread poverty, unemployment as high as 80% in some estates, and inadequate public services. It is also the site on which some of the most violent conflict between the state and the republican movement has been fought.

This poverty and violence not only aggravate the conditions encouraging crime but also the community's reaction to crime and offenders. Around 50% of all cars stolen in Northern Ireland are recovered in West

Belfast. In 1991, 1159 stolen cars were recovered in the area targeted by Turas. Much delinquency goes unchecked due to ineffective policing. Politically motivated offences and the personal security of the police took precedence over normal policing. Many people do not see the RUC as a legitimate police force and consequently are reluctant to report crimes and cooperate with the police.

The community pressurizes paramilitary organizations to deal with offenders. The republican movement acted as a police force, court and agent of punishment. Sanctions involve a tariff of warnings, beatings, curfews, banishments and shootings. The effect of this system of punishment, like any other which stigmatizes, rejects and ostracizes, is to reinforce the processes through which offenders commit crime. It restricts their access to resources, marginalizes them and strengthens their dependence upon crime and other offenders.

Institutional Obstacles to Change

In recent years the Probation Service has been invited to assume a more central role in the criminal justice system. To achieve this status it has been required to improve its competence in management, adopt a more punitive approach in its work with offenders, and be better 'value for money'. There is little evidence to suggest that this strategy has served to increase the Service's status and influence. In any case, it is hardly likely to make the task of reducing offending any easier. The primary reason for this pessimistic perspective is that governmental policy on probation is aimed at managing problems within the system, and not at engaging in the outside realities such as those I have described in West Belfast and which apply equally to many other communities in which offenders and victims live.

The criminal justice system is generally in a state of crisis which has made it turn in on itself and exclude the authentic experience of the community, of victims and of offenders. Miscarriages of justice, racism, sexism, homophobia, and in Northern Ireland sectarianism, have all contributed to the isolation of the system from the community. Crime statistics rising in spite of overcrowded prisons, fear and distrust of the police, the courts and the probation service are all symptoms of this crisis and serve to highlight the ineffectiveness of the system.

The Probation Service is no exception. We are perceived by the public, and particularly by those most vulnerable and most in need of our help as bureaucratic, elitist and more concerned about our own status in the system than with justice. Too often we attempt to force offenders to become clients of a service whose methods are more relevant to the organization's values and needs than to their own.

Our 'clients' are selected fairly arbitrarily by an inefficient system and proceed through a decision-making process rife with prejudice before we receive them. Our programmes are designed to appeal to courts and to reduce custody rather than crime. We set about challenging an offence which they probably committed over six months previously and which they hardly remember, as they may have committed many more since. Our centre- or office-based work makes it very difficult to gain a real insight into the causes, the nature and volume of offending of a high-risk offender. The precedence we now give to achieving defined levels of contact lead us to rely increasingly on our authority and the threat of breach to engage with offenders rather than the quality and relevance of our work.

Personal Obstacles to Change

The ways in which the community and the criminal justice system attempt to manage joyriding, far from acting as a deterrent, actually create a sense of crisis for the joyrider from which he or she is inclined to run away. Attempts to stigmatize, ostracize and oppress reinforce the low self-esteem, the alienation and the fatalism which caused the offending in the first place. They also result in an elaborate subculture which both glamorizes joyriding and denies its negative consequences. What represents a social problem to the community is to the joyrider an individual solution to the personal problems of living in that community.

Like many adolescent activities, joyriding is part of the process of growing up or, more accurately, putting off growing up. Most joyriders are young men, who appear to have greater problems maturing than young women, particularly when there are no jobs and when popular male role models typically value aggression, competition and egocentric and sexist attitudes. They become stuck in a role in which valuable items of private property designed for adult use are treated as 'toys' to be played with until they are broken or boredom sets in.

Many people, including joyriders, often refer to the activity of driving stolen cars as an addiction. At first the project resisted this concept as it implied personal pathology and consequently a lack of personal respon sibility for rational decision-making. However, we have adopted some of the techniques that have proved effective in reducing addictive behaviour. We would describe joyriding as an activity on which young people can become highly dependent. Stealing cars provides excitement, status, identity, a sense of achievement and power, escape, attention and companionship, money and sex. Few activities offer so much immediate gratification to a young person growing up in a deprived and oppressive environment. Far from deterring joyriders, a punitive response by the community and the state reinforces this dependency by further reducing the resources available to the offender.

To summarize, there are three 'systems' in a state of permanent and deepening crisis: the communities in which offenders reside and often commit their offences; the criminal justice system; and the offenders themselves as individuals. Each of these systems is doing its best to manage its own crisis and to resist threats to its survival. The difficulty is that each system's strategy for survival represents a threat to the others, and is then detached from the realities faced by them.

Commitment to Change

Turas was set up to attempt to get closer to the reality of joyriding and to intervene actively in the tensions between these three systems. It is jointly managed by the Probation Board for Northern Ireland and the West Belfast Parents and Youth Support Group, a local community group. The team is led by a senior probation officer and made up of two probation officers and five community youth workers. One of the workers is an ex-joyrider and another is the mother of a joyrider. There are five men and three women in the team. Five of the team come from West Belfast and three are from the protestant tradition. None is black.

The workers thus have one foot in the criminal justice system and one foot in the community network. In West Belfast, as in other deprived and oppressed communities there is a distance or credibility gap between these two systems. To straddle them is uncomfortable and at times painful. At times when they are actively in conflict over issues of justice, of resources or of a political nature, it can be a very vulnerable space in which to work. And as the casualties of this conflict fall around the staff team, it can become very distressing. Yet it is the tension within this space that can generate the dynamics of change and creativity.

Programme of Change

The programme of change that Turas is using is still evolving. It attempts to be integrated and progressive. *Turas* is the Irish word for journey. The programme emphasizes movement and stages in change. In this the staff group have been influenced by work in the field of addictions (Miller, 1983; Miller & Rollnick, 1992).

The activity programme is shown in Table 6.1. The first task is to make contact with identified joyriders. This outreach work is done through home visits, street-corner work, prison visits and so on. Statutory authority is not employed. Once contact has been made, individuals are invited to participate in activities organized at times when they are most likely to offend. The aim at this point is directly to reduce

Table 6.1. The Turas programme.

Programme structure	Process of change	Method

Outreach
• To identify high-risk joyriders
• To make contact with them and invite them to participate
• To engaged them in late-night activities
	Precontemplation
	• Developing the conditions, awareness and relationships necessary for change
	• Self-directed groupwork in specific locations:
	
	Key themes
	• Social action and cooperation
	• Empowerment
	• Responsiveness to the community
		• Community partnerships
		• Outreach contact
		  1. Twinbrook/Poleglass
		  2. Lenadoon/Andersonstown
		  3. Westrock
		  4. Lower Falls
		• Young Women's groups
		• Crisis management
		• Parents' support groups
		• Facing Up to Car Crime course
		• Problem Solving course
		• Personal Development Plan (Duke of Edinburgh/Endeavour Award Scheme)

Personal planning • To develop a plan for each participant leading away from joyriding	**Contemplation/determination** • Helping participants think about change and make choices on how they can change *Key themes* • Vulnerability • Empathy • Thinking/choice	

Core programmes
• To facilitate and maintain personal change
	Action/maintenance
	• Supporting the individual's efforts to change
	
	Key themes
	• Challenge
	• Personal effort and responsibility
	• Development of skills
	• Achievement
	• Service and caring for others
	• Public recognition
		• Football—senior
		          —junior
		• Wheels—go-karting
		       —mechanics
		       —driving lessons
		       —scrambling
		• Outdoor pursuits
		• Creative—art
		        —drama
		        —video
		• Volunteer training

opportunities to offend and to begin to undermine the patterns that make offending routine.

Activities need to be very attractive and to offer choice. We organize go-karting from midnight to 3.00 a.m. on Friday nights. We invite joyriders to a restaurant late at night. We stand with them at the street corner as they drink. We have a drop-in centre which stays open every Sunday night until 2.00 a.m.

When we first encounter them, most joyriders have no intention of changing. They are at the 'precontemplative stage' of change. We do not attempt to challenge their offending directly at this stage. We are simply developing trust, breaking down barriers to communication and getting to know our participants. We are trying to develop within them some kind of identification with Turas and to start them thinking that change might be possible.

The next stage is to involve the participant in thinking seriously about their offending. This is done through a formal course, 'Facing up to Car Crime'. This is aimed at those at the contemplative stage and is based upon cognitive skills such as self-awareness, taking a social perspective, anticipating consequences and empathy. On completion they are invited to construct a personal development plan reinforcing their decision to reduce their offending.

As they begin to think that there might be a viable alternative to joyriding, we offer a range of programmes designed both to divert them from crime and to encourage them to view themselves differently. We have a football team which meets three times a week to train and compete. It also travels to England and Scotland to watch matches. Others are involved in the Duke of Edinburgh Award scheme, regularly going on outdoor expeditions. A women's group meets once a week. Our creative programme has proved most effective at changing self-image and increasing self-esteem. Participants have mounted a photographic exhibition, devised a drama and performed it in public and painted a mural on the Falls Road. We also run car mechanics' courses and help participants through their driving tests. In these ways participants are actively engaged in activities leading them away from crime.

As participants progress out of offending we offer training for voluntary work and to increase their job prospects. Two of our participants are now working with the project under a government work experience scheme. Three others are volunteers. We organize a preventive programme for younger participants using ex-joyriders as supervisers.

The overall aim is help individuals to move through the stages of change significantly more quickly than they would have done if left to their own devices. The focus is on the efforts and achievements of the participants rather than those of the workers. In the process, the participants are developing a different image of themselves, increasing their sense of personal responsibility and respect for themselves and others and learning that there are alternatives to crime. Essentially the programme is about growing up, a task that society makes increasingly difficult, particularly for young men.

Evaluation of Change

Turas has been evaluated by an independent research organization (Marks & Cross, 1992). The project also monitors its performance on a monthly basis. As a result the following conclusions can be drawn.

1. The 'outreach' approach of targeting serious offenders had the following outcomes:
    *   58 high-risk joyriders were identified
    *   25% reported that they had regularly been in over 20 stolen cars per month
    *   68% reported involvement in over six stolen cars per month
    *   The team were consistently in contact with over 90% of all identified joyriders every month.
2. It is possible to engage serious offenders in constructive activities leading away from crime on a voluntary contract:
    *   The team consistently engaged over 60% of identified joyriders in programmes run late at night and at the weekends
    *   Examples of the many achievements by participants include six Duke of Edinburgh silver awards, a drama production that has been performed over 20 times, five ex-joyriders being accredited as volunteers to work towards preventing others from joyriding
    *   Since the project started over 70 joyriders have been engaged in the programme. Over 30 of these have left because they had stopped stealing cars. We continue to work with the rest until they too have stopped.
3. Such a programme can demonstrate an impact on the overall rates of offending in the target areas:
    *   According to police statistics the incidence of car theft increased by 4% in the targeted areas in the first year of operations. Reassuringly, the statistics increased by 57% in the neighbouring police subdivision in the same time
    *   Recent statistics show around 30% reduction in the incidence of joyriding when we organize the late-night go-karting.

Turas has, then, a contribution to make to the overall reduction of joyriding in the community, but it obviously cannot provide a solution on its own. To reduce joyriding and other crimes in deprived communities to manageable levels requires the will of government to change policies that deprive communities of the resources, opportunities and power that they need to help all their young men to mature into responsible citizens.

REFERENCES

Davies, H. (1993). *Evaluation of Motor Offender Projects*. Birmingham: West Midlands Probation Service.

Gow, J. & Peggrem, A. (1991). *Car Crime Culture? A Study of Motor Vehicle Theft by Juveniles*. Cardiff: Barnardo's.

Greater Manchester Probation Service (1992). *Car Crime Survey*. Manchester: GMPS.

Light, R., Nee, C. & Ingham, H. (1993). *Car Theft: The Offender's Perspective*. Home Office Research Study 130. London: HMSO.

Mair, G. & Nee, C. (1992). Day Centre reconviction rates. *British Journal of Criminology*, **32**, 329–339.

Marks, J. & Cross, G. (1992). *An Evaluation of the Turas Project*. Belfast: The Extern Organisation.

McCaghy, G., Giordano, P. & Henson, T. (1977). Auto theft: offender and offense characteristics. *Criminology*, **15**, 367–385.

McCullough, D., Schmidt, T. & Lockhart, B. (1990). *Car Theft in Northern Ireland: Recent Studies on a Persistent Problem*. CIRAC Paper No. 2. Belfast: The Extern Organisation.

McGillivray, M. (1993). *Putting the Brakes on Car Crime: A Local Study of Auto-related Crime among Young People*. London and Cardiff: The Children's Society and Mid Glamorgan Social Services Department.

Miller, W. R. (1983). Motivational interviewing with problem drinkers. *Behavioural Psychotherapy*, **11**, 147–172.

Miller, W. R. & Rollnick, S. (1992). *Motivational Interviewing: Preparing People to Change Addictive Behavior*. New York: Guilford Press.

Spencer, E. (1992). *Car Crime and Young People on a Sunderland Housing Estate*. Police Research Group, Crime Prevention Unit Series, Paper No. 40. London: Home Office.

Webb, B. & Laycock, G. (1992). *Tackling Car Crime: The Nature and Extent of the Problem*. Crime Prevention Unit Paper 32. London: Home Office.

CHAPTER 7

Teaching Self-risk Management to Violent Offenders

Jack Bush

Correctional Treatment Associates, Barre, Vermont, USA

CRIMINAL VIOLENCE

Criminal violence is not associated with any single disease or disorder. It does not have a single cause and it cannot be cured with any single treatment. Some dangerously violent people use violence frequently, others very rarely. Some are mentally ill. Others show no sign of mental or emotional disturbance. Many have experienced abuse themselves as children, but others have grown up under apparently normal and healthy circumstances.

Within this diversity there are certain generalizations that have particular relevance for treatment:

1. *Criminal violence is not an isolated and distinct form of criminal behaviour.* Broadly speaking, criminals are characterized more by the diversity of their criminal conduct than by their specialization. In one large study of offenders who reoffended while on parole, those who had been originally convicted of property crimes were just as likely to reoffend with a violent offence as were those who had originally ben convicted of violent crimes. (Beck, 1987).

2. *Violence is a learned behaviour* (Bandura, 1973; Goldstein, 1988). Violent people learn to use violence as a coping response to a wide

What Works: Reducing Reoffending—Guidelines from Research and Practice.
Edited by J. McGuire. © 1995 John Wiley & Sons Ltd.

range of stressful experiences. It is often their most familiar and, from their point of view, most effective means of responding to threatening or stressful circumstances. They may have learned to use violence or the threat of violence as a coping response to a whole spectrum of life's stresses and challenges. Violence may be experienced as the only reliable means of experiencing their own power and efficacy. Violence for these people is rewarding. Non-violence is not.

3. *Patterns of violence and criminal behaviour are embedded in habits of thinking* (Andrews, 1990). Attitudes, beliefs and thinking patterns in the minds of violent individuals support and promote their violent behaviour. Violent people may truly believe, for instance, that if they abandon violence the world will overwhelm them. They may form the habit of thinking of themselves as victims. They may nurture underlying feelings of righteous anger and resentment toward the world. They may believe that they are entitled to hurt others because of the hurt they have suffered. These kinds of attitudes, beliefs and thinking patterns can make violence seem to be a normal, justified and necessary behaviour.

Thoughts and Actions

The Cognitive Self Change programme in Vermont aims to change violent behaviour by targeting the attitudes, beliefs and thinking patterns that support that behaviour. The programme does not assume that violent offenders are emotionally ill, and they are not treated as patients. Our premise is that, with few exceptions, violent offenders commit crimes and acts of violence because they want to. We focus our attention on those attitudes, beliefs and automatic habits of thinking that make them want to. We do not try to force them to change, but we challenge them to change themselves.

The Cognitive Self Change programme is a specifically correctional intervention. Authority, limits and accountability are fundamental to the programme. Groups are delivered by prison staff (uniformed officers and caseworkers) and parole officers, in addition to a limited number of contracted treatment specialists. The combination of authority with treatment is a critical element of programme strategy. While we are setting limits and exercising authority, we are also communicating to offenders that we respect their right and their ability to control their own lives. Our objective is to replace the adversarial relationship between authority and offender—'us versus them'—with a relationship of cooperation.

Offenders are taught how to control their own risk to reoffend by controlling the attitudes, beliefs, and automatic thinking patterns that *put* them at risk to reoffend. Offenders in the programme become part of their own 'supervision team'. Decisions involving each offender's release and level of supervision are based on a combination of objective risk factors (e.g. severity and extent of offence history) and the offender's mastery of the methods of cognitive self-change.

The programme does not demand that offenders comply their thinking to any specified norm. (This is both impossible and undesirable: impossible, because we have no access to how offenders think other than what they tell us, undesirable because coerced compliance is not real or lasting change.) Instead, we teach offenders to observe their own thinking, to recognize the consequences of that thinking, and to learn specific skills for controlling that thinking. In place of automatic patterns of thinking and acting, offenders learn to be aware of their thinking and to recognize that they can control it. They learn that how they think has a powerful influence on how they act. They learn that their thoughts are in fact also behaviours, and that (like physical behaviours) they can be brought under their conscious control. We teach them the ability to control their own lives by taking control of the cognitive foundations of their lives. Ultimately, we challenge them to choose what their lives will be.

The programme is presented in three phases. Phase I and Phase II are presented in prison. Phase III takes place in the community following release from prison.

Phase I comprises the introduction and orientation to the programme. Offenders learn the basic concepts of cognitive change and learn specific skills for observing and reporting the content of their thinking. We teach a technique that we call 'thinking reports', based on the process of phenomenological reporting described by Yochelson and Samenow in *The Criminal Personality* (1976). Phase I groups meet twice a week for 8 to 10 weeks.

Phase II is devoted to three primary tasks. Each offender must: (1) identify the patterns of thinking that have led him or here to perform acts of crime and violence in the past and that pose a risk of such behaviours in the future; (2) learn specific skills for intervening in and controlling these patterns of thinking; and (3) summarize these patterns and interventions in the form of a plan for controlling their high-risk thinking in the community. This becomes his or her 'relapse prevention plan' (Marlatt & Gordon, 1985). Groups meet two to four times a week for at least 4 months but no longer than 2 years.

In Phase III offenders apply their relapse prevention plans in the community. Offenders describe the situations they encounter and their thoughts in response to those situations. Most importantly, they report and evaluate their efforts to control that thinking. Phase III groups meet twice a week for 1 year.

TARGETING COGNITIVE BEHAVIOUR

Treatment groups begin with an offender writing his or her 'thinking report' on a blackboard or flip-chart. The report begins with a brief description of a situation, and proceeds to list every thought they can remember having during that situation. The report is strictly objective, without interpretations, justifications, or censorship. They report their feelings along with their thoughts. The feelings they report often reveal the basic meaning of the experience and the 'logic' of their thinking.

One offender with a long history of minor assaults had been given an early release from prison. Two weeks after his release, he was clearly at risk of violating his conditions. Because of his special early release status, these conditions were very strict and specific. His daily schedule and list of approved activities were specified on a weekly 'pass sheet'. He had been pushing the limits of these conditions without doing anything that constituted a major or overt violation. He was frequently a few minutes late to appointments, he took circuitous routes to and from work, and would casually meet and converse with individuals with whom he was not approved to socialize.

We asked him to report his thinking about his release conditions and his behaviours that put him at risk of being in violation of his conditions. He presented this report:

My thoughts:

>   I know that if I do these things I will be going back to jail.
>
>   It's really starting to get to me.
>
>   I feel locked up in my own apartment.
>
>   I really resent this.
>
>   I shouldn't have to follow these rules.
>
>   Maybe it would be better to just go back to jail and get my sentence over with.
>
>   I feel like I'm not in charge of my life anymore.
>
>   I can't stand it.

My feelings:

>   uncomfortable, angry, controlled, threatened.

After an offender presents a thinking report, they and the other group members and the staff facilitator review the report to find the key elements of thinking and feeling that increase the risk of reoffending. The group's attitude is objective, not condemning or defensive. The atmosphere is one of solving a puzzle. At its best the group process feels like an exciting game. Everyone is an equal participant.

It is important that the whole group understand and accept this task. It is all too easy to fall into unproductive debates about the 'right and wrong' of situations, or to 'problem solve' the situation with practical advice about 'what he or she could or should have done'. As important as such discussions may be, they are clearly defined as outside the scope of the group's primary task—to discover the elements of thinking that increase this individual's risk to offend.

We begin by reviewing all the reported thoughts and feelings and assuring ourselves that we understand just what this person was experiencing. We may ask for more information or clarification. The group's attitude remains objective and descriptive. For example, this client was asked to explain what he meant by 'feeling threatened'. He explained this as feeling 'belittled and discounted', as if he was being told he was worthless and did not count.

In situations that involve a specific 'trigger event', we ask clients to describe in detail their very first thoughts and feelings after the event occurred. This focuses their (and our) attention on the concrete details of the experience, and starts us on the process of tracking the development of their thinking leading to increased risk. In this group we focused on the 'trigger event' of the client picking up his pass sheet at the parole office. He remembered reading these conditions while standing at the front desk at the parole office.

He described his very first reaction as 'feeling uncomfortable'. The next thing he remembered was thinking about how miserable his situation was. He felt trapped. Then he started thinking about how unfair it was. As he described the sequence of his thoughts and feelings, it began to be clear how each part of his experience led to the next. His sense of discomfort became a sense of injustice, which led in turn to righteous rage, entitlement, and eventually to the thought that he absolutely had to defy these rules if he was going to preserve any sense of dignity or self-worth. At this point and in his mind, offence behaviour was not only permissible, it was imperative.

The group identifies each piece of 'subjective logic' and attempts to see the connections between the pieces. We use a circle diagram to display the key steps of the overall cognitive–emotional process. This thinking report resulted in a diagram such as Figure 7.1.

This kind of diagram is the typical outcome of a thinking report group. The diagram displays how each step of thought and feeling gives rise to the next in an escalating logic of criminal behaviour.

This offender will need to present a series of thinking reports to confirm or disconfirm the steps displayed in this circle diagram. Has his past violent

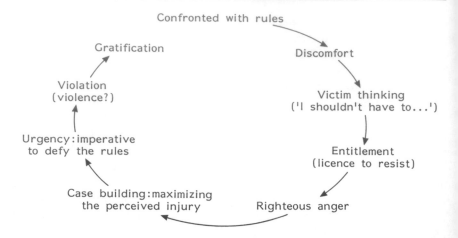

Figure 7.1. Circle diagram to show key steps of cognitive-emotional process leading to rule violation.

behaviour resulted from the same 'subjective logic' that we see here? Our assessment of the risk in his thinking depends exclusively on uncovering the historical connections between his thoughts and his acts of crime and violence.

There is often just one core pattern behind hundreds of criminal acts. Most serious criminals have a small set of cognitive habits that define their orientation toward life, and their licence to commit crime. But we never presuppose to know an offender's way of thinking, or to know in advance the risk in that thinking. Our approach is strictly empirical. Offenders report their experiences and we examine them to detect whatever patterns they reveal. Only when a pattern is clearly displayed as posing a real risk of offence behaviour do we take it up as a target for intervention and change.

The offender in this example practiced an essentially similar pattern of thinking and feeling whenever his sense of pride was challenged—and his sense of pride was challenged whenever his desires of the moment were denied. Sometimes the result was a violent assault. At other times, he just 'broke the rules'.

Like many offenders, this man's cognitive patterns were intimately involved with his experience of self-worth (Corson, 1989). They rest on a simple and primitive logic: first, he interprets constraints and limits on his freedom as insults to his autonomy. He takes an accusatory stance toward those he deems responsible. In so doing, he converts his experience of being victimized into licence to do whatever he pleases, without regard to rules or injury to others. He feeds this sense of licence by dwelling on the perceived injustice and working up feelings of righteous indignation and rage. Finally, his acts of defiance or violence provide powerful feelings of gratification: 'When I break the rules, I feel like I'm back in charge of my own life'.

His crimes and assaults are not always direct reactions to a specific encounter with authority. His perception of authority and rules has become a pervasive and permanent aspect of his orientation toward life. Authority is a standing threat. Rule breaking is a standing gratification. When he assaulted someone, the feelings of righteousness, power and fulfilment were intoxicating. In both kinds of cases (violent or merely criminal), self-gratification is achieved through power and domination, i.e. through essentially antisocial means. It is only because these means are antisocial that they work. Criminality provides his primary source of self-worth.

This is an 'antisocial logic' common to many offenders. It is based on thinking of oneself as a victim, taking an accusatory stance toward whoever is responsible, and giving oneself licence to do as one pleases. The elements of this logic mutually support each other, i.e. because he is victimized, the offender has the right to act however he pleases, and because he grants himself the licence to do as he pleases, any interference is by definition unfair and victimizing. In this dreadful logic, punishment and the imposition of social controls have the consequence of validating the offender's licence to break the law. The more punitive we are, the more he feels entitled to defy our authority (Figure 7.2).

This way of thinking effectively eliminates any concern for the rights or feelings of other people. One offender in the programme had many of the characteristics of the classic psychopath. He said he had absolutely no remorse for any of his crimes, which included many acts of brutal violence. (In one report he had described torturing two victims—a man and his wife—by squeezing their fingers with pliers until their skin burst. 'But I honestly don't feel bad about that', he said.) We asked this man if there was ever in his life a situation in which he felt bad for something he had done. At first he said no, but then we asked him if he had ever hurt his mother's feelings by doing something wrong. (He had described

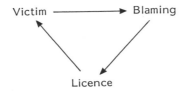

Figure 7.2. Circular logic of victimization and licence.

his mother as a good and kind and honest woman.) He gave this report of a time when he was less than 8 years old:

> I don't remember what I had done but I remember my mother crying. She was upset over something I had done. I felt bad because she was crying. I felt guilty. Then I thought, 'Why is she making me feel this way? What right has she got to make me feel bad?' Then I felt better.

Several members of the treatment group described similar memories of thinking of themselves as victims in order to escape the pangs of conscience. They had discovered a simple cognitive act that eventually covered a multitude of sins.

These cognitive patterns of licence, accusation and being a victim are clearly learned behaviours. In these examples, the particular cognitive behaviour was reinforced by the relief it provided from feelings of guilt and the discomforts of responsibility. They learned to use these patterns whenever they were made to feel uncomfortable by practically any situation, and these same patterns soon came to provide the positive reinforcement of personal power and the absolute freedom to do as they pleased. The patterns eventually dominated their lives.

The rewards of criminal behaviour reinforce not just the criminal behaviour itself, but the cognitive behaviour that provides the meaning and motive for that criminal behaviour. It is the offender's way of thinking that makes criminal behaviour rewarding. The offenders described above have learned to think of themselves as victims in almost every situation in which their own immediate gratification is denied. They feel—and think and truly believe—that they are entitled to whatever would make them feel good. This belief is not the product of conscious reflection, but is an habitual attitude and mind-set. They are quick to take personal offence and quick to use their well learned patterns of cognition, feeling and behaviour to redress the perceived injury, and they hold on to these habits of thinking as if their lives depended on them. The tragic irony is that, in the subjective domain of their experience of self, they are right.

The strategy of cognitive self change is to control the cognitive patterns that make crime and violence rewarding. We target those cognitive behaviours that determine the meanings and the 'reinforcement values' of their social behaviours. The clients' first task is to identify these cognitive patterns, and to recognize them as their own. Their next task is to learn how to control them. We do not try to do this for them by manipulating their rewards and punishments. They are responsible for their own motivation. We challenge them to take their reinforcers into their own conscious control, i.e. to teach themselves ways of thinking that make crime and violence aversive and responsible behaviour rewarding. We attempt to make them as conscious as possible of their own control over their own life, and we challenge them to choose.

INTERVENTIONS FOR CHANGE

We teach techniques for controlling thinking only after the patterns have been clearly identified and their scope and consequences are vividly clear in the mind of the offender. We want the offenders to see that their habitual way of thinking is part of their own behaviour—i.e. it is something they do, that they are responsible for doing, and that they can do differently. This self-awareness is the foundation of their motivation to change.

Offenders keep individual daily journals in which they track each and every occurrence of their high-risk thinking. Our objective is so to sensitize them to these patterns that they cannot occur without their conscious awareness. Then we teach simple thought-stopping techniques. These are brief pieces of self–self talk that interrupt the train of thoughts and make the offender aware of his or her ability to control those thoughts. An example might be the phrase, 'Here I go again, feeling victimized'. Offenders might practise saying these words to themselves every time they notice the slightest trace of victim stance thinking. They would record these instances in their daily journals. We want these patterns of thinking to move from being automatic habits to being conscious and deliberate actions.

We do not tell the offenders how they are supposed to think. We challenge them to find their own alternative ways of thinking. Each offender is required to devise his or her own methods for interrupting their key patterns and for imposing new direction to their thinking. This project includes identifying beliefs and general attitudes that promote their criminality and violence, and defining alternative beliefs and attitudes that do not put them at such risk. We do not require that they believe what we think they should believe. (It would be ludicrous to make the attempt.) We do require that they become conscious of their own cognitive behaviour and acquire the ability to control it.

At this stage of the process we teach pro-social thinking skills, e.g. problem solving, negotiation, expressing emotions, seeing another person's point of view. We use the skill-training methods developed by Arnold Goldstein (Goldstein, 1988; Goldstein and Glick, 1987). In our longer-term institutions we present the programme of cognitive skill training developed by Bob Ross and Elizabeth Fabiano, called Reasoning and Rehabilitation (Ross et al., 1986). These programmes teach pro-social thinking as a set of discrete cognitive–behavioural skills. Such skills are the ideal alternatives to the antisocial patterns exposed in the thinking report process.

In place of the habitual thinking that puts offenders at risk of crime or violence, they can practise the skills of pro-social thinking. Their acquired sensitivity to their old patterns of thinking provides the cues for them to apply the new cognitive skills.

The tasks assigned to the offender are kept simple and concrete. The larger issues of motivation, self-worth and self-identity are reduced to a series of practical tasks. Our communication with offenders is always focused on concrete details of thinking, feeling and behaviour, and on concrete tasks they can easily understand and perform. Offenders complete Phase II of the programme by writing a 'relapse prevention plan' that describes their key thinking patterns and the cognitive actions they have learned for controlling them. Each target pattern is identified with a specific method for interrupting that pattern (e.g. self talk), and an alternative way of thinking (e.g. a new cognitive skill).

Cognitive self-change is a form of 'cognitive restructuring'. It can be described equally well (though less fashionably) as 'volitional restructuring'. We promote change by challenging the offender to choose.

COMMUNICATING LIMITS AND AUTHORITY

The programme is not voluntary. Violent offenders in Vermont must complete the first two phases of the programme in order to be considered for parole. They are then required to complete Phase III in the community as a condition of their release. (Earlier versions of the programme were voluntary. This avoided the resentment that comes from being forced to participate, and many prisoners volunteered to take the programme. Unfortunately, they tended to lose this motivation when they were released from prison. When the community phase of the programme was not required as a condition of parole, offenders tended to lose their determination to keep up the daily grind of maintaining their self-awareness.)

The attempt to force offenders to change triggers automatic resistance to change. Offenders are quick to interpret external control as an attempt to deny them the power of self determination—the basic right to be who they are. It is a perfectly human kind of response. The trouble is, of course, that many offenders experience assaults against their integrity when most of us would simply experience a manageable level of discomfort.

Offenders jealously guard their attitudes, beliefs and ways of thinking.

> Everything can be taken from a man but one thing: the last of the human freedoms—to choose one's attitudes in any given set of circumstances, to choose one's own way. (Victor Frankl, quoted in Ross & Fabiano, 1985).

With prisoners, the power to control their own thoughts is often their last refuge of self-determination. Their efforts to protect that power of self-determination generates (among other things) the prison culture of resentment and defiance of authority.

The process of cognitive self examination begins to instil motivation for self-change. It does this by challenging each offender to make conscious choices, not only about his or her behaviour but about the attitudes and thinking patterns that underlie it. They begin to view change, not as submission to external control, but as an act of self-determination.

We nurture that experience of self-determination. The offender's resistance to external control is triggered every time he or she encounters our authority. We attempt to convert these inevitable encounters with authority into experiences of choice and self-determination. Staff are trained to make offenders make a conscious and deliberate decision every time we exercise our authority over their behaviour. This is practised as a communication skill intrinsic to our exercise of authority. Our ultimate objective is to create a relationship of cooperation with each offender based on responsible behaviour and mutual respect.

Our strategy is to combine the exercise of authority with respect for the offender's right to make his or her own decisions. The guiding principle is that it is possible to respect a person's right to make their own decisions without thereby granting them the right to break the law. Our message is: 'You have the right and the power to direct your own life, but that is not a licence to do as you please'. And the other side of the coin: 'You do not have the right to break the rules, but we respect your right to make your own choices'.

Every situation that calls for limit setting is taken as an opportunity to convey these meanings. We never threaten. We do clearly define limits and the consequences of breaking those limits. Rules and limits are presented as the conditions of the offender's participation in the social group. The rules of the programme are presented as the conditions of participation in the programme. The rules of an individual's supervision status are presented as the conditions of his or her present level of freedom. The rules of society are presented as the conditions of participation as a free person in society. Instead of threatening we take the time to define a choice. We convey to the offenders that they have the sole control over how they are going to respond to these conditions: 'These are the conditions of participation. You must now decide how you will respond to them'.

Conveying this message is not a mere courtesy. Our strategy is not merely to offer a choice, but to force one. We attempt to make offenders make conscious and deliberate decisions each and every time they encounter our authority. It is a message intrinsic to the exercise of authority in general, and not just within a treatment programme. It is as applicable when we apply physical force as it is when we 'just talk'. (Klugiewicz, 1990).

Staff are trained by role playing realistic situations in which limits must be set and consequences imposed. Staff play the parts of offenders, as well as their own roles of authority. Choice of words, tone of voice, time, place and situation all affect the message heard by the offender. Each situation is played and replayed until everyone is satisfied that the essential dual message is effectively conveyed:

1. These are the limits and conditions of your participation.
2. You have the control and the choice over how you are going to respond to those conditions.

The advantages of getting offenders to make conscious choices are clear and immediate. Deliberate action takes the place of blind reaction. Offenders are forced to take a degree of responsibility in situations where they would otherwise simply feel victimized. We avoid the deepest level of interpersonal conflict—i.e. conflict based on their perception that we are trying to deny them their most basic experience of self-determination. Most important, the strategy promotes mutual respect and the conditions of genuine cooperation between 'us' and 'them'.

RISK MANAGEMENT: AN INTEGRATED STRATEGY

The Cognitive Self Change programme is just one element of a broader strategy of correctional supervision delivered by the Vermont Department of Corrections. Supervision on parole is provided by a team composed of the parole officer, the staff who deliver the programme and the offender. The offender does not take part in all discussions or all the decisions made by this team, but is expected to provide meaningful input in decisions affecting their level of supervision and their freedom.

The supervision team is responsible for monitoring and evaluating the offender's risk to reoffend and taking action to minimize that risk. External controls such as surveillance, alcohol and drug testing, and reincarceration are balanced against the internal risk controls practised by the offender.

An offender may begin to show small signs of irresponsibility without actually breaking the law or violating the conditions of parole. They may be late to a series of appointments, for instance, as in the example described above. The principles of relapse prevention demand that this risk be controlled early, before it becomes a full-fledged relapse into criminal behaviour. The offender's behaviour is reviewed by the supervision team and considered together with all other information affecting the offender's risk to reoffend. This includes their participation in the programme. Is the offender reporting their thinking connected with these high-risk behaviours in their Phase III group? Are they identifying their own high-risk thinking patterns? Are they applying the cognitive interventions and controls defined in their relapse prevention plan? The offender will be asked to provide their own input to the supervision team. How does the offender interpret his or her own risk behaviour? Does he or she minimize the seriousness of such behaviour? Do they accept appropriate responsibility? All of these factors are taken into account by the supervision team in assessing the offender's risk and planning a response to that risk. External controls are applied in inverse proportion to the internal controls exercised by the offender.

When an offender breaks a law or violates the conditions of parole, the principles of risk management continue to be applied. Offence behaviours are measured in conjunction with the offender's own efforts at self-risk management. If offenders are reincarcerated, they are expected to continuo participating in the programme while back in prison. They will be expected to learn from the experience of their failures. They will be required to do new thinking reports on their violation behaviours and the circumstances that led up to them. They will design new interventions and new controls for these thinking patterns. They will be required to demonstrate that these new controls hold genuine promise of being effective by putting them into practice before they are released, and making them work. The offender remains in a position to affect the degree of external control imposed on them. If at any point the offender chooses to drop out of the programme, the supervision team is left with the need to control their risk to reoffend by the application of external controls alone. These external controls include maximum periods of incarceration and the highest levels of surveillance and supervision on probation or parole.

The Vermont Department of Corrections is in the process of implementing this comprehensive system of risk management. The power of the programme to effect change will depend ultimately on our ability to implement this broader strategy. The Department of Corrections also provides specialized programmes for sexual offenders and for substance abuse. The techniques of treatment vary, but the strategy of risk management is universal. Correctional treatment is conceived not as an alternative to correctional control, but as an intrinsic part of mainstream correctional practice.

This concept entails radical changes from our traditional thinking. Instead of a dichotomy and competition between 'treatment' and 'control' approaches to managing offender risk, we are developing an integrated strategy that combines elements of both and transforms the nature of each. The project is described by the Commissioner of the Vermont Department of Corrections, John Gorczyk, as 'creating a behavioural science of corrections'.

A BRIEF LOOK AT OUTCOME

The Cognitive Self Change programme began in 1988 in one long-term prison at St Albans, Vermont. It has since expanded to six institutions and eight probation and parole offices. While we have planned for outcome evaluation since the beginning, we have not constrained the delivery of the programme to meet the conditions of rigorous experimental design. The programme was originally voluntary, meaning that offenders did not earn automatic credit toward their release by taking the programme and were not denied release for failing to take it. In 1991 this policy was changed so that offenders convicted of violent offences must now partic- ipate in the programme in order to earn recommendation for parole. The programme has also evolved in other details of its delivery, though not in its basic methods or theory.

In our largest outcome study, we are tracking all the offenders who were incarcerated at the St Albans institution since the programme began in 1988 (Henning, 1994). The recidivism of offenders who participated in the programme is compared with the recidivism of offenders who did not. The programme group and the non-programme group are compared on various characteristics previously associated with recidivism. Table 7.1 and Figure 7.3 report recidivism as defined by new accusations, meaning that recidivists have been accused but not necessarily convicted of violating the conditions of their parole or committing a new crime.

At the time of writing the data are promising but are not final or conclu- sive. The differences in rates of recidivism between the programme and non-programme groups are statistically significant, and are of an order of magnitude that we are led to expect based on the results of other well

Table 7.1. Recidivism rates as a function of participation in the programme.

Length of time on (months)	New accusations (%) after (years)		
	1	2	3
7+	25.0	42.1	45.5
	($n = 24$)	($n = 19$)	($n = 11$)
1–6	53.9	66.7	80.0
	($n = 13$)	($n = 9$)	($n = 5$)
0	49.2	70.8	76.7
	($n = 118$)	($n = 96$)	($n = 73$)

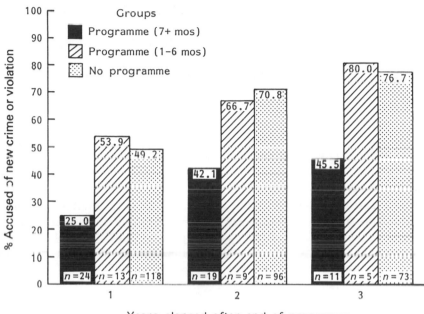

Figure 7.3. New accusations by fixed time samples.

designed and well implemented treatment programmes. The programme and non-programme groups are comparable in their offence histories. The programme group had committed slightly more serious past offences. The programme group was slightly older than the non-programme group, and this may be influencing recidivism in the same direction as programme participation.

Of those offenders who were convicted of (and not merely charged with) new crimes after release, 18% of the convictions for the non-programme group were for violent crimes against persons. None of the convictions for the programme group were for violent crimes.

Note that offenders with less than 6 months in the programme fare no better than those with no time in the programme. This is consistent with the 'drop out' phenomena reported in other correctional outcome studies and may reflect a screening effect that eliminates some of the most defiant and resistant (and highest risk) offenders from the programme before they complete it. At the same time, it should be noted that offenders who dropped out for reasons of non-compliance or their own choice form a relatively small proportion of total drop-outs: 70% of programme drop-outs were due to administrative transfer to another institution; 17% were removed by staff for lack of performance; 9% were because the offender chose to quit. Note too that the recidivism rates are quite high for all the reported categories. This is consistent with the fact that the St. Albans institution houses the most serious and highest risk offender population in Vermont.

The comprehensive system of risk management that integrates treatment with external control is just beginning to be implemented by the Vermont Department of Corrections. The effects of that system are not reflected in these data. The majority of offenders in this study were transferred to other institutions, for periods of time ranging from a few weeks to several years before their eventual release to the community. Most of them did not take part in the programme after leaving the St Albans institution and had no aftercare programming in the community. During most of the duration of this study there were no such programmes available. At the time of writing, the programme is available at all institutions. Follow-up community treatment—of the programme 'Phase III'—is now widely available and is in fact mandatory for all programme participants. We expect these evolving features of programme design to affect future rates of recidivism.

REFERENCES

Andrews, D. (1990). *The Role of Antisocial Attitudes in the Psychology of Crime*. Paper presented to the Canadian Psychological Association, Ottawa.
Bandura, A. (1973). *Aggression: A Social Learning Analysis*. Englewood Cliffs: Prentice Hall.
Beck, A. J. (1987). *Recidivism of Young Parolees*. Washington, DC: Bureau of Justice Statistics Special Report.
Corson, J. (1989). *Stress, Self-concept, and Violence*. New York: AMS Press.
Goldstein, A. (1988). *The Prepare Curriculum*. Champaign: Research Press.
Goldstein, A. & Glick, B. (1987). *Aggression Replacement Training*. Champaign: Research Press.
Henning, K. (1994). *Violent Offender Programe Outcome Study*. Burlington: University of Vermont.
Klugiewicz, G. (1990). *Crisis Management Strategies*. Greenfield, WI: ACMi Systems.
Marlatt, A. & Gordon, J. (1985). *Relapse Prevention*. New York: The Guilford Press.
Ross, R. & Fabiano, E. (1985). *Time to Think: A Cognitive Model of Delinquency Prevention and Offender Rehabilitation*. Johnson City: Institute of Social Sciences & Arts.
Ross, R., Fabiano, E. & Ross, R., (1986). *Reasoning and Rehabilitation: A Handbook for Teaching Cognitive Skills*. Ottawa: The Cognitive Centre.
Yochelson, S. & Samenow, S. (1976). *The Criminal Personality*, Vols I & II. New York: Aronson.

CHAPTER 8

A Rationale for the Treatment of Sex Offenders: Pro Bono Publico

Robert Prentky

Joseph J. Peters Institute, Philadelphia, USA

Over the past several decades, the escalation of sexual violence has become an increasingly acute health problem, manifested in costs to both victims and society at large. The long-term psychological impact of sexual assault on victims has been documented many times and includes a wide range of manifestations: general psychological distress and impaired self-esteem (Finkelhor, 1984; Golt 1986; Norris Feldman-Summers, 1981; Resick, 1993; Stein et al., 1988; Wirtz & Harrell, 1987), Borderline Personality Disorder and other character disorders (Briere & Zaidi, 1989; Brown & Anderson, 1991), symptoms of dissociation and Post-Traumatic Stress Disorder (Anderson et al., 1993; Briere, 1992; Krager & Green, 1991; Resick, 1993), suicidality (Briere, 1992; Briere & Zaidi, 1989; Brown & Anderson, 1991), sexual problems (Briere, 1992; Briere & Zaidi, 1989; Gold, 1986; Resick, 1993; Stein et al., 1988), substance abuse (Briere, 1992; Briere & Zaidi, 1989; Brown & Anderson, 1991; Peters, 1988; Stein et al., 1988), greater number of hospitalizations and general impaired health (Moeller et al., Nash et al., 1993).

The costs incurred by society include a network of medical and psychological services provided to aid victim recovery and the investigation, trial and incarceration of offenders—often in segregated units or special facilities. The actual monetary cost of sexual violence was determined for the

What Works: Reducing Reoffending—Guidelines from Research and Practice.
Edited by J. McGuire. © 1995 John Wiley & Sons Ltd.

Commonwealth of Massachusetts in a study that examined the cost effectiveness of rehabilitation of child molesters (Prentky & Burgess, 1992). Although space does not permit a detailed explication of the cost–benefit model or the procedures used for calculating costs, I will briefly overview some of our findings. We compared the reoffence rates for treated and non-treated child molesters, using a sample of 129 treated offenders who had been discharged from the Massachusetts Treatment Center between 1960 and 1985. We used as our recidivism rate for treated offenders the number of men who were charged with a sexual offence during the first 5 years after discharge (25%). The comparable figure for non-treated offenders was 40%. We then identified as many of the relevant offender-related and victim-related expenses as we could and obtained average cost estimates for each item. The main categories for offender-related expenses included: (a) apprehension and pretrial investigation, (b) trial, (c) incarceration, and (d) parole supervision. The main categories for victim-related expenses included: (a) Department of Social Services investigation, (b) hospital medical expenses, (c) victim evaluation, (d) Victim Witness Services, and (e) victim treatment. The model proposed that in the treated case, a convicted child molester spends 5.1 years (the average length of time that the 129 men were at the Treatment Center) at a treatment facility. The cost of residential treatment was determined to be US$118 146 (5.1 years × US$23 166/year). The man is released to the street with a 0.25 risk of reoffending within the first 5 years. The cumulative costs of a sexual offence (all offender-related and victim-related expenses) came to US$183 333. Thus, the expected cost in the case of a treated offender was: US$118 146 + (US$183 333 × 0.25) = US$163 979. The model further proposed that in the case of a non-treated child molester, the man is convicted, receives a 10–15-year sentence, and serves two-thirds of his minimum sentence (7 years) at a cost of US$158 634 (7 years × US$22 662/year). He is released to the street with a 0.40 risk of reoffending within the first 5 years. Again, the cost of a reoffence is US$183 333. Thus, the expected cost in the case of a non-treated offender would be: US$158 634 + (US$183 333 × 0.40) = US$231 967. The difference between US$231 967 and US$163 979 (US$67 988) represents the additional cost of one victim in the event of a reoffence by one offender.

In deriving costs for this model, one area of disparity is the time of incarceration (7 years) versus the time of treatment (5.1 years). Although these two figures were independently and objectively derived, they nevertheless represent a major cost difference. If we control for this difference by setting treatment time equal to 7 years, then the principal cost difference must be attributable to reoffence risk. The 'time-adjusted' difference between the treated case and the non-treated case is now US$23 973. When the added 'cost' of a given offence (US$24 000 if one uses the revised estimate) is multiplied by an estimate of the number of offences within a given time period, the magnitude of the potential 'savings' becomes evident.

Beyond the obvious psychological impact of sexual violence on victims and the high costs associated with such victimization, perhaps the most dramatic, if not the most widespread, impact of sexual violence is the invisible but tangible blanket of fear that forces all potential victims to schedule normal daily activities around issues of safety. Simple questions such as when to go to the laundromat, when to leave work in the evening, what mode of transportation to use, where to park the car, where it is safe to walk or jog, and whether to use your first name on your mail box or in the phone book become major concerns, especially in larger cities. Questions that now concern parents, such as choosing day care or babysitters, permitting unsupervised outside play, and providing chaperons reflect a fear that is so widespread that it has become, quite literally, the 'norm'.

Society's recognition of this danger is reflected in the special legislation passed by many states in the United States to deal specifically with such offenders as well as a number of recent commissions and a seemingly endless array of regional and national conferences. The evidence that has provoked such concern, however, appears to be only the tip of the iceberg. If survey-based victimization estimates are reliable, the actual number of rapes is about four times the number reported, or about 683 000 rapes per year in the United States (National Victim Center, 1992). Whatever the 'real' victimization rates are for adult women (incidence estimates vary considerably), the incidence of child molestation may be considerably greater. It has been estimated, for instance, that the incidence of child sexual assault may be 20 times greater than the incidence of adult sexual assault (Abel, 1982). Because so many cases of child sexual assault are 'hidden' or otherwise go unreported, the estimates of incidence vary widely, ranging from 500 000 to 5 000 000 incidents per year. Russell (1982) reported, in her random sample of 930 women, that 38% experienced unwanted sexual contact before the age of 18 and 28% before the age of 14. The figure reported by Koss and colleagues (1987) in their study of 6159 college students was 27.5%. The figure reported by Gavey (1991) in her study of 347 college students was 51.6%. At this point, a crude estimate of incidence suggests that between 25% and 35% of all adult women were sexually exploited by an adult male during their childhood or adolescence (Russell & Howell, 1983). It would not be hyperbolic to suggest that the problem has reached epidemic proportions.

Given the apparent magnitude of the human and monetary costs incurred by society as a result of sexual violence, the response has been remarkably ambivalent. Because the problem of sexual violence is unlikely to abate, the necessity of identifying offenders or potential offenders and making discretionary decisions about convicted offenders will remain. Thus, the options of predictive neutrality and dispositional uncertainty are not viable, and new methods for enhancing predictive accuracy and treatment efficacy must be sought. Treatment, in this context, is a potentially efficacious secondary intervention strategy for reducing victimization rates.

In this chapter, I attempt to provide the rudiments of the theoretical underpinning for sex offender treatment. The literature on sex offender treatment has been reviewed quite thoroughly (e.g. Freeman-Longo & Knopp, 1992; Marshall, 1993; Marshall & Barbaree, 1990; Marshall et al., 1991; Murphy, 1990; Pithers, 1993), and I will not attempt to restate what has been extensively discussed elsewhere. Instead, I will focus on the rationale for sex offender treatment. The rationale for the modification of any unwanted behaviour stems from the informed consideration of those factors that are most importantly associated with the emergence and the sustenance of the behaviour. In a relatively simple case, such as Reactive or Acute Depression, we attempt to identify the precursors of the depression. Although sexual aggression derives from a substantially more complex amalgam of factors and typically reflects a chronic pattern of maladaptive behaviours, the principles remain the same. That is, before designing strategies for modifying sexually aggressive behaviour, we first must identify those factors that are most importantly related to the behaviour. Some of those factors were reviewed by Prentky and Knight (1991). In the present chapter, I briefly discuss those factors and the most commonly employed treatment modalities that have been utilized for each of them. Although the factors presented here are by no means inclusive, they do represent the core components of most contemporary treatment programmes.

FACTORS THAT DIFFERENTIATE AMONG SEX OFFENDERS

Space does not permit an adequate differentiation between factors uniquely associated with child molestation (e.g. degree of sexual preoccupation with children and amount of contact with children) and rape (e.g. misogynistic anger). The factors that are discussed, however, generally apply, in varying degrees of importance, to all sex offenders.

Figure 8.1 provides a hypothetical model that depicts childhood precursors of different adult outcomes which, in turn, are precursors of sexual assault. The childhood precursors are obviously highly simplified. Developmental history of abuse, for example, must be examined with respect to types of abuse, age of onset of abuse, duration of abuse, severity of abuse,

Childhood   Adult   Outcome

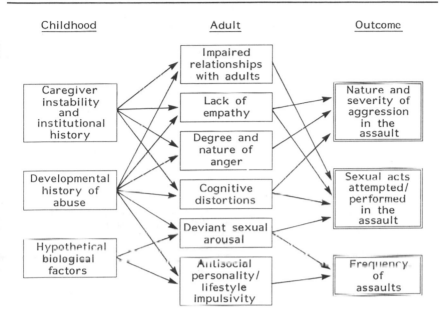

Figure 8.1. Hypothetical interrelation among factors: longitudinal perspective.

relation of victim to perpetrator, and the co-occurrence of other forms of developmental pathology such as history of institutionalization and caregiver instability (Prentky et al., 1989). The focus of this chapter, however, is on the middle column, the putative adult outcomes that place someone at high risk for sexual assault. These are the outcomes, or factors, that are the focus of the treatment interventions listed in Figure 8.2. Although the treatment modalities provided in Figure 8.2 are not inclusive, they do represent most of the commonly employed techniques.

Impaired Adult Relationships

Impaired relationships with adults reflect a broad dimension of social competence that is temporally stable and multiply determined. Becker and colleagues (1978), for instance, identified three components of social skills: (a) heterosexual behaviour, (b) assertive behaviour, and (c) empathetic behaviour. Although social skills training is one of the most frequently included components of treatment for sex offenders (McFall, 1990), its role in relation to sexual aggression remains unclear. Because there are many facets to social competence, it is critical to specify which aspect one is assessing. For instance, there is reasonable support for the

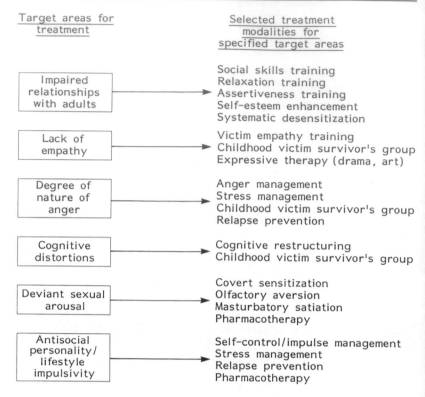

Target areas for treatment	Selected treatment modalities for specified target areas
Impaired relationships with adults	Social skills training Relaxation training Assertiveness training Self-esteem enhancement Systematic desensitization
Lack of empathy	Victim empathy training Childhood victim survivor's group Expressive therapy (drama, art)
Degree of nature of anger	Anger management Stress management Childhood victim survivor's group Relapse prevention
Cognitive distortions	Cognitive restructuring Childhood victim survivor's group
Deviant sexual arousal	Covert sensitization Olfactory aversion Masturbatory satiation Pharmacotherapy
Antisocial personality/ lifestyle impulsivity	Self-control/impulse management Stress management Relapse prevention Pharmacotherapy

Figure 8.2. Modes of treatment for adult precursors of sexual assault.

conclusion that rapists have assertiveness problems (e.g. Stermac & Quinsey, 1986), but differences in other areas of social competence are less evident. Some child molesters, such as 'paedophiles' (i.e. those with a long-standing sexual preoccupation with children), are often acutely deficient in their social and interpersonal skills (e.g. initiating and sustaining conversations with adults), feel socially awkward around adults and are generally more comfortable with younger companions (e.g. Araji & Finkelhor, 1986). Segal and Marshall (1985) found that child molesters were more heterosocially inadequate than rapists, and Williams and Finkelhor (1990) concluded that social isolation and poor social skills were noteworthy features of incestuous fathers.

Although the aetiological importance of social competence remains inconclusive, the inclusion of techniques to address social skills deficits may still be clinically appropriate (Segal & Marshall, 1985; Whitman & Quinsey, 1931). In addition to social skills training, the modalities that are most often used to improve relationships with adults include assertiveness training, relaxation training, systematic desensitization, sex education and self-esteem enhancement. Despite a long tradition of social skills training, however, the available evidence that supports its efficacy remains questionable (McFall, 1990). Understanding the role of social competence may ultimately only be deciphered in the context of typological analyses that are more differentiated than simply comparing rapists and child molesters with non-offender controls.

Lack of Empathy

In all domains of interpersonal violence, a general lack of empathic relatedness for one's victim can be regarded as a powerful disinhibitor. Alternatively, the presence of empathic concern will serve to inhibit aggression. As Hildebran and Pithers (1989: 238) stated, 'Victim empathy gives [the sex offender] the pivotal reason for not reoffending, for, with empathy, he can no longer not perceive his victim's pain'. Although these two statements are hypotheses, ample data have been generated over the years to support them (e.g. Bandura, 1973; Bandura et al., 1975; Feshbach, 1987; Feshbach & Feshbach, 1982; Mehrabian & Epstein, 1972; Parke & Slaby, 1983). Thus, although the empirical evidence of specific deficits in empathy among subgroups of sex offenders is inconclusive, there is a clear clinical rationale for assuming the presence of such deficits and targeting interventions to enhance empathy (Freeman-Longo & Pithers, 1992; Marshall, 1993; Pithers, 1993).

Although capacity for emotional relatedness and empathic concern have long been a focus of treatment for sex offenders, these issues have, until recently, been included in the larger topic of social skills deficits. As noted, for example, the third component of the assessment of social skills by Becker and colleagues (1978) was empathetic behaviour. More recently, however, it has been argued that deficits in empathy not only characterize many sex offenders, but such deficits may be of critical aetiological importance (Marshall, 1993; Marshall & Barbaree, 1990; Williams & Finkelhor, 1990). Hildebran and Pithers (1989) described the importance of developing empathy for all victims of sexual abuse as an essential first stage of treatment, followed by the development of empathy for one's own victims. At this point most sex offender treatment programmes include a separate component for increasing victim empathy. Indeed, Knopp and co-workers (1992) found in their survey of treatment programmes in North America that 94% included victim empathy training. In addition to the standard exercises and tapes (video and audio) used in victim empathy training (cf. Freeman-Longo & Pithers, 1992), expressive therapy may be used to increase the offender's emotional or affective response to the distress of the victim. Some programmes introduce victim advocates, victim counsellors and occasionally victims to increase further the emotional ante. Moreover, increasing the offender's affective appreciation of his own child-hood experiences of victimization can instil a greater awareness of his victim's experience of abuse. The generalized importance of empathy was captured by Pithers' conclusion that, 'If empathy can be established, signif-icant effects may be observed in sexual arousal, cognitive distortions, inti-macy within interpersonal relationships, realistic self-esteem, and motivation to change and maintain change,' (Pithers, 1993: 190).

Degree and Nature of Anger

The degree and nature of anger evidenced in the assault have long been assumed to differentiate between offenders who were—and those who were not—willing to use extreme force to gain victim compliance. Anger, or its behavioural manifestation—aggression—that is used only to force victim compliance, sometimes referred to as 'instrumental' aggression, may vary according to victim resistance, the use of alcohol or drugs, the presence of other offenders or victims, and situational or offender-specific factors (e.g. Prentky et al., 1985). Thus, sex offenders who intend only to force victim compliance are likely to vary widely in the amount of aggres-sion evident in their offences. When the aggression clearly exceeds that necessary to force victim compliance, sometimes referred to as 'expres-sive' aggression, the motivation and manifestation may also vary consid-erably (cf. Prentky et al., 1985). In the case of expressive aggression, the anger may be undifferentiated with respect to victims (i.e. the offender may be globally angry and express his anger at any available target), or the offender may be focally angry at the subgroups represented by his victims. Sex offenders may be generally angry at women (i.e. misogynistic anger) or they may displace their anger on specific groups of women (e.g. elderly women). Similarly, child molesters who intentionally inflict consid-erably physical injury on their victims may be generally angry at children.

Regardless of how 'expressive' the aggression is and how it is mani-fest, we must assume that in a battery offence, such as sexual assault, aggression must have been present. It is thus impossible to dismiss a component of sexual assault that is obviously so prominent and critical a feature of the behaviour. The recognition of the importance of anger as a driving force in sexual offences has resulted in the inclusion of treat-ment techniques to reduce and contain anger. The most commonly employed of these techniques is an anger management group which uses cognitive–behavioural strategies to increase self-control as well as the timely and appropriate expression of angry feelings. In addition, Relapse Prevention, which also focuses on increasing self-management skills, and

Stress Management can assist the offender to gain control over chronic and situationally induced anger. Lastly, early life experiences of victimization can fuel lifelong anger that is periodically triggered by real or imagined provocations. A group that focuses on childhood victimization can help the offender to master these traumatic events.

Cognitive Distortions

Cognitive distortions are 'irrational' ideas, thoughts, and attitudes that serve to: (a) perpetuate denial around sexually aggressive behaviour, (b) foster the minimization and trivialization of the impact of sexually aggressive behaviour on victims, and (c) justify and sustain further sexually aggressive behaviour. Cognitive distortions are presumed to be learned attitudes that are instilled at an early age by caregivers, reinforced by peers during childhood and adolescence, and further strengthened in adulthood by the prevailing social climate.

The social and cultural forces that have been hypothesized to contribute to sexual violence include the permissive responses of a wide variety of social systems and institutions that function to perpetuate rape myths and misogynistic attitudes, the objectification and exploitation of children and women in pornography, and the often similar but more subtle messages conveyed in advertising that support, or at least condone, sexual harassment (cf. Stermac et al., 1990). Indeed, many facets of sexual aggression represent institutionalized, normative behaviour that is deeply ingrained in the social fabric.

The causal relation among demeaning and misogynistic attitudes, attributions, moral evaluations and sexual violence is, arguably, one of the more important areas of inquiry in research on sexual aggression (cf. Marshall, 1993; Murphy, 1990; Segal & Stermac, 1990). This area of research, emerging both from the laboratories of experimental social scientists and from the writings of feminist theorists, dovetails nicely with the clinical and experimental psychopathology research on cognitive distortions. Whereas social and feminist research has tended to focus on rape-supportive attitudes and rape myths held by a cross-section of society (i.e. non-offenders), clinical research has focused on the irrational and offence-justifying attitudes expressed by offenders (i.e., child molesters and rapists).

The importance of cognitions in moderating sexual arousal has been repeatedly demonstrated. Moreover, clinical observations have suggested that many sexual offenders harbour offence-justifying attitudes and that these attitudes are importantly related to the maintenance of the 'sexual assault cycle'. Thus, the modification of irrational attitudes has been a major focus of treatment intervention. Although there are a variety of treatment modalities that may impact these distortions, the most commonly employed technique is cognitive restructuring. For cognitive restructuring to be most effective, it is critical that cognitive *and* affective components be addressed. That is, it is insufficient merely to confront the 'distorted' nature of the attitudes, to discuss the role that such distortions play for the individual, or to provide accurate information about sexual abuse (all cognitive components). It is equally important to create discomfort by focusing on the victim's response (e.g. fright, pain, humiliation)—the affective component. This latter exercise is also integral to victim empathy training.

In addition to cognitive restructuring, a group that focuses on childhood victimization can also be very helpful. Since the origin of these distorted attitudes is often a primary caregiver who was an influential role model, as well as exposure to peer role models—often in institutional settings—a group that focuses on these early life experiences can help to trace the cognitions to their source, thereby challenging their generality and diminishing their sense of 'truth' or 'reality'.

Sexual Fantasy and Deviant Sexual Arousal

Sexual fantasy refers to cognitive activity that focuses on thoughts and images having sexual content, and deviant sexual arousal refers to an arousal response that is prompted by thoughts, stimuli (visual or auditory) or behaviours that are defined as unconventional or antisocial by society. Studies investigating the relation of sexual fantasy to sexual aggression have typically employed plethysmography to assess sexual arousal to auditory and visual stimuli that purportedly tap specific sexual preferences. The guiding premise of these studies has been that deviant sexual fantasy is highly correlated with deviant sexual arousal and that both deviant fantasy and deviant arousal patterns are important precursors of deviant sexual behaviour (Abel & Blanchard, 1974).

Substantial evidence has emerged supporting the relation between phallometrically assessed sexual preferences and sexually deviant behaviour (cf. Quinsey & Earls, 1990). For instance, differential arousal patterns to specific sexual/aggressive stimuli have discriminated rapists from non-rapists and differentiated among rapists (Quinsey et al., 1984). Moreover, more recent studies have provided evidence that deviant sexual arousal patterns are an important identifier of sexually coercive males in non-criminal samples (e.g. Malamuth, 1986, 1989). Finally, phallometrically measured sexual interest in non-sexual violence has been found to be a predictor of both sexual and violent offence recidivism (Rice et al., 1990).

The frequent targeting of such fantasies for therapeutic intervention (e.g. Quinsey & Earls, 1990) reflects the widely held belief that the modification of deviant sexual fantasies and deviant sexual arousal patterns is critical for the successful treatment of sex offenders. Indeed, the presence of deviant sexual fantasies does appear to increase the likelihood of subsequent deviant sexual behaviour (Abel & Blanchard, 1974). Moreover, the moderate success at increasing non-deviant arousal and behaviour by applying techniques aimed solely at modifying arousal to deviant sexual fantasies (Marshall et al., 1983) supports the hypothesis that deviant fantasies not only lead to and maintain deviant sexual behaviour but also impede normal sexual adaptation.

Behavioural techniques for modifying sexual arousal patterns are grouped into two categories, those that decrease deviant arousal (e.g. covert sensitization, aversion, masturbatory satiation, biofeedback, shame therapy) and those that increase appropriate arousal (e.g. systematic desensitization, fantasy modification and orgasmic reconditioning, 'fading' techniques, exposure to explicit appropriate sexual material). Although over 20 different behavioural techniques have been reported in the literature, the most widely used method has involved some variant of aversive therapy. Kelly (1982) found, for instance, that 78% of the 32 studies he reviewed employed aversive techniques. Furthermore, most research on methods for reducing deviant sexual arousal has focused on covert sensitization and/or aversion therapy (Grossman, 1985).

Both of these procedures follow a standard classical conditioning paradigm in which a noxious stimulus is paired with auditory or visual stimuli of deviant sexual content. In aversion therapy, the deviant stimuli are typically paired with noxious odours. In covert sensitization, the deviant stimuli are typically paired with negative mental images (e.g. a physically unpleasant experience such as vomiting or having a cavity filled, or a psychologically unpleasant experience such as being apprehended by the police and going to prison). Aversive stimuli may be combined with mental images (e.g. presenting a noxious odour with an image of vomiting). The relative efficacy of the different aversive techniques with different types of offenders remains an empirical question. Moreover, the extent to which response inhibition is situation-bound after repeated exposure to aversive experiences remains to be demonstrated.

In addition to the repertoire of behavioural interventions, organic treatment has become increasingly popular as a complement to psychological treatment. These organic or drug treatments consist primarily of antiandrogens (Bradford, 1990) and antidepressants (Kafka, 1991; Kafka & Prentky, 1992). The antiandrogens (e.g. medroxyprogesterone acetate and cyproterone acetate) reduce sexual drive by reducing the level of testosterone. The antidepressants that are used are primarily the selective serotonin reuptake inhibitors such as fluoxetine. Although the neuroregulation of sexual drive remains unclear, there is some evidence that enhanced central serotonin neurotransmission inhibits sexual arousal (Segreaves,

1989). In addition, there is clinical evidence that uncontrollable sexual urges and compulsive sexual behaviours are associated with dysthymia and major depression (e.g. Kafka & Prentky, 1992).

Antisocial Personality/Lifestyle Impulsivity

Impulsivity has long been a cynosure for the general criminal literature and, more recently, the sexual assault literature. In research on sexual offenders, lifestyle impulsivity has proven to be a significant discriminator (e.g. Hall, 1988; Prentky & Knight, 1986; Prentky et al., 1995; Rice et al., 1990). In his postdictive study of the offence histories of 342 non-psychotic sex offenders who were examined at a state hospital, Hall (1988) found that the frequency of sexual offending against adults was related to a wide range of other criminal offences, suggesting the presence of anti-social personality. Rice and colleagues (1990) found that the degree of psychopathy predicted both sexual and violent (sexual and non-sexual) recidivism. In a 25-year follow-up of 106 rapists released from a maximum-security treatment facility, Prentky and co-workers (1995) found that the hazard rate for the high impulsivity offenders was at least twice as great as the hazard rate for the low-impulsivity offenders across all domains of criminal behaviour. For non-sexual, victimless offences, the hazard rate was almost four times as great.

There is increasing evidence even within non-criminal samples (e.g. college students) that the likelihood of engaging in sexually aggressive behaviour is greater among those who are more impulsive (e.g. Lisak & Roth, 1988; Rapaport & Burkhart, 1984). Lisak and Roth (1988) found, for instance, that college men who reported having been sexually aggressive rated themselves as more impulsive than did non-aggressive college men. The sexually aggressive men also reported having less respect for society's rules.

Clinicians have long recognized the importance of impulsivity for relapse and have introduced self-control and impulsivity management modules into treatment. In addition to groups that focus specifically on impulse control, most treatment programmes include components of Relapse Prevention. Relapse Prevention begins by identifying the chain of events and emotions that lead to sexually aggressive behaviour. Once this 'assault cycle' is described, two interventions are employed: (a) strategies that help the offender avoid high-risk situations, and (b) strategies that minimize the likelihood that high-risk situations, once encountered, will lead to relapse. This is an 'internal self-management' system (cf. Pithers, 1990) that is designed to interrupt the seemingly inexorable chain of events that lead to an offence. Relapse Prevention is potentially helpful for interrupting patterns of behaviour that eventuate in specific outcomes, such as sexual assault, as well as patterns of behaviour that are more global, such as impulsive, antisocial behaviour.

Lastly, there is reasonable evidence in the literature that supports the efficacy of selective serotonin reuptake inhibitors for impulse disorders (e.g. Benarroche, 1990; McElroy et al., 1991). It was speculated, in this regard, that impulse disorders may ' . . . share a common perturbation of central serotonin pathophysiology and a diathesis for mood disorder,' (Kafka & Prentky, 1992).

CONCLUSION

Given the failure of more traditional correctional remedies, such as deterrence and incapacitation, for reducing the level of sexual violence, other interventions must be actively sought. One potentially effective intervention is offender treatment. The verdict as to the efficacy of treatment for sexual offenders will inevitably be a complex one that addresses: (a) optimal treatment modalities for specific subtypes of offenders; (b) optimal conditions under which treatment and follow-up should occur; and (c) selection (or exclusion) criteria for treatment candidates. At the present time, the most informed and dispassionate conclusion must be that the jury is still out. The evidence submitted thus far, however, is encouraging. After describing a comprehensive treatment programme Marshall stated, 'I believe the utilization of the above programme will produce far greater benefits in the rehabilitation of rapists than have been achieved heretofore,' (Marshall, 1993: 156).

As Prentky and Burgess (1992) noted, we resist treating sexual offenders because it is perceived to be a 'humane' response to egregious behaviour. If the overriding goal is reducing the number of victims, as well as the costs incurred by such victimization, and if rehabilitation can be demonstrated to reduce the likelihood of reoffence, then it is imperative that we overcome our resistance to treatment and work toward the optimization of treatment interventions and treatment conditions that reduce risk of reoffence. Clearly, the most compelling motive for offender treatment is the presumptive reduction in victimization rates. To that end, the treatment of sex offenders may be viewed, quite legitimately, as *pro bono publico*, and not *pro bono privato*.

ACKNOWLEDGEMENTS

The research reported in this chapter was supported by the National Institute of Justice (82-IJ-CX-58) and the National Institute of Mental Health (MH 32309).

Portions of this chapter that describe the results of a cost–benefit study for treatment of child molesters were abstracted from an article that was first published by the *American Journal of Orthopsychiatry*, 1990, **60**, 108–177, and subsequently reprinted in Burgess (Ed.) (1992). *Child Trauma I: Issues and Research*. New York: Garland, pp. 417–442.

REFERENCES

Abel, G. (1982). Who is going to protect our children? *Sexual Medicine Today*, July, 32.

Abel, G. G. & Blanchard, E. B. (1974). The role of fantasy in the treatment of sexual deviation. *Archives of General Psychiatry*, **30**, 467–475.

Anderson, G., Yasenik, L. & Ross, C. A. (1993). Dissociative experiences and disorders among women who identify themselves as sexual abuse survivors. *Child Abuse and Neglect*, **17**, 677–686.

Araji, S. & Finkelhor, D. (1986). Abusers: A review of the research. In D. Finkelhor & Associates (Eds). *A Sourcebook on Child Sexual Abuse*. Newbury Park: Sage Publications, pp. 89–118.

Bandura, A. (1973). *Aggression: A Social Learning Analysis*. Englewood Cliffs: Prentice-Hall.

Bandura, A., Underwood, B. & Fromson, M. E. (1975). Disinhibition of aggression through diffusion of responsibility and dehumanization of victims. *Journal of Research in Personality*, **9**, 253–269.

Becker, J. V., Abel, G. G., Blanchard, E. B., Murphy, W. D. & Coleman, E. (1978). Evaluating social skills of sexual aggressives. *Criminal Justice and Behavior*, **5**, 357–367.

Benarroche, C. L. (1990). Trichotillomania symptoms and fluoxetine response. In *New Research Program and Abstracts of the 143rd Annual Meeting of the American Psychiatric Association*, New York. Abstract NR 327.

Bradford, J. M. W. (1990). The antiandrogen and hormonal treatment of sex offenders. In W. L. Marshall, D. R. Laws & H. E. Barbaree (Eds). *Handbook of Sexual Assault: Issues, Theories, and Treatment of the Offender*. New York: Plenum Press, pp. 297–310.

Briere, J. N. (1992). *Child Abuse Trauma*. Newbury Park: Sage Publications.

Briere, J. N. & Zaidi, L. Y. (1989). Sexual abuse histories and sequelae in female psychiatric emergency room patients. *American Journal of Psychiatry*, **146**, 1602–1606.

Brown, G. R. & Anderson, B. (1991). Psychiatric morbidity in adult inpatients with childhood histories of sexual and physical abuse. *American Journal of Psychiatry*, **148**, 55–61.

Feshbach, N. D. (1987). Parental empathy and child adjustment/maladjustment. In N. Eisenberg & J. Strayer (Eds). *Empathy and its Development*. New York: Cambridge University Press, pp. 271–291.

Feshbach, N. D. & Feshbach, S. (1982). Empathy training and the regulation of aggression: Potentialities and limitations. *Academic Psychology Bulletin*, **4**, 399–413.

Finkelhor, D. (1984). *Child Sexual Abuse: New Theory and Research*. New York: Free Press.

Freeman-Longo, R. E. & Knopp, F. H. (1992). State-of-the-art sex offender treatment: Outcome and issues. *Annals of Sex Research*, 5, 141–160.

Freeman-Longo, R. E. & Pithers, W. D. (1992). *A Structured Approach to Preventing Relapse: A Guide for Offenders.* Orwell, Vermont: The Safer Society Program.

Gavey, N. (1991). Sexual victimization prevalence among New Zealand university students. *Journal of Consulting and Clinical Psychology*, 59, 464–466.

Gold, E. R. (1986). Long-term effects of sexual victimization in childhood: An attributional approach. *Journal of Consulting and Clinical Psychology*, 54, 471–475.

Grossman, L. S. (1985). Research directions in the evaluation and treatment of sex offenders: An analysis. *Behavioral Sciences and the Law*, 3, 421–440.

Hall, G. C. N. (1988). Criminal behavior as a function of clinical and actuarial variables in a sexual offender population. *Journal of Consulting and Clinical Psychology*, 56, 773–775.

Hildebran, D. & Pithers, W. D. (1989). Enhancing offender empathy for sexual abuse victims. In D. R. Laws (Ed.). *Relapse Prevention with Sex Offenders.* New York: Guilford, pp. 236–243.

Kafka, M. P. (1991). Successful antidepressant treatment of nonparaphilic sexual addictions and paraphilias in males. *Journal of Clinical Psychiatry*, 52, 60–65.

Kafka, M. P. & Prentky, R. A. (1992). Fluoxetine treatment of nonparaphilic sexual addictions and paraphilias in men. *Journal of Clinical Psychiatry*, 53, 351–358.

Kelly, R. J. (1982). Behavioral reorientation of pedophiles: Can it be done? *Clinical Psychology Review*, 2, 387–408.

Knopp, F. H., Freeman-Longo, R. E. & Stevenson, W. (1992). *Nationwide Survey of Juvenile and Adult Sex-offender Treatment Programs.* Orwell, Vermont: Safer Society Press.

Koss, M. P., Gidycz, C.A. & Wisnieski, N. (1987). The scope of rape: Incidence and prevalence of sexual aggression and victimization in a national sample of higher education students. *Journal of Consulting and Clinical Psychology*, 55, 162–170.

Kramer, T. L. & Green, B. L. (1991). Posttraumatic stress disorder as an early response to sexual assault. *Journal of Interpersonal Violence*, 6, 160–173.

Lisak, D. & Roth, S. (1988). Motivational factors in nonincarcerated sexually aggressive men. *Journal of Personality and Social Psychology*, 55, 795–802.

Malamuth, N. M. (1986). Predictors of naturalistic sexual aggression. *Journal of Personality and Social Psychology*, 5, 953–962.

Malamuth, N. M. (1989). The Attraction to Sexual Aggression Scale: Part 2. *Journal of Sex Research*, 26, 324–354.

Marshall, W. L. (1993). A revised approach to the treatment of men who sexually assault adult females. In G. C. Nagayama Hall, R. Hirschman, J. R. Graham, & M. S. Zaragoza (Eds). *Sexual Aggression: Issues in Etiology, Assessment, and Treatment.* Washington, DC: Taylor & Francis, pp. 143–165.

Marshall, W. L. & Barbaree, H. E. (1990). Outcome of comprehensive cognitive–behavioral treatment programs. In W. L Marshall, D. R. Laws & H. E. Barbaree (Eds). *Handbook of Sexual Assault: Issues, Theories, and Treatment of the Offender.* New York: Plenum Press, pp. 363–385.

Marshall, W. L., Abel, G. G. & Quinsey, V. L. (1983). The assessment and treatment of sexual offenders. In S. Simon Jones (Ed.). *Sexual Aggression and the Law.* Burnaby, BC: Criminology Research Centre, Simon Fraser University, pp. 43–52.

Marshall, W. L., Jones, R., Ward, T., Johnston, P. & Barbaree, H. E. (1991). Treatment outcome with sex offenders. *Clinical Psychology Review*, **11**, 465–485.

McElroy, S. L., Pope, H. G., Hudson, J. I., Keck, P. E. & White, K. L. (1991). Kleptomania: A report of 20 cases. *American Journal of Psychiatry*, **148**, 652–657.

McFall, R. M. (1990). The enhancement of social skills: An information-processing analysis. In W. L. Marshall, D. R. Laws & H. E. Barbaree (Eds.). *Handbook of Sexual Assault: Issues, Theories, and Treatment of the Offender*. New York: Plenum Press, pp. 311–330).

Mehrabian, A. & Epstein, N. (1972). A measure of emotional empathy. *Journal of Personality*, **40**, 525–543.

Moeller, T. P., Bachmann, G. A. & Moeller, J. R. (1993). The combined effects of physical, sexual, and emotional abuse during childhood: Long-term health consequences for women. *Child Abuse and Neglect*, **17**, 623–640.

Murphy, W. D. (1990). Assessment and modification of cognitive distortions in sex offenders. In W. L. Marshall, D. R. Laws & H. E. Barbaree (Eds.). *Handbook of Sexual Assault: Issues Theories and Treatment of the Offender*. New York: Plenum Press, pp. 331–342.

Nash, M. R., Hulsey, T. L., Sexton, M. C., Harralson, T. L. & Lambert, W. (1993). Long-term sequelae of childhood sexual abuse: Perceived family environment, psychopathology, and dissociation. *Journal of Consulting and Clinical Psychology*, **61**, 276–283.

National Victim Center (1992). *Rape in America. A Report to the Nation*. Arlington National Victim Center.

Norris, J. & Feldman-Summers, S. (1981). Factors related to the psychological impacts of rape on the victim. *Journal of Abnormal Psychology*, **90**, 562–567.

Parke, R. D. & Slaby, R. G. (1983). The development of aggression. In E. M. Hetherington (Ed.). *Manual of Child Psychology. Socialization, Personality and Social Development*, Vol. 4. New York: John Wiley, pp. 549–641.

Peters, S. D. (1988). Child sexual abuse and later psychological problems. In G. E. Wyatt & G. J. Powell (Eds.). *Lasting Effects of Child Sexual Abuse*. Newbury Park: Sage Publications, pp. 101–117.

Pithers, W. D. (1990). Relapse prevention with sexual aggressors: A method for maintaining therapeutic gain and enhancing external supervision. In W. L. Marshall, D. R. Laws & H. E. Barbaree (Eds.). *Handbook of Sexual Assault: Issues, Theories and Treatment of the Offender*. New York: Plenum Press, pp. 343–361.

Pithers, W. D. (1993). Treatment of rapists: Reinterpretation of early outcome data and exploratory constructs to enhance therapeutic efficacy. In G. C. Nagayama Hall, R. Hirschman, J. R. Graham & M. S. Zaragoza (Eds.). *Sexual Aggression: Issues in Etiology, Assessment, and Treatment*. Washington, DC: Taylor & Francis, pp. 167–196.

Prentky, R. A. & Burgess, A. W. (1992). *Rehabilitation of child molesters: A cost–benefit analysis. In A. W. Burgess (Ed.).* Child Trauma I: Issues and Research. New York: Garland Press.

Prentky, R. A. & Knight, R. A. (1986). Impulsivity in the lifestyle and criminal behavior of sexual offenders. *Criminal Justice and Behavior*, **13**, 141–164.

Prentky, R. A. & Knight, R. A. (1991). Identifying critical dimensions for discriminating among rapists. *Journal of Consulting and Clinical Psychology*, **59**, 643–661.

Prentky, R. A., Cohen, M. L. & Seghorn, T. K. (1985). Development of a rational taxonomy for the classification of sexual offenders: Rapists. *Bulletin of the American Academy of Psychiatry and the Law*, **13**, 39–70.

Prentky, R. A., Knight, R. A., Sims-Knight, J. E., Straus, H., Rokous, F. & Cerce, D. (1989). Developmental antecedents of sexual aggression. *Development and Psychopathology*, **1**, 153–169.

Prentky, R. A., Knight, R. A., Lee, A. F. S. & Cerce, D. (1995). Predictive validity of lifestyle impulsivity for rapists. *Criminal Justice & Behaviour*, **22**, 106–128.

Quinsey, V. L. & Earls, C. M. (1990). The modification of sexual preferences. In W. L. Marshall, D. R. Laws & H. E. Barbaree (Eds.). *Handbook of Sexual Assault: Issues, Theories, and Treatment of the Offender*. New York: Plenum Press, pp. 279–295.

Quinsey, V. L., Chaplin, T. C. & Upfold, D. (1984). Sexual arousal to nonsexual violence and sadomasochistic themes among rapists and non-sex offenders. *Journal of Consulting and Clinical Psychology*, **52**, 651–657.

Rapaport, K. & Burkhart, B. R. (1984). Personality and attitudinal characteristics of sexually coercive college males. *Journal of Abnormal Psychology*, **93**, 216–221.

Roioo, A. J. & Roth, J. A. (Eds,) (1993). *Understanding and Preventing Violence*. National Research Council. Washington, DC: National Academy Press.

Resick, P. A. (1993). The psychological impact of rape. *Journal of Interpersonal Violence*, **8**, 223–255.

Rice, M. E., Harris, G. T. & Quinsey, V. L. (1990). A follow-up of rapists assessed in a maximum-security psychiatric facility. *Journal of Interpersonal Violence*, **5**, 435–448.

Russell, D. E. (1982). The prevalence and incidence of forcible rape and attempted rape of females. *Victimology*, **7**, 81–93.

Russell, D. E. H. and Howell, N. (1983). The prevalence of rape in the United States revisited. *Signs: Journal of Women in Culture and Society*, **8**, 688–695.

Segal, Z. V. & Marshall, W. L. 1985). Heterosexual social skills in a population of rapists and child molesters. *Journal of Consulting and Clinical Psychology*, **53**, 55–63.

Segal, Z. V. & Stermac, L. E. (1990). The role of cognition in sexual assault. In W. L. Marshall, D. R. Laws & H. E. Barbaree (Eds.). *Handbook of Sexual Assault: Issues, Theories and Treatment of the Offender*. New York: Plenum Press, pp. 161–174.

Segreaves, R. T. (1989). Effects of psychotropic drugs on human erection and ejaculation. *Archives of General Psychiatry*, **46**, 275–284.

Stein, J. A., Golding, J. M., Siegel, J. M., Burnam, M. A. & Sorenson, S. B. (1988). Long-term psychological sequelae of child sexual abuse. In G. E. Wyatt & G. J. Powell (Eds.). *Lasting Effects of Child Sexual Abuse*. Newbury Park: Sage Publications, pp. 135–154.

Stermac, L. E. & Quinsey, V. L. (1986). Social competence among rapists. *Behavioural Assessment*, **8**, 171–185.

Stermac, L. E., Segal, Z. V. & Gillis, R. (1990). Social and cultural factors in sexual assault. In W. L. Marshall, D. R. Laws & H. E. Barbaree (Eds.). *Handbook of Sexual Assault: Issues, Theories, and Treatment of the Offender*. New York: Plenum Press, pp. 143–159).

Whitman, W. P. & Quinsey, V. L. (1981). Heterosocial skill training for institutionalized rapists and child molesters. *Canadian Journal of Behavioral Science*, **13**, 105–114.

Williams, L. M. & Finkelhor, D. (1990). The characteristics of incestuous fathers: A review of recent studies. In W. L. Marshall, D. R. Laws & H. E. Barbaree (Eds.). *Handbook of Sexual Assault: Issues, Theories, and Treatment of the Offender*. New York: Plenum Press, pp. 231–255.

Wirtz, P. W. & Harrell, A. V. (1987). Effects of postassault exposure to attack-similar stimuli on long-term recovery of victims. *Journal of Consulting and Clinical Psychology*, **55**, 10–16.

CHAPTER 9

Diversion from Prosecution: A Scottish Experience

David Cooke
Glasgow Caledonian University and Douglas Inch Centre, Glasgow, Scotland

In this chapter there will be a focus upon a particular type of service rather than a particular type of treatment; namely a service based on diversion from prosecution. Within the context of the criminal-justice system the term diversion is used to describe any process by which an offender, or alleged offender, is diverted—redirected or re-routed—from the normal process of prosecution into another system. Diversion may take many forms and it may occur at different stages of the process of prosecution. Traditionally, the distinction is made among primary, secondary and tertiary diversion depending on the stage at which the individual is re-routed.

Primary diversion occurs at, or before, the decision to prosecute is taken; primary diversion would include being given a verbal warning by a police constable, receiving a parking ticket from a traffic warden, being referred to an Intermediate Treatment programme or being referred for psychological help.

Secondary diversion occurs after the process of prosecution has begun but before conviction; the offender would avoid a court appearance and might be expected, for example, to provide restitution to their victim or attend an alcohol addiction clinic.

Tertiary diversion occurs after conviction and generally represents an alternative to imprisonment; tertiary diversion may include Community Service or participation in a sex offenders' treatment group.

What Works: Reducing Reoffending—Guidelines from Research and Practice.
Edited by J. McGuire. © 1995 John Wiley & Sons Ltd.

This chapter focuses on the development and operation of the first scheme in Scotland—and perhaps the first in the United Kingdom—where alleged offenders are offered psychological assistance rather than prosecution. I will attempt to provide a broad view of this service by considering six aspects of diversion schemes, namely, why diversion schemes exist, how this particular diversion scheme developed, how it operates, the type of people that are referred and the criminal-justice outcome of referral. Sixth and finally, I will consider the policy implications which may be derived from this particular diversion scheme and highlight issues which may assist in the creation and operation of new diversion schemes.

WHY DO DIVERSION SCHEMES EXIST?

Why do we have diversion schemes, and why does the procurator fiscal (independent state prosecutor) not merely proceed to prosecution? There are essentially two major arguments in support of diversion schemes: an economic argument and a humanitarian argument. The Stewart Committee (HMSO, 1983) indicated that both the overall increase in criminal activity and the general widening of the application of the criminal law had resulted in an increased and increasing burden on the court system. Diversion schemes may reduce this burden. Others have argued that, not only do diversion schemes reduce the burden on the courts, but in addition, they may represent best value for money (Ancram, 1985). Bonta & Motiuk (1992) argued that diversion schemes have become more than merely a humane response, they have become an economic necessity. These practical and economic considerations may have merit in relation to certain types of diversion—diversion through warning letters, diversion through procurator fiscal fines or reparation—but have little relevance to schemes where disturbed or distressed individuals are diverted for treatment (Cooke, 1989; 1991a). Diversion for psychological reasons occurs in relatively few cases and the level of administration demanded by these cases is similar to that for cases that proceed to prosecution.

The second argument for diversion is based on a humanitarian principle. Sue Moody (Moody, 1983) in her study of diversion to social work care, argued that many people were diverted from prosecution because the causes of their alleged offences appeared to be linked to such things as mental disorder, marital difficulties or addiction to alcohol, rather than to greed or other negative motivations. Thus, the procurator fiscal felt that in a humane society these individuals should not be punished but should be helped.

The Development of Diversion Schemes

Blackburn (1993) argued that the influence of labelling theorists led directly to the growth of diversion schemes in the 1960s. Labelling theory predicted that juveniles who came in contact with formal court processes, and were thereby labelled as offenders, would be propelled onto a pathway of deviancy and crime. One radical approach to the diversion of juveniles within Scotland was the effective abolition of juvenile courts with the creation of the Children's Panel system in 1971. Children who committed offences were to be regarded as similar to those who needed compulsory care because of educational problems or inadequate parenting. Under the Children's Panel system a group of lay people decides what is the most appropriate way to care for and manage the child (Nicholson, 1990).

In England and Wales juvenile courts still exist; however, magistrates have the option of imposing a supervision order as an alternative to custody and the juvenile may be enrolled in an Intermediate Treatment pro gramme designed to provide educational and recreational facilities in a community setting.

The effectiveness of diversion schemes for juveniles is not clear. Whitehead & Lab (1989) in their meta-analysis of treatment programmes for juvenile offenders distinguished between two types of diversion schemes: 'non-system diversion' programmes, which result in the complete termination of links with the criminal-justice system, and 'system diversion' schemes, which operate as an extension of the formal criminal-justice system. Whitehead & Lab (1989) found that while 'non-system' diversion schemes had little positive effect on recidivism, 'system diversion' schemes had a modest positive effect.

The failure of these diversion schemes to show clear effects may, as Blackburn (1993) suggested, be because of the limited treatment integrity of many of the programmes: good quality services do appear to reduce recidivism.

Diversion schemes are not purely the domain of juvenile offenders. Brown & Crisp (1992) described Public Interest Case Assessment (PICA) schemes in which the Crown Prosecution Service may decide to discontinue a case on a variety of grounds including ' . . . the attitude of the complainant; the extent of the defendant's involvement in the offence; the defendant's health, age and personal circumstances' (p. 88). Cases are most commonly discontinued either because the likely penalty is minimal or because of the mental health of the defendant. Rauma (1984) described a diversion scheme wherein offenders received treatment as an alternative to prosecution for spousal assault.

Although diversion schemes have their proponents, they have not met with universal approval. Pratt (1986) argued that diversion, rather than liberating juveniles from the control of the criminal-justice system, acts to impose greater regulation on their lives. Austin and Krisberg (1981) indicated that in some cases diversion results in the criminal-justice system casting its net wider, capturing children who would not normally come under its jurisdiction.

In summary, diversion schemes have historically focused on the needs of juvenile offenders. In the rest of this chapter I wish to consider diversions for another group of offenders, namely adult offenders with mental health problems.

THE DEVELOPMENT AND OPERATION OF THE DOUGLAS INCH CENTRE DIVERSION SCHEME

In 1984, in direct response to the publication of the Stewart Committee report (HMSO, 1983), a diversion scheme was established at the Douglas Inch Centre in Glasgow. The Douglas Inch Centre is a National Health Clinic that provides a service for offenders who have psychological difficulties.

The process of diversion begins when individuals are apprehended by the police on suspicion that they have committed an offence (see Cooke, 1991b for a fuller description of this process). At this stage the police officer prepares a report, which may include descriptions of the alleged offence, eye-witness accounts of the offence, comments of the accused and, perhaps, an account of any unusual or abnormal behaviour displayed by the accused. The police officer would not question the accused about psychiatric or psychological difficulties but, in his or her report, may refer to any pertinent information which has been acquired during inquiries.

The police report, together with information about previous criminal behaviour, is screened by members of the procurator fiscal's department. Depute fiscals screen this information in an attempt to identify individuals who may be suitable cases for diversion. Depute fiscals look for cases in which there are suggestions of odd or unusual behaviour, behaviour which might be indicative of psychiatric disturbance (See Cooke 1994a for a detailed analysis of the decision-making process of procurators fiscal). In some police reports there may be clear references to current or previous psychiatric problems, in other cases the depute fiscals make their decisions on the basis that there are unusual circumstances surrounding the alleged offence.

At this stage the papers will be forwarded to the assistant procurator fiscal responsible for diversion cases. If the assistant procurator fiscal comes to the view that the case is suitable for diversion—suitable from the legal point of view—then a letter offering diversion is sent to the

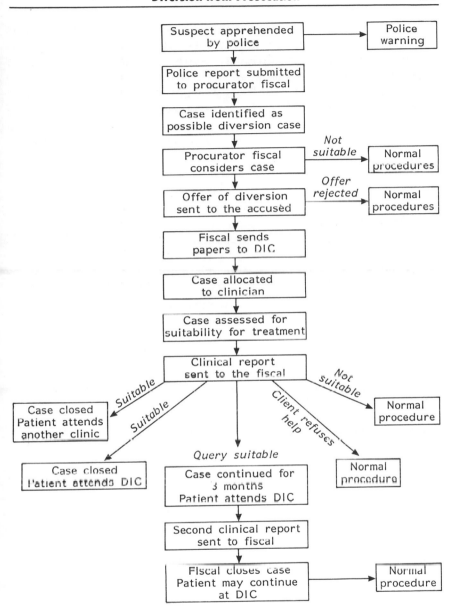

Figure 9.1. The process of diversion.

accused. In this letter the procurator fiscal indicates to the accused that although he or she believes that there is sufficient evidence to justify proceeding with a prosecution, the circumstances of the offence justify an alternative to prosecution. The alleged offender is then given the option of attending the Douglas Inch Centre for 'treatment, advice or other assistance'. At this stage, it is made clear that the procurator fiscal may continue proceedings following attendance at the Centre, or may defer this decision for a period until the individual has attended the clinic for treatment over a period of a few months.

In this letter the procurator fiscal strongly advises the alleged offender to seek advice—perhaps from a lawyer, or other trusted adviser—regarding the offer of diversion from prosecution. It is made clear that attendance is voluntary; if the alleged offender declines the offer of assistance from the Douglas Inch Centre then the case is considered on its merits. When an individual receives an offer of diversion they have 14 days to reply. Failure to reply is interpreted as a rejection of the offer. At this stage the process diverges depending on whether the individual accepts or rejects the offer of diversion.

If the accused rejects the offer of diversion the procurator fiscal may exercise several other options, namely, mark the case 'no proceedings', issue a conditional offer of a fixed penalty under Section 56 of the Criminal Justice (Scotland) Act 1987, issue a warning letter, administer a personal warning, or indeed, institute proceedings against the accused.

If the individual accepts the offer of diversion then the procurator fiscal will forward copies of the police report, information concerning any previous convictions and any other relevant information to the Douglas Inch Centre. Clinical staff attend allocation meetings at which all cases are allocated to either clinical psychologists, psychiatrists or social workers depending on the nature of the apparent problem and the particular skill or expertise of the clinician involved.

The patient will then be offered an assessment interview: at this interview it is made clear to the patient that the clinician is concerned with whether the accused has some psychological or psychiatric difficulty rather than with questions of guilt or innocence. The clinician tries to answer three questions: first, is there a problem? second, is this problem amenable to change? third, is the patient motivated to change? The question of guilt or innocence is not of importance to the clinician, whereas the questions of treatability and motivation are of central importance.

Following the assessment interview the clinician provides the procurator fiscal with an account of his or her opinion of the patient and the alleged offence. Generally, an attempt is made to describe the role which psycho-social factors may have played in the alleged offence. The person's apparent state of mind at the time of the offence, contemporaneous stresses or difficulties in his or her life, and perhaps, problems of addiction would be described. The clinician tries to help the procurator fiscal understand the offence from a psychological viewpoint. In addition, the clinician will guide the procurator fiscal, not only about the availability of suitable treatment, but also about the patient's apparent motivation to comply with treatment.

If suitable treatment facilities are not available at the Douglas Inch Centre patients may be referred to other treatment centres. If a patient is already receiving treatment elsewhere, then a recommendation will be made regarding whether treatment should be continued at the original centre, or whether the more specialized help available at the Douglas Inch Centre would be more appropriate. Patients in need of specialized and intensive treatment for particular problems such as drug addiction may be referred to centres dealing with these problems. If the patient is clearly in need of help but appears to have poor motivation, then the clinician may suggest to the procurator fiscal that the decision to prosecute might be delayed for some 3 months.

When the procurator fiscal receives the clinician's assessment report he or she may deal with the case in several ways: proceed with a prosecution, issue a warning letter, terminate the process and advise the accused to attend for treatment or, finally, inform the accused that the decision about prosecution will be deferred for 3 months until the impact of treatment can be determined. At this stage in the process the accused has the option of refusing treatment and returning to the normal prosecution process.

If the procurator fiscal has decided to defer the decision concerning prosecution, when the 3 month deadline is approaching, a further report from the clinician who is treating the individual will be requested. Depending on the content of this report, and other relevant information, at this stage he or she may end the process, issue a warning letter or proceed to prosecution.

Frequently, indeed generally, when the diversion process is terminated the client will continue to come to the Douglas Inch Centre for advice or treatment.

In summary, it can be observed that the process by which an alleged offender becomes a patient at the Douglas Inch Centre is complex. Complexity is inevitable: diversion schemes must be sufficiently flexible to ensure that a balance is maintained between the rights of the accused, the rights of the public and clinical effectiveness. Because of the differing professional backgrounds and concerns, it is vital that any diversion scheme should evolve through discussion amongst the legal practitioners and clinicians who will operate the scheme. These discussions should ensure that checks and balances are maintained.

WHAT TYPE OF PEOPLE ARE REFERRED TO THE DOUGLAS INCH CENTRE DIVERSION SCHEME?

In order to provide a detailed description of those who were diverted to the Douglas Inch Centre, a consecutive cohort of individuals, referred by the procurator fiscal, were interviewed by a research psychologist, either immediately before or after their interview with the clinician who was assessing their suitability for treatment (see Cooke, 1991a for a fuller description of this study). The interview, which was developed for this particular study, was semi-structured in form. The interview lasted between one and two hours and the following information was collected:

1. Demographic characteristics were assessed using the techniques of government social surveys (Atkinson, 1971). The distribution of the cohort in terms of sex, age, socio-economic status, employment status, marital status, size of household, educational level and religious affil-iation was collected.

2. The presence and nature of psychiatric disturbance or personality disorder were assessed using the Schedule for Affective Disorders—Life Time Version (SADS—L).

3. Given that the principal justification for referral to this type of diver-sion scheme is that the offence was prompted or influenced by psycho-logical factors, a 60 item semi-structured interview was developed to examine opportunity and motivation. The Opportunity and Moti-vation for Offence Questionnaire was developed to measure the following motivations for offending; impulsivity, peer pressure, tension reduction, self-esteem, accidental offending, disinhibition, excitement and material gain. Opportunity for offending was assessed in terms of objective risk of detection and the ease of committing the offence.

4. Information pertaining to current and ongoing stresses was collected using the Life Events and Difficulties Schedule (Brown & Harris, 1978; 1989).

Demographic Characteristics of the Cohort

A total of 111 people were interviewed, of whom 52% were men. It would appear, therefore, that women are over-represented in those who are diverted from prosecution. This sex ratio of virtually 1 : 1 should be contrasted with a male : female ratio of 8 : 1 for those who are proceeded against in Scotland (HMSO, 1987). The large proportion of women in the diverted sample is consistent with other findings, which suggest that female offenders are more likely to be referred for psychiatric examina-tion and treatment (Allen, 1988; Carlen, 1983; Eaton, 1986; Heidensohn, 1987; Steadman et al., 1988).

The age distribution of the cohort also suggests that the cohort contains an unusual group of offenders. While 36% of the cohort were 50 years old or over, only 18% were 19 or under. It is clear that older individuals are over-represented when the distribution of those diverted is compared with the distribution of convictions in Scotland (HMSO, 1987) ($\chi^2 = 57.95$, d.f. $= 1$, $p < 0.001$). The majority of these patients (58%) were first offenders, most having taken to criminal behaviour later in life.

Even in simple demographic terms this would appear to be an *unusual* process for *unusual* offenders. Of what offences were they accused? The Stewart Committee indicated that, in general, diversion schemes should be restricted to those accused of committing minor offences. More than a third of the cases were accused of theft by shoplifting, just under a third were accused of breaches of the peace, while the remaining third were distributed among four other offence categories.

Examination of Figure 9.3 indicates that the majority (84%) of those accused of shoplifting were women while the majority (78%) of those accused of a breach of the peace were men. All those accused of shoplifting were over the age of 35 years while the majority (60%) of those accused of breach of the peace were under 35. This pattern of referral is consistent with the view of the Stewart Committee that only minor offences should be referred.

The psychiatric status of those referred was assessed using the Research Diagnostic Criteria (RDC) (Endicott & Spitzer, 1978). In all, 70% of the cohort had one or more formal psychiatric diagnoses; 58% of the cases had a single RDC diagnosis, while the remaining 42% had multiple diagnoses. Schizophrenic disorders were infrequent, with only two cases being identified. Of the single diagnoses, anxiety and depressive disorders were the most common (Table 9.1).

Psychologically disturbed offenders tend to have high rates of comorbidity, that is, they have more than one disorder at a time or have a history of more than one disorder (e.g. Abram, 1989; Abram & Teplin, 1991). When

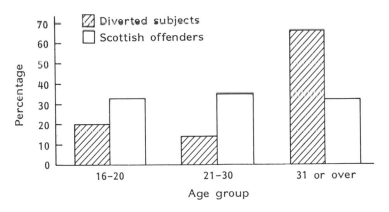

Figure 9.2. Age distribution of the cohort compared with that for all Scottish offenders.

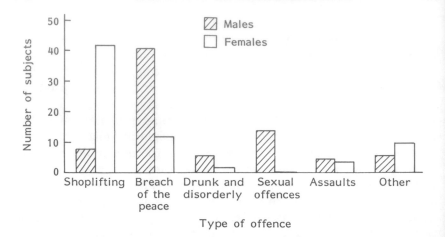

Figure 9.3. Distribution of offences of which men and women in the cohort were accused.

multiple diagnoses were considered cases of alcoholism in combination with anxiety or depression were most frequent. Personality disorder in combination with various other difficulties such as depression, drug abuse and alcoholism was the next most common pattern of disorder.

It would appear, therefore, that the Procurator Fiscal's department is

Table 9.1. Distribution of diagnostic categories of those interviewed.

Diagnostic category	Number	(%)
Single diagnoses		
Schizophrenia	2	(2)
Depressive disorders	12	(11)
Anxiety disorders	18	(16)
Personality disorder	3	(3)
Alcoholism	8	(7)
Drug abuse	4	(4)
Multiple diagnoses		
Anxiety with depression	5	(5)
Alcoholism with anxiety	5	(5)
Alcoholism with depression	12	(11)
Personality disorder with depression	3	(3)
Personality disorder with other diagnosis	6	(5)
No diagnosis	33	(30)
Total	111	

successful in selecting people who are suffering from significant psychological or psychiatric disturbance. Many of them had long-standing psychological difficulties and had not received treatment previously.

Psychological Factors and Offending

People are diverted for psychological treatment because it is assumed that they were either psychologically disturbed at the time of the alleged offence or that psychological factors, in some sense, caused them to commit the offence. The interview measured the following motivations for offending: impulsivity, peer pressure, tension reduction, self-esteem, accidental offending, disinhibition, excitement and material gain. In addition, opportunity for offending was assessed in terms of the objective risk of detection and the ease of committing the offence.

These psychological factors are not mutually exclusive: several may be operating within one offender while he or she is carrying out one offence. This point can be illustrated if we consider a bank robber whom I treated over many years. He described an occasion when he was going shopping with his wife, and on passing a bank he developed a powerful urge to rob the bank. He stopped the car, removed a gun from the boot of his car, and proceeded to rob the bank. He reported that afterwards he felt 'on top of the world' and that he got a 'buzz' which was stronger than that which he obtained when he went rock climbing or parachuting. From this account it would appear that many psychological factors were involved. The act was impulsive but it led to feelings of excitement, mastery and boosted self-esteem. He achieved significant financial gain. Many offences are less complex than this, but none the less, it is not uncommon for more than one factor to be involved.

The distribution of psychological factors was examined across the cohort (Figure 9.4). It appears that the majority of offences in this group of offenders were related to one cluster of factors namely impulsivity, lack of control, and disinhibition due to substances. There was little evidence that the offences resulted from emotional needs including excitement, tension reduction, improvement of self-esteem or reduction in peer pressure. The desire for material or financial gain appeared to be significant in only 4% of the cases.

Some may find it difficult to understand the finding that although one-third of the cohort were accused of shoplifting, material gain was not the primary motive for their offence. It is now well recognized that significant cognitive changes including memory lapse, retardation of thought, confusion, preoccupation with negative thoughts and poor concentration are characteristic of people who are suffering from anxiety and depression. This may have significance for psychologically disturbed shoplifters.

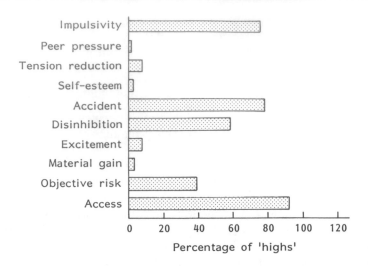

Figure 9.4. Psychological factors in offending.

Reason & Lucas (1984) examined the reports of individuals who claimed that they had been wrongly accused of shoplifting. Over half the sample said that they had been confused or absent-minded at the time of the offence. Using a sample of individuals who were not accused of shoplifting—or any other offence—Reason & Lucas (1984) found that 18% of this sample admitted that they had inadvertently left a shop with an article for which they had not paid: this group also attributed their behaviour to distractability or absent-mindedness. Reason & Lucas argued that certain types of shoplifting can be attributed to distractability and preoccupation because these individuals are

> ... no longer able to monitor their largely routine actions with sufficient vigilance, and risky errors pass unnoticed. Moreover, since the layout of supermarkets is specifically designed to elicit taking behaviour, it is not unreasonable to suppose that such environmental factors play a part in 'shaping' unintended actions. (Reason & Lucas, 1984: 16).

This may go some way to explaining this apparently contradictory result.

When opportunity for offending was considered, 93% of the cohort found the offence was simple to commit, there was 'easy access' and no significant barriers to committing the offence. In 40% of the cases the probability of being detected—the objective risk—was low.

THE CRIMINAL-JUSTICE OUTCOME OF REFERRAL— DOES IT WORK?

It is well established that there are major difficulties in assessing therapeutic outcome when assessing a treatment procedure—these difficulties are even greater when assessing a therapeutic service and, in particular, when it is a forensic service. These difficulties are based, first, on the range of the psychological difficulties displayed by those who are referred and second, on the variety of therapeutic techniques which have to be employed. In the present study, the psychological difficulties treated range from memory disturbance due to depressive illness, through poor anger control, alcohol addiction and psychotic experiences to phobias, mental handicaps and deviant sexual fantasies. With such a broad range of psychological problems, it is difficult to generate a measure which will chart psychological or behavioural change in a meaningful manner. This difficulty is further compounded by the range of therapeutic approaches that had to be adopted: the therapeutic approaches ranged from cognitive–behavioural therapy, through the prescription of psychotropic medication to counselling and family therapy. Depending on the approach adopted, different therapists would look for, and emphasize, different types of change.

The second issue to consider is the aim of treatment. Are we trying to make people feel better and cope more effectively—while continuing their life of crime—or are we trying to stop them reoffending? Treatment programmes for offenders, both within and outwith prisons, are often evaluated using reconviction as a criterion of outcome (e.g. Farrington, 1978; Gunn & Robertson, 1982; Scott, 1964). Critics of the reconviction criterion such as West (1980) have argued that reducing criminal activity is rarely the goal of treatment, and thus, reconviction rate can at best be an oblique measure of treatment outcome. West's argument may have less force in relation to diversion schemes: the procurator fiscal has a duty to protect the public interest and might legitimately expect that the therapist will endeavour to reduce the rate of reoffending.

There is a pragmatic reason for adopting the reconviction criterion as a measure of outcome; for the reasons outlined above, it is difficult to choose any other appropriate outcome measure when evaluating the effectiveness of a diversion scheme. It can be argued that the reconviction criterion is a useful measure of success. Offending behaviour, or the accusation of offending behaviour, is the *sine qua non* for referral under the diversion scheme. Reconviction is the one objective criterion that can be applied irrespective of the presenting psychological problem, or the therapeutic approach adopted in tackling this problem. It can be used to determine whether the public interest is being well served; do people who are diverted continue to offend? It may reassure the procurator fiscal that the risks which he or she is taking are worthwhile, and it may assist in the identification of appropriate and non-appropriate referrals.

In order to assess reconviction rate, 120 cases were followed up with an average period of follow-up of 31 months (range 23–34 months) (See

Cooke, 1992 for further details). Of those referred for treatment during this period, 25% ($n = 30$) were reconvicted during the follow-up period. Not all cases who were referred under the diversion scheme were accepted for treatment: only 69% were accepted. Clinicians tended not to accept patients when they denied the alleged offence, when they denied having any significant psychological difficulties or when they admitted to having difficulties but displayed little or no willingness to tackle these difficulties. Thus, given that there was a degree of patient selection—perhaps the selection of 'good bets'—it is difficult to determine whether treatment had an impact on reconviction or not (Figure 9.5).

There was a significant relationship between treatment and reconviction ($\chi^2 = 9.63$, d.f. $= 1$, $p < 0.01$). Of those treated, 15% were reconvicted, compared with 41% of those who were not treated. Clearly this result could be explained either in terms of selection or in terms of a positive treatment effect.

The lack of comparability between the treated and non-treated groups means that it is difficult to determine whether selection factors or treatment effects are responsible for the differences in post-treatment conviction. Stepwise logistic regression was carried out in an attempt to establish the impact of treatment on post-treatment conviction with the effects of other variables being controlled (Nerlove & Press, 1973). Terms relating to previous convictions, age, offence type and sex were forced into the regression equation prior to the treatment term. The risk ratio associated with the treatment term represents the effect of treatment on reconviction after the other variables have been controlled (Table 9.2).

The apparent effect of treatment on reconviction rate observed when

Figure 9.5. Reconviction during a mean follow-up period of 31 months (range 23–34 months) after diversion for offenders ($n = 120$) accepted for treatment (69%) and refused entry to the scheme.

Table 9.2. Log linear regression of reconviction rate.

Factor	Risk ratio	t value
Treatment	1.32	0.41
Previous age	7.69	3.27*
21–30 vs 16–20	1.75	0.62
31–40 vs 16–20	2.63	1.10
41+ vs 16–20	2.86	1.05
Offence		
Breach of the peace vs shoplifting	1.92	0.70
Drunk and disorderly vs shoplifting	1.26	0.20
Other vs shoplifting	2.08	0.76
Sex	3.25	1.54

* $p < 0.01$, $n = 110$.

those who were treated were compared with those who were not treated disappeared when selection factors were controlled for in the logistic regression analysis. While there was a trend that suggested that treatment might have an effect, it failed to reach statistical significance. Given that the reconviction rate is at best an oblique measure of treatment effects and the fact that the sample size was small, any treatment effect would have to be extremely powerful to achieve conventional levels of statistical significance (Cohen & Cohen, 1983; West 1980). Perhaps the most appropriate verdict on the proposition that treatment affects reconviction rates in this diversion scheme is the Scottish verdict of 'not proven'. A larger cohort is required. Even if the worst case is accepted that we have no effect on reconviction rate then it would not justify abandoning our attempts. As West noted: '... An important minority of offenders manifest such serious personal problems or actual illness that their need for help is too pressing to be ignored on account of the uncertain effect on reconviction rates' (1980: 630).

POLICY IMPLICATIONS OF THESE STUDIES

If we are to set up more schemes of this type, what policy issues should we consider? First, I believe that all schemes must be flexible; flexible in the way in which they are set up and flexible in the way in which they operate. I do not think that the Douglas Inch model can necessarily be imposed in other places. The scheme has got to develop within existing facilities. Many professional groups are involved, who have different priorities and different concerns. It is necessary for a degree of trust and understanding to develop through frequent discussions, in particular while the scheme is being established.

Flexibility is also important when the scheme is up and running.

Schemes have to find the delicate balance between the public interest, the rights of the accused and clinical effectiveness. The system which has evolved in Glasgow, in my opinion, allows us to safeguard these competing interests. If the accused person is using diversion as an easy option, then the decision to prosecute can be held over until we are certain that he or she is properly engaged in treatment. If the threat of prosecution is so anxiety-provoking that it interferes with treatment then the threat can be removed. Equally, where the threat of prosecution may enhance motivation to change then it can be used to that end.

The second issue which I would like to consider is that of saving money. I do not believe that diversion schemes of this type can be justified on the basis that they will save money. I understand from the fiscal who oversees the scheme that the amount of administration involved is not dissimilar to that involved in the normal court processes. If there is any saving in costs it results because the costs are transferred from the criminal justice system to the National Health Service. I would argue that this is quite appropriate. In total 70% of the referrals are psychiatric cases—a significant proportion of these people have not received help before. Thus the fiscal's department is merely acting as a channel through which disturbed people make contact with the appropriate services.

DIVERSION FOR MORE DISORDERED OFFENDERS

Looking to the future, I would hope that diversion schemes will grow not only in terms of geographical spread but also in terms of the seriousness of cases that can be considered suitable for diversion rather than prosecution. The offenders diverted within the current scheme can be characterized as having relatively minor disorders—the offences which they allegedly committed were not overly serious. This is consistent with the policy espoused by the Stewart Committee (HMSO, 1983). While valuable, this may not address the most pressing need.

Toch (1982) argued that there is a group of disordered offenders who are treated with 'bus therapy': these disruptive individuals are shuttled between mental health, criminal-justice and social service facilities. They fail as patients by being labelled 'difficult'; they fail as prisoners by accumulating disciplinary offences; they fail to obtain care. Freeman & Roesch (1989: 114) characterized the problem as follows:

> The mentally ill ex-offender presents with a complex set of needs and problems, ranging from basic requirements for food, shelter and employment to the need for mental health treatment. Responsibility for provision of such a range of services seldom falls to a single agency, and the mentally ill are

poorly equipped to untangle the skein of disparate and at times competitive jurisdictions. Too often they fall between the cracks of the social net.

Coid (1988) demonstrated that these multidisordered people have difficulty in gaining admission to psychiatric hospitals; they fall through the net of the mental health services and end up within the prison system. Cooke (1994b), in a recent study of psychological disturbance in the Scottish prison system, identified 6% of the prison population as being multiproblem prisoners; they displayed high levels of comorbidity—in particular, personality disorder together with depression, drug dependence and alcohol dependence—prior to imprisonment they were homeless, they had long histories of offending and were serving frequent short sentences. These individuals do life sentences by instalments because of the absence of other approaches to their care and management.

One approach to this problem that has been proposed—and more importantly, implemented—is an integrated service for psychologically disturbed offenders that cuts through the traditional boundaries between the health, social and criminal-justice systems (Corrado et al., 1989; Durham, 1989; Eaves, 1991; Greene, 1988; Jemelka et al., 1989; Pinder & Laming, 1991).

Eaves (1991) described the Inter-Ministerial project funded by the Correctional service and the Mental Health service in British Columbia. This project is designed to provide services to this group of difficult prisoner–patients and has the dual aims of extending their community tenure and improving their quality of life. The support is provided by social workers who work intensively with 10 to 12 patients each at 'street level'. The social workers aim to achieve the above goals by helping patients obtain and maintain access to the existing community support networks and facilities. By their very nature these patients are difficult to deal with and much of the workload of the social workers appears to be advocacy on behalf of their clients with supporting criminal-justice and housing agencies. The case worker has the explicit focus of preventing reincarceration and rehospitalization. They may achieve this by ensuring that their clients are diverted from prosecution when they commit minor offences. The social workers provide their service by having frequent contact with their clients. The project is now being expanded to take on people who have just been released from prison. The project is currently under evaluation and preliminary results indicate that both community tenure and quality of life are enhanced. Eaves (personal communication) suggested that although the staff costs of running this project are high, they are low when compared with the costs of incarceration or hospitalization.

The precursor of this project, the Multi Service Network Project, has been formally evaluated. Corrado and co-workers (1989) demonstrated that this co-ordinated approach not only ensured that clients had access to services but also produced a cost saving of C$3520 per client.

In conclusion, there can be little doubt that the diversion from prosecution of the psychologically disturbed represents a more humane response; the diversion of the multidisordered individual may also represent a more cost effective approach to the management of this challenging group.

ACKNOWLEDGEMENTS

This research was funded by the Criminological and Legal Research Group of the Scottish Home and Health Department. I would like to thank Mrs Valerie Gray and Mrs Sheila McDaid for collecting the data on which this study is based. The project would not have been possible without the support and guidance of Mr Barry Heywood, Mr Ian Murray and Mr Chris Donnely of the Glasgow and Strathkelvin Procurator Fiscal's Department and of my clinical colleagues at the Douglas Inch Centre. The views expressed in this paper are those of the author and do not necessarily represent the views of the Scottish Home and Health Department.

REFERENCES

Abram, K. M. (1989). The effects of co-occuring disorders in criminal careers: interaction of antisocial personality, alcoholism and drug disorders. *International Journal of Law and Psychiatry*, **12**, 133–148.

Abram, K. M. & Teplin, L. A. (1991). Co-occurring disorders among mentally ill jail detainees. *American Psychologist*, **46**, 1–10.

Allen, H. (1988). *Justice Unbalanced: Gender, Psychiatry and Judicial Decisions*. Milton Keynes: Open University Press.

Ancram, M. (1985). Opening address on alternatives to criminal justice. In B. Williams (Ed.). *Proceedings of a SACRO Conference on Alternative Criminal Justice: Decriminalisation, Diversion, Depenalisation*. Edinburgh: SACRO.

Atkinson, J. (1971). *A Handbook for Interviewers: A Manual for Social Survey Interviewing Practice and Procedures on Structured Interviewing*. London: HMSO.

Austin, J. & Krisberg, B. (1981). Wider, stronger and different nets: the dialectics of criminal justice reform. *Journal of Research in Crime and Delinquency*, **18**, 165–196.

Blackburn, R. (1993). *The Psychology of Criminal Conduct: Theory, Research and Practice*. Chichester: Wiley.

Bonta, J. & Motiuk, L. L. (1992). Inmate classification. *Journal of Criminal Justice*, **20**, 343–353.

Brown, A. J. & Crisp, D. (1992). Diverting cases from prosecution in the public interest. *Research Bulletin*, **32**, 7–12.

Brown. G. W. & Harris. T. O. (1978). *Social Origins of Depression: A Study of Psychiatric Disorder in Women*. London: Tavistock.

Brown, G. W. & Harris. T. O. (1989). *Life Events and Illness*. London: Unwin Hyman.

Carlen, P. (1983). *Women's Imprisonment: A Study of Social control*. London: Routledge & Kegan Paul.

Cohen, J. & Cohen. P. (1983). *Applied Multiple Regression/Correlation Analysis for the Behavioural Sciences*. London: Lawrence Erlbaum Associates.

Coid, J. (1988). Mentally abnormal prisoners on remand: I—Rejected or accepted by the NIHS? *British Medical Journal*, **296**, 1779–1782.

Cooke, D. J. (1989). *Treatment as an Alternative to Prosecution; Diversion to the Douglas Inch Centre*. Edinburgh: SHHD, Central Research Unit Papers.

Cooke, D. J. (1991a). Treatment as an alternative to prosecution: offenders diverted for treatment. *British Journal of Psychiatry*, **158**, 785–791.

Cooke, D. J. (1991b). Psychological treatment as an alternative to prosecution: a form of primary diversion. *The Howard Journal of Criminal Justice*, **30**(1), 53–65.

Cooke, D. J. (1992). Reconviction following referral to a forensic clinic: the criminal justice outcome of diversion. *Medicine, Science and the Law*, **32**, 325–330.

Cooke, D. J. (1994a). Primary diversion for psychological treatment: The decision making of Procurators Fiscal. *International Journal of Law and Psychiatry*, **17**, 211–223.

Cooke, D. J. (1994b). *Psychological Disturbance in the Scottish Prison System: Prevalence, Precipitants and Policy*. Edinburgh: SHHD.

Corrado, R. R., Doherty, D. & Glackman, W. (1989). A demonstration program for chronic recidivists of criminal justice, health, and social service agencies. *International Journal of Law and Psychiatry*, **12**, 211–229.

Durham, M. L. (1989). The impact of deinstitutionalization on the current treatment of the mentally ill. *International Journal of Law and Psychiatry*, **12**, 117–131.

Eaton, M. (1986). *Justice for Women?: Family, Court and Social Control*. Milton Keynes: Open University Press.

Eaves, D. (1991). *The Management of Mentally Disordered Persons in Conflict with the Law*. (unpublished paper).

Endicott, J. & Spitzer, R. L. (1978). A diagnostic interview: the schedule for affective disorders and schizophrenia. *The Archives of General Psychiatry*, **35**, 837–844.

Farrington, D. P. (1978). The effectiveness of sentences. *Justice of the Peace*, **142**, 68–71.

Freeman, R. J. & Roesch, R. (1989). Mental disorder and the criminal justice system: a review. *International Journal of Law and Psychiatry*, **12**, 105–115.

Greene, R. T. (1988). A comprehensive mental health care system for prison inmates: retrospective look at New York's ten year experience. *International Journal of Law and Psychiatry*, **11**, 381–389.

Gunn, J. & Robertson, G. (1982). An evaluation of Grendon Prison. In J. Gunn & D. P. Farrington (Eds). *Abnormal Offenders, Delinquency and the Criminal Justice System*. Chichester: John Wiley.

Heidensohn, G. (1987). *Gender Crime and Justice*. Milton Keynes: Open University Press.

HMSO (1983). *Keeping Offenders Out of Court: Further Alternatives to Prosecution. Cmnd 8959*. Edinburgh: HMSO.

HMSO (1987). Criminal proceedings in Scottish courts in 1986. *Statistical Bulletin*, 9.

Jemelka, R., Trupin, E. & Chiles, J. A. (1989). The mentally ill in prison: a review. *Hospital and Community Psychiatry*, **40**, 481–491.

Moody, S. (1983). *Diversion from the Criminal Justice Process*. Edinburgh: Scottish Office Central Research Unit.

Nerlove, M. & Press, S. J. (1973). *Univariate and Multivariate Log-linear and Logistic Models*. Santa Monica: Rand.

Nicholson, G. (1990). The courts and law in Scotland. In R. Bluglass & P. Bowden (Eds). *Principles and Practice of Forensic Psychiatry*. London: Churchill Livingstone, pp. 55–60.

Pinder, M. & Laming, H. (1991). Time to re-think. In K. R. Herbst & J. Gunn (Eds). *The Mentally Disordered Offender*. Oxford: Butterworth-Heinemann, pp. 186–195.

Pratt, J. (1986). Diversion from the Juvenile court: a history of inflation and a critique of progress. *British Journal of Criminology*, **26**, 212–233.

Rauma, D. (1984). Going for gold: prosecutorial decision making in cases of wife assault. *Social Science Research*, **13**, 321–351.

Reason, J. T. & Lucas. D. (1984). Absentmindedness in shops: its correlates and consequences. *British Journal of Clinical Psychology*, **23**, 121–131.

Scott, P. D. (1964). Approved school success rates. *British Journal of Criminology*, **4**, 525–556.

Steadman, H. J., Rosenstein, M. J., MacAskill, R. L. & Manderscheid, R. W. (1988). A profile of mentally disordered offenders admitted to inpatient psychiatric services in the United States. *Law and Human Behavior*, **12**, 91–99.

Toch, H. (1982). The disturbed disruptive inmate: where does the bus stop? *The Journal of Psychiatry and Law*, **10**, 327–349.

West, D. J. (1980). The clinical approach to criminology. *Psychological Medicine*, **10**, 619–691.

Whitehead, J. T. & Lab, S. P. (1989). A meta-analysis of juvenile correctional treatment. *Journal of Research in Crime and Deliquency*, **26**, 276–297.

PART III

Practice, Research and Programme Delivery

CHAPTER 10

The Meaning and Implications of 'Programme Integrity'

Clive R. Hollin

University of Birmingham and Glenthorne Youth Treatment Centre, Birmingham, UK

While much has been written on the content of effective programmes for working with offenders (for reviews see Hollin, 1990, 1993; Mulvey et al., 1993; Ross & Fabiano, 1985), it is only comparatively recently that attention has turned to management of such programmes. Thus the focus in this chapter is not on programme content, but on management issues in ensuring the integrity and quality of programmes for offenders.

THE IMPORTANCE OF INTEGRITY

A perfect example of the importance of integrity is provided by Quay's discussion (1987) of a project he had undertaken a decade earlier. In this earlier work, Quay had examined in detail an evaluation of a programme of group counselling with adult offenders. This study, originally reported by Kassenbaum et al. (1971), had found that the intervention, group counselling, had not had any impact on rates of recidivism. The design of the study, Quay continues, was exemplary, even involving random allocation of participants to treatment and control conditions. At face value we have a well designed piece of outcome research that found, like so many others, that a caring, therapeutic programme does not affect recidivism: more fuel, it seems, for the proponents of the 'nothing works' position. However, when Quay began to look at the minutiae of the intervention it appeared

What Works: Reducing Reoffending—Guidelines from Research and Practice.
Edited by J. McGuire. © 1995 John Wiley & Sons Ltd.

that all was not as might have been wished. The treatment protocol was poorly defined and the delivery of the counselling itself was not well planned. Yet further:

> The majority of the practitioners responsible for carrying out the treatment were not convinced that it would affect recidivism (the major dependent variable of the study), and the group leaders (*not* professional counselors) were poorly trained. The treatment was clearly *not* well implemented. (Quay, 1987: 246).

Indeed, to quote Quay yet again, 'What was striking was the serious lack of what we termed "program integrity"' (Quay, 1987: 245–246). Nevertheless, in spite of these operational factors, which would clearly have diluted the impact of the programme, the study itself entered the annals of similar studies that fail to show any effect of intervention on recidivism. The final product of a string of such 'failures' is, of course, the view that 'nothing works'; this view, in turn, produces disenchantment among practitioners and poor services (Hollin & Henderson, 1984). What, then, are the factors that threaten programme integrity, and what are the unwanted consequences?

THREATS TO INTEGRITY

That the effectiveness of an intervention is dependent upon the rigour with which that intervention is conducted is an obvious point. No one should really be surprised that this was one of the main points to emerge from the meta-analysis studies (e.g. Lipsey, 1992). It is now clear that the most effective programmes, in terms of reducing recidivism, have high treatment integrity: they are carried out by trained practitioners, and the treatment initiators are involved in all the operational phases of the programme. In other words, effective programmes with high treatment integrity are characterized by sound management, tight design and skilled practitioners.

It is important to note that treatment integrity applies equally to all interventions, whatever their theoretical base, method of working or client group. Treatment integrity simply means that the programme is conducted in practice as intended in theory and design.

As Moncher and Prinz (1991) note, with only occasional exceptions (as exemplified by Quay's work), concern about treatment integrity has only recently surfaced in the outcome literature. However, this is now changing rapidly, so that it is not impossible to see a position where to be taken seriously programmes will have to show that they have a high level of integrity. Given this, in order to begin to suggest a way forward, it is useful to identify the potential threats to integrity. There are at least three threats to programme integrity: (1) programme drift; (2) programme reversal; and (3) programme non-compliance.

Programme Drift

As described by Johnson (1981), programme drift is characterized by the gradual shift over time of the aim of a programme. Johnson describes how a psychodynamic programme for offenders gradually moved over time from an emphasis on therapeutic issues to a concern with routine administration. Johnson suggests that a lack of management and the immediacy of routine matters as opposed to longer-term therapeutic goals gradually changed the nature of the programme.

Programme Reversal

This is perfectly illustrated by Schlichter and Horan (1981) in their account of a self-control programme to help young offenders control their anger and aggression. They record how some staff worked to reverse and undermine the self-control approach: 'Some modeled aggressive behavior in response to anger provocations. Others operating from a different theoretical perspective encouraged the subjects to experience and express their "pent up" anger' (Schlichter & Horan, 1981: 34).

Clearly this is less than satisfactory for all concerned, particularly the unfortunate young people for whom the experience must have been entirely confusing and counterproductive.

Programme Non-compliance

With non-compliance there is a situation in which the practitioners conducting the programme elect, for reasons of their own, to change or omit parts of the programme. At the whim of the individual practitioner, some sessions are dropped, new methods introduced, fresh targets for change added, the original material chopped about, and so on. The final product of all this, especially if the programme has been 'handed down' through several sessions of in-service training, is rather like the last murmur in a game of Chinese Whispers. There may be some vestige of the original message, but the original meaning is lost forever.

MAXIMIZING INTEGRITY

How can these threats to integrity be minimized? What needs to be done to maximize the chances of programme integrity? The starting point in answering this question must be to devise a way to monitor and measure integrity: without a system of measurement it is impossible to tell what is happening. There are two ways to look at the issue of monitoring and measurement: the first from the perspective of applied psychology, the second from a management viewpoint.

A Psychological Approach

If the issue of measuring integrity is viewed as a problem in applied psychology, then several conditions must be met to conform with the rules of good empirical practice. The first prerequisite of a sound empirical approach is a correctly formulated and defined experimental *aim*, perhaps including one or more hypotheses, which encapsulates the purpose of the study. To achieve that aim and test the hypotheses, the experimenter needs a *methodology* that must, in turn, be accompanied by a precise experimental *procedure* and *design*. To give meaningful data, the procedure and design must, of course, include clearly defined *independent* and *dependent variables*. Finally, the implementation of the procedure must be of demonstrable methodological rigour, so that there must be some assessment of programme reliability.

Now if this all sounds rather too scientific, what if the jargon is changed. As shown in Table 10.1, the experimental metaphor translates reasonably well into contemporary management terminology.

In management terms, the experimental aim might be thought of as, say, a strategic or corporate objective, or even a mission, which expresses a purpose for the service. This mission might, for example, be expressed as: 'By best practice to reduce recidivism among offenders placed on probation'. To turn this mission into practice, a management system (i.e. methodology) is needed. Thus, the mission may be translated into several objectives, for example: 'To introduce programmes for working with offenders consistent with "what works"'. To achieve this service objective it will be necessary to introduce (through training) a standard

Table 10.1. Interplay between psychological and management terminology.

Experimental terms	Managerial terms
Aim	Mission
Methodology	Management system/objectives
Procedure	Programme
Design	Strategy/targets
Dependent and independent variables	Performance indicators
Reliability	Audit

programme (i.e. procedure) for practitioners to follow, while this must be accompanied by a strategy (i.e. design) by which to introduce the programme, monitor its running and evaluate its effectiveness. This strategy will then generate targets such as: 'Using trained staff, to run x groups for $y\%$ of offenders on probation'. Finally, to ensure that the programme is being run as planned, it will be necessary to have an audit (i.e. estimate of reliability). An audit needs performance indicators (PIs), here of two types: process measures during the programme, and outcome measures after the programme (i.e. two classes of independent variable). These measures must be defined; they might include, for example, the number of sessions attended, change in attitude towards offending, and recidivism (i.e. dependent variables). Of course, one of these dependent variables may be more important than the others: given the aim of the programme, recidivism may be monitored as a 'key performance indicator' (KPI)

Treatment integrity really depends on the satisfactory completion of all these management tasks, but with an emphasis on audit: is the programme running in practice as intended in design? Now, clearly, the factors that ensure best practice are not going to happen of their own accord: those individuals responsible for research and management must be aware of a number of practical factors.

PROGRAMME INTEGRITY: IN PRACTICE

To achieve high programme integrity it is necessary to set the scene by paying attention to several areas well before a client is seen.

Treatment Definition

It is an obvious point, but worth stating, that to be able to follow a programme, it is first necessary to define what is to be done during that programme. In practice this means a statement of quantity and content: for example, planning the number and length of sessions; knowing which techniques will be used; planning and detailing the content of sessions; and the selection and justification of the measures that will be used to evaluate changes in the client's behaviour. This whole procedure is made much easier when programmes are guided by a treatment manual.

A good manual is one that is firmly based on a respectable theory, and is itself meticulously researched and evaluated by proficient researchers and practitioners. A sound manual will contain detailed guidelines for the design, setting up, running and evaluation of a given treatment programme. For example, take the ideal social skills training manual. This manual would have to contain a discussion of the theoretical basis of social skills training; details of skills training techniques; information on the equipment that will be needed; suggestions for practice, say how to construct a role-play and some vignettes around which to construct role-plays for different situations; information on the ordering of components of the programme—typically modelling, role-play, practice, feedback; how to handle tricky situations, such as someone not coming 'out of role' after a role-play; and scales for evaluation of outcome.

Having set up the programme, the active part of the process needs to be considered, that is, the strategies that can be used to monitor and inform the management of programme integrity. Needless to say, this is enormously time-consuming.

Assessing Quantity and Quality

There are three sources of information on the quality and quantity of a programme: (1) outside observers of programmes; (2) client report; and (3) practitioner report. While there is room for all three, it is generally agreed that outside observers are the most objective and reliable judges, especially of the quality of an intervention.

Observer Recording

To be effective recorders of programme integrity, outside observers must be in a position to examine the actual work, not just rely on verbal reports from practitioners and clients. To maximize the utility of outside observers, several conditions must be met. The observers, note the plural, must themselves be skilled and trained in the treatment approach, and be familiar with the particular planned programme they are going to observe. The periods of observation, using live and/or videotaped observation, must be substantial and, ideally, follow a prearranged sampling schedule. For example, the decision could be made to sample, say, 50% of sessions, or to observe all the components of the treatment programme. The observers should be trained to follow the same procedures in recording their observations. There are several rating procedures available that can be adapted for most purposes (e.g Marziali et al., 1981).

The final product of the observational evaluation will be a statement of the match between what was planned at the outset and what was delivered in practice. Such a statement of quality and quantity has a number of uses (for both managers and practitioners): it can be used to answer questions about the client's experience of treatment, it can be helpful in informing the design of future treatment programmes, it can be a useful method of performance feedback to practitioners, and it should be an essential component of statements of outcome.

Practitioner and Client Report

While observer information is important, the need to consider the views of practitioners and clients should not be ignored in measuring programme integrity. A system should be developed to allow practitioners and clients systematically to record their judgements of the progress and integrity of the programme. A record should be kept of the quantitative aspects— length of sessions, number of sessions, etc.—of the programme. Periodic debriefing interviews should be held with both practitioners and clients, while practitioners should be encouraged to keep a log of contacts, recording both quantitative and qualitative information (Johnson, 1981). Armed with information on the progress of the programme from observer ratings, practitioner logs and client feedback, it should be possible to establish the degree of programme integrity. Basically, this statement of integrity will be across several dimensions, some of which might be as follows: (1) was the quantity of treatment as planned?; (2) did the practitioner stay on course or was there a drift away from the planned focus of the programme?; (3) was there significant client change, in the anticipated direction, on the evaluation measures?; (4) did the clients feel that their expectations had been met?

There are several examples of schedules designed to assess overall programme integrity. For example, the STOP Programme run by the Mid Glamorgan Probation Service in Wales produced a document for practitioners, *Achieving Programme Integrity*, which not only make the case for integrity but give their Programme Integrity Checklist (Mid Glamorgan Probation Service, 1991). This checklist, completed during the STOP programme by session leaders and programme consultants, produces several ratings, such as the extent to which session focus was maintained, and deviations from the planned session. The first report on the STOP programme was not only able to comment generally on maintenance of integrity, but could pinpoint where and how integrity was threatened (Lucas et al., 1992). Thus, the eventual outcome figures of the STOP programme evaluation will be informed by the assessment of integrity. In a similar vein, the Correctional Programme Evaluation Inventory (Gendreau & Andrews, 1991) is a highly sophisticated psychometric instrument that looks at a range of programme characteristics, including integrity.

What happens when we go to this amount of trouble in thinking about integrity? My view is that once one begins to consider issues of integrity, then one is forced to think about quality. There are three specific areas— ethics, practice, research—that immediately suggest themselves as important when considering the interplay between programme integrity and quality.

INTEGRITY AND QUALITY

Ethical Issues

If as practitioners we enter an agreement with a client to undertake a specific piece of work, then there is a strong argument to say that we are ethically bound to be in a position to give clients some facts. We should be able to inform the client what that work entails, how long it will last, how it will be carried out, and what they might reasonably expect as an outcome if they participate fully. It is important to note that the definition of 'client' can be extended to include not only those individuals seen on a face-to-face basis, but also the courts with whom agreements are made about what will happen in given cases. As noted, a clear statement of the programme's aims and methods is a prerequisite for high levels of integrity, which goes some way towards satisfying ethical demands.

The monitoring of programme integrity further extends our ability to respond to ethical demands. Not only should we be able to start what we plan to do, we should be able to state whether the planning has turned into practice. Armed with this level of knowledge, we can inform clients, courts and anyone else who is interested, that the agreement has been kept (and if not, why not).

Practice Issues

Leaving aside ethical issues, there are practical benefits to be gained from working towards high levels of integrity through monitoring the effects of a programme. At a broad level, concern about integrity as part of a management system is an important component in setting quality standards (e.g. CCETSW, 1992). At a practitioner level, concern with the details of practice can have beneficial effects on delivery of services. Bruggen and Pettle offer an excellent example of monitoring integrity:

> When considering the initial contact with a family attending a first appointment, a team decided that it was good practice for the therapist to:
> (i)   Extend a hand and offer eye contact with each member of the family;
> (ii)   Introduce her- or himself;
> (iii) Describe and explain the equipment in use;
> (iv)   Answer questions asked by the family relating to equipment;
> (v)   Make a clear statement about the structure and length of the session;
> (vi)   Describe the team and method of live supervision. (Bruggen & Pettle, 1993: 89).

Through observation, an audit was carried out focusing on the extent to which the actual practice matched the intentions expressed above. It was found that two factors lowered integrity: 'Good practice was not occurring when the therapist was a trainee, or on the one day in the week when the team was very rushed' (p. 89). This discovery, in turn, led to a fresh emphasis on training new therapists, and to a reorganization of the appointment booking system.

Indeed, there are many potentially beneficial consequences of monitoring integrity. For example, many programmes last for lengthy periods of time, and although the intervention is successful the rate of change can be slow. A record of the progress and effects of the programme can serve both to remind the practitioner and client of what has been achieved, and to reinforce their working relationship. Another practical reason for monitoring progress is that if a programme is failing, then this can be detected at an early stage and appropriate steps taken. In truth, these practical reasons are simply different sides of the same coin: systematically looking to see whether what we are doing is what we set out to do, and whether we are having the desired effect. Armed with this knowledge, practitioners and managers should be in a position to improve the quality of practice.

Research Issues

It is probably true to say that most practitioners are not researchers in the formal, academic sense of the term. However, there is most certainly research taking place—in Manchester and Mid Glamorgan Probation Services, for example—that has the potential to have a substantial impact on probation work. Knowledge of programme integrity, as Quay so graphically described, is essential when it come to reading the results of studies such as those in Manchester and Mid Glamorgan. For research findings to be of impact, it must be shown that all participants followed the same programme, using trained and skilled practitioners, and with similar outcome measures.

While structured programmes will go some way towards setting the scene for high programme integrity, clearly they will not be sufficient on their own. Attention must also be paid to the needs of the practitioners who are going to be delivering the programme.

Practitioners

Selection, Training and Support

It is true to say that most practitioners have a preferred style of working and like a particular client group. Thus, some practitioners like working with groups, others prefer working with individuals; some practitioners like one style of counselling, some like another; some prefer active methods of working, like role-play and modelling, others prefer more contemplative, less directive methods; some people like working with adolescents, others prefer adults. There is, of course, room for all styles and approaches, but it makes sense at the onset to match the practitioner to their preferred style of intervention. This is particularly true when it comes to the type of work being advocated here: for reasons I will return to, it seems likely that not all practitioners will be happy for some of their work to be guided by a manual.

For those practitioners who elect to use a structured approach, training is essential, and likely to increase programme integrity. A trained practitioner is more likely to be a competent practitioner, one who understands why they are doing what they are doing and stays with the programme.

It would be wrong, however, to assume that training is all that is needed. The availability of good supervision is a vital ingredient to maintaining programme integrity. Through supervision by an experienced individual, practitioner performance can be monitored and feedback offered. Needless to say, supervisory arrangements should be negotiated before treatment begins.

PROBLEMS AND PITFALLS

By this stage, it will be evident that the monitoring of programme integrity faces many obstacles: there are (at least) three potential sources—the organization, the client and the practitioner.

Organizational Resistance

The concept of organizational resistance refers to the obstacles, whether in a community or institutional setting, that hinder and impede the development of programmes with high integrity. In a classic paper Laws (1974) described the barriers he faced when attempting to set up a residential treatment programme with offenders. Essentially these barriers were about who exercised control over the programme to safeguard treatment integrity: who had control over admission of offenders to the programme; who had control over the timing of offenders leaving the programme; who had control over the finances and resources; and who had control over practitioner training to run the programme. Laws, in common with other authors, documented professional clashes with both administrators and fellow practitioners.

Of course it would be foolish to suggest that such organizational issues will be easily resolved. However, if we turn to the principles described by Reppucci (1973) some solutions begin to appear. In essence, Reppucci suggested that the chances of high levels of integrity are greatly increased if policies can be formulated along the following lines: (i) a clear guiding philosophy that is understood by all those involved in the process of rehabilitation; (ii) an organizational structure that facilitates communication and accountability; (iii) an involvement of all staff in decision-making; (iv) setting time restraints in developing and 'tuning' programmes, thereby resisting the pressure to try to do too much in too short a space of time.

Clearly the formulation of policies around these points is a highly involved task. One pitfall that it is easy to fall into is that training will solve all the problems. However, as Ziarnik and Bernstein (1982) point out, there are many reasons other than a lack of training that can account for poor organizational performance. There may not be any clear criteria by which staff and management can judge performance; poor performance may be reinforced socially by the organizational culture, or tangibly by the award of incentives such as pay rises and promotion on criteria other than practitioner skills; or practitioner skills are not reinforced in an organization that places greater priority on other matters. In other words, if the organization is not committed to programme integrity, even the most highly trained, highly skilled practitioners will have little impact. No amount of training is going to change an organizational climate that only pays lip service to the importance of integrity. Training is a strategy to be used within, not instead of, a coherent organizational structure.

Client Resistance

In the same way that clients may be reluctant to engage in programmes, so they may similarly be reluctant to engage in evaluation. However, this may be a matter of presentation: if an expectation of contributing towards evaluation is part of the programme, rather than being presented as an optional extra, then client compliance is much more likely. Indeed, with today's consumer-led ethos, clients might well welcome the chance to offer an appraisal of the service they are offered!

Practitioner Resistance

I can see two dimensions to practitioner objections to monitoring of programme integrity: one at a philosophical level, the other at a practical level.

Philosophical Objections

To engage in measurement of treatment integrity, one has to accept two related underlying principles. The first is that one adopts a scientist–practitioner approach to one's work; the second is that one accepts that an empirical approach should inform one's practice. In other words, one is committed to the principle that practice will be informed by data gathered, as much as possible, according to the rules of scientific enquiry (Barlow et al., 1984). If this sounds rather imposing, there are several excellent guides that will help practitioner evaluation of their work (e.g. Herbert, 1990).

Related to this empirical approach is the partial surrender of professional autonomy. When practice is based on an established programme, it becomes much more difficult to sustain the position that each practitioner knows what is best for their client and works along those lines, doing what they feel they and their client will relate to. It is true that when guided by rigorous assessment the practitioner will be uniquely placed to judge their client's needs. However, once the decision is made, say, to use a Reasoning and Rehabilitation programme (Ross & Fabiano, 1985), it has to be accepted that one will follow the programme manual. It has to be agreed at the onset that the package has been designed as a package, not something to borrow from and change as one might see fit. Tinkering with programme design and procedures is a recipe for low integrity, which is not conducive to a good outcome.

Everyday experience says that practitioners will differ in their response to this: some will happily and creatively work within a programme, while others will be unable to accept these principles. This is not to say who is right and who is wrong: it must be recognized, of course, that there are other equally valid philosophies in this area. However, my personal view is that each approach must maintain its own standards of integrity: I fail to see any role for mix and match eclecticism.

Practical Objections

The practical objections are those objections that arise every time evaluation is mentioned, namely, that the evaluation can be intrusive, and that the information gathered during evaluation could be misused. Both are surely true, but neither is insurmountable. Practice teachers sit in on their student's work, so why should it be impossible to make acceptable arrangements for others to sit in on, or even videotape, our work? It is the case that evaluation data can be used in way for which it was not intended, say by management to appraise practitioner performance to inform promotion decisions. To prevent this, stringent conditions must be detailed at the onset about who has access to evaluative information and what purpose this information will serve.

SUMMARY

There can be little doubt that at present we are seeing the re-emergence of a treatment ethos in the field of working with offenders (Palmer, 1992). The meta-analyses have pointed us in the direction we should move towards to construct effective programmes (e.g. Lipsey, 1992; this volume, Chapter 3). However, this knowledge should guide not only the content of programmes, but also focus attention on the need to monitor treatment integrity. It is plain that there are many issues to be struggled with before programme integrity becomes an accepted part of everyone's practice. In my view the struggle is worthwhile for several reasons, the most important of which is that with high levels of integrity programmes have a greater chance of success. Successful programmes with offenders that reduce criminal behaviour are to the obvious benefit of all concerned.

REFERENCES

Barlow, D. H., Hayes, S. C. & Nelson, R. O. (1984). *The Scientist Practitioner: Research and Accountability in Clinical and Educational Settings*. Boston: Allyn & Bacon.

Bruggen, P. & Pettle, S. (1993). RUMBASOL: Audit in practice. *Journal of Family Therapy*, **15**, 87–92.

CCETSW (1992). *Setting Quality Standards for Residential Child Care*. London: Central Council for Education and Training in Social Work.

Gendreau, P. & Andrews, D. A. (1991). *Correctional Program Evaluation Inventory* (2nd edn). New Brunswick: University of New Brunswick.

Herbert, M. (1990). *Planning a Research Project: A Guide for Practitioners and Trainees in the Helping Professions*. London: Cassell.

Hollin, C. R. (1990). *Cognitive–Behavioral Interventions With Young Offenders*. Elmsford: Pergamon Press.

Hollin, C. R. (1993). Advances in the psychological treatment of delinquent behaviour. *Criminal Behaviour and Mental Health*, **3**, 142–157.

Hollin, C. R. & Henderson, M. (1984). Social skills training with young offenders: False expectations and the 'failure of treatment'. *Behavioural Psychotherapy*, **12**, 331–341.

Johnson, V. S. (1981). Staff drift: A problem in treatment integrity. *Criminal Justice and Behavior*, **8**, 223–232.

Kassenbaum, G., Ward, D. & Wilner, D. (1971). *Prison Treatment and Parole Survival: An Empirical Assessment*. New York: Wiley.

Laws, D. R. (1974). The failure of a token economy. *Federal Probation*, **38**, 33–38.

Lipsey, M. (1992). Juvenile delinquency treatment. A meta-analytic inquiry into the viability of effects. In T. Cook, H. Cooper, D. Corday, H. Hartman, L. Hedges,

R. Light, T. Louis & F. Mosteller (Eds). *Meta-Analysis for Explanation: A Casebook*. New York: Russell Sage Foundation.
Lucas, J., Raynor, P. & Vanstone, M. (1992). *Straight Thinking on Probation: 1 Year On*. Bridgend: Mid Glamorgan Probation Service.
Marziali, E., Marmar, C. & Krupnick, J. (1981). Therapeutic alliance scales: Development and relationship to psychotherapy outcome. *American Journal of Psychiatry*, **138**, 361–364.
Mid Glamorgan Probation Service. (1991). *S.T.O.P Probation Order: Achieving 'Programme Integrity'*. Bridgend: Mid Glamorgan Probation Service.
Moncher, F. J. & Prinz, R. J. (1991). Treatment fidelity in outcome studies. *Clinical Psychology Review*, **11**, 247–266.
Mulvey, E. P., Arthur, M. W. & Reppucci, N. D. (1993). The prevention and treatment of juvenile delinquency: A review of research. *Clinical Psychology Review*, **13**, 133–167.
Palmer, T. (1992). *The Re-emergence of Correctional Intervention*. Newbury Park: Sage Publications.
Quay, H.C. (1987). Institutional treatment. In H. C. Quay (Ed.). *Handbook of Juvenile Delinquency*. New York: Wiley.
Reppucci, N. D. (1973). Social psychology of institutional change: General principles for intervention. *American Journal of Community Psychology*, **1**, 330–341.
Ross, R. R. & Fabiano, E. A. (1985). *Time to Think: A Cognitive Model of Delinquency Prevention and Offender Rehabilitation*. Johnson City: Institute of Social Sciences and Arts.
Schlichter, K. J. & Horan, J. J. (1981). Effects of stress inoculation on the anger and aggression management skills of institutionalized juvenile delinquents. *Cognitive Therapy and Research*, **5**, 359–365.
Ziarnik, J. P. & Bernstein, G. S. (1982). A critical examination of the effect of inservice training on staff performance. *Mental Retardation*, **20**, 109–114.

CHAPTER 11

Practitioner Evaluation in Probation

Gill McIvor
University of Stirling, Scotland

THE CASE FOR PRACTITIONER RESEARCH

Research and evaluation have tended to be little-used terms in the vocabulary of social workers and probation officers. Broadly speaking, evaluative research has had limited impact upon probation policy and practice (e.g. Jenkins, 1987). There are several notable exceptions, an obvious one being the erosion of rehabilitative aspirations in response to the pessimistic conclusions of Martinson (1974) and others (e.g. Brody, 1976; Sechrest et al., 1979) in the 1970s.

There are several reasons why effectiveness research appears to have had a limited impact upon probation practice. Researchers (and especially academic researchers) have often been accused of addressing issues that are of limited relevance to day-to-day practice; of producing reports that are indigestible and obscure; and of failing to recognize the mechanisms by which, in organizations such as probation departments, policies and practices are developed and changed. Educators responsible for pre- and postqualifying training have likewise come under fire (e.g. Sheldon, 1987) for failing to equip practitioners with an appreciation of research and its applicability to practice.

It is also widely believed that social work and probation practice emerge badly when subjected to research. It has, until recently, been more common, for example, for social work to be reported for its lack of impact on

What Works: Reducing Reoffending—Guidelines from Research and Practice.
Edited by J. McGuire. © 1995 John Wiley & Sons Ltd.

delinquent activity than for its achievements: more positive accounts of probation practice have tended, though not always, to be ignored, though there is good reason for this to change (Sheldon, 1994).

Evaluative research does, none the less, have a crucial contribution to make to the development of effective methods of working with offenders. Without the many carefully conducted evaluations of practice that have been carried out over the past few years we would not now be in the position to identify which types of approaches are most effective with which types of offenders in reducing offending behaviour. Our understanding of 'what works' can only be further refined and the quality and impact of services enhanced if probation practice is more widely subjected to systematic evaluation of its effectiveness.

The concepts of evaluation and effectiveness have gained wider currency in a political climate of accountability, efficiency and value for money. Intrinsic evaluation may be a specific requirement of the funding of innovative projects and may be a necessary means of ensuring the continuation of established services. Increasingly, practitioners have begun to take a more active role in monitoring and evaluating the services they provide. The starting point of this Chapter is the twofold belief that practitioners should be encouraged to engage in the evaluation of their own practice, and that they possess many of the skills necessary to undertake the evaluative task. Evaluative research has traditionally been regarded as the proper domain of the 'experts'—the academic and in-house researchers—but as Collett and Hook (1991) have argued, there are various reasons why practitioners should be encouraged to become involved in the evaluation of their practice.

On a purely pragmatic level, it is likely to be the case that if practitioners do not evaluate the effectiveness of their work with clients then no one else will. There simply are not enough in-house (agency-based) and academic researchers available to evaluate the numerous innovative projects that have been developed over recent years. In-house researchers are usually limited in their ability to undertake evaluative research by demands to provide management information for their organization. Researchers in academic institutions are under increasing pressure to undertake work of a more 'strategic' nature while financial constraints upon universities and colleges mean that researchers in these settings are likely only to be able to provide their services at a cost.

Practitioners are, furthermore, often better placed then external evaluators to design and conduct evaluative studies that maximize their usefulness and minimize their intrusiveness into day-to-day practice. External researchers, by virtue of their independence, may bring additional objectivity to the evaluative task but they may also be less sensitive to the additional demands that the evaluation places upon practitioners and may not share with them the priorities attached to different aspects of their practice. As Steve Collett and Richard Hook point out in their discussion of practitioner evaluation in a group care setting, 'there is nothing more deflating than operating a monitoring system which is time-consuming for both workers and residents and amasses information which is either inaccessible or useless' (Collett & Hook, 1991: 113).

Further, if evaluative research is to occupy a more prominent position in relation to the development of effective policies and practice it will be necessary to create a 'culture of evaluation' in agencies. This will require that managers and practitioners come to regard evaluation as an integral component of practice and as a means of positively influencing service provision. Within such a framework, probation officers would, for example, be encouraged as a matter of course to review systematically their work with clients and assess jointly with their clients the extent to which the objectives of intervention identified in individual cases have been achieved. The incorporation of evaluation into day to day practice can facilitate the setting of objectives in work with individual offenders and can improve the quality of services offered to clients. The creation of a culture of evaluation should, in addition, facilitate the development of an informed approach to management and to service development.

Practitioners who need further convincing that evaluation should be an integral component of probation practice may be finally persuaded by McGuire's comment that:

> Numerous, ingenious programmes have been carefully nurtured into existence and steered through to their conclusions, only to disappear—because not one shred of evidence had been gathered about their clientele, their functioning or their effectiveness. Systematic programme planning involves the notion of 'what to evaluate and how' being embedded into the thinking of the staff group from the outset of the enterprise. (McGuire, 1991a: 50).

THE PROCESS OF EVALUATIVE RESEARCH

Having argued the case for increased practitioner research, I will now turn briefly to consider how practitioners might go about evaluating the effectiveness of their work with clients. Before doing so, some clarification is in order. Sometimes the terms 'monitoring' and 'evaluation' are used as though they are interchangeable. Monitoring is, however, a much more limited exercise, though it can serve evaluative purposes (if, for example, a primary concern is with how effectively services have been targeted). It has been defined by Mair as follows:

> Essentially, monitoring is the collection of basic information which will enable one to recognise any changes which are taking place and thus when

there may be a problem with a practice or system, or when certain standards do not appear to be being met, or inequalities or inconsistencies seem
to be occurring. (Mair, 1991: 88).

Evaluation, on the other hand, entails an assessment of the impact of a
service against some previously defined criteria or goals. In the scientific
tradition, effectiveness is normally assessed through the use of control
groups, where individuals are randomly allocated either to a 'treatment'
group or to a 'no treatment' control or, alternatively, to two different forms
of 'treatment'. For both practical and ethical reasons, the experimental
paradigm cannot, however, be readily applied to the probation setting and
other methods of evaluation are therefore usually required.

SMART
objectives
 In project or group evaluation, effectiveness can be most fruitfully examined by exploring the extent to which service objectives have been achieved
(though this may beg the question of how appropriate the objectives were
in the first case or, put another way, how much value should be attached
to them). The first step in the evaluative process involves a careful and
clear definition of the purposes of the research and the questions that it
seeks to address. Since the research questions as initially defined will influence the nature of information collected and, as a consequence, the conclusions that can be drawn, it is crucial that the purposes of the evaluation
are clearly defined from the outset. This in turn requires that the objectives of intervention are defined in ways that enable their achievement
to be assessed (Stecher & Davis, 1987). The process of translating project
objectives into 'researchable questions' for which appropriate outcome
measures can be identified can be informative in itself. Sometimes this
will be relatively straightforward: if, for example, a practice objective is
to reduce the severity or range of personal problems experienced by
offenders, then methods of measuring problem reduction (such as the
administration of problem checklists before and after intervention) can
be easily applied. If an objective is so vague or intangible that it cannot
be cast into operational terms and subjected to some form of measurement, this may call into question the appropriateness of the objective itself.
If a project embraces a number of objectives, it may be necessary to proceed
on an incremental basis or to focus primarily or exclusively upon those
which are held as central to its philosophy or aims. The selection of
outcome measures will be determined by the objectives of the evaluation.
Some outcome measures (such as those which indicate whether successful
targeting has been achieved) will relate to broader project or agency objectives while others (such as those which address problem reduction, attitudinal change or reductions in offending behaviour) will be concerned
with the impact of intervention upon clients.

 Sources of data might include existing agency records and monitoring
systems which are suitably adapted to provide the information required.
Client feedback, on a sessional basis or at the end of intervention, can

provide valuable insights into the perceived usefulness of different programme components and their impact upon clients. Attitudinal and other measurement scales (such as problem checklists) can be introduced at the beginning and end of the programme to assess change over the course of intervention and to provide a focus for review. It should be clear, therefore, that with a bit of imagination and with little adaptation to existing practice, a range of information can be drawn upon by practitioners to evaluate the effectiveness of the services and programmes they provide.

Although the preceding discussion has focused upon group evaluation, similar principles can also be applied in the evaluation of practice with individual clients. The single-case design offers practitioners a methodology for measuring client change over the course of intervention. Some of the more sophisticated designs enable the researcher to separate out the specific contribution of intervention (as opposed to other factors) to the process of change. Single-case designs have most commonly been applied to behavioural methods, where outcomes can be measured repeatedly over the course of intervention. In the offender literature, single-case designs have been employed across a range of behaviours, such as alcohol abuse, anger management and sexual offending. The outcomes to be measured need not be behavioural in nature but could include attitudinal change, problem reduction and improvements in cognitive or reasoning skills. Useful descriptions of the single-case design and its application can be found in Sheldon (1983), McGuire (1991b) and Morley (1989).

SOME PRACTICAL CONSIDERATIONS

A number of useful methodological texts exist, some of which are more general in nature (e.g. Cheetham et al., 1992; Jupp, 1989; Lishman, 1984) and some of which are more specifically geared towards the practitioner researcher (e.g. Addison, 1988; Everitt et al., 1992; Robson, 1993). Since these texts can usefully steer a researcher around the methodological obstacles which have to be contemplated when designing a piece of evaluative research, I will concentrate instead on highlighting some of the important practical considerations that need to be addressed before embarking upon a study. Some are peculiar to practitioner research: others are more pervasive, but may raise particular problems for practitioners engaged in the evaluation of their practice.

When to Evaluate?

New services or projects invariably undergo modification and development as teething problems are encountered and resolved. Policies and practices as originally defined may be revised in the light of experience in order that effectiveness may be enhanced. Researchers engaged in detailed evaluation early in the life of a project are likely to find themselves attempting to keep track of a moving target. More significantly, evaluation which is undertaken before a project has had the opportunity to learn from experience and adjust its practices accordingly may fail to reflect its true potential once initial difficulties have been identified and resolved.

It is important, on the other hand, to introduce appropriate systems for monitoring and evaluation from the outset. This might, for instance, involve the systematic recording of information about offenders referred to the project (What are their ages, gender and ethnic origins; What types of offences have they been convicted of; Do they have previous custodial experience?) and their progress through the programme (How many sessions were attended? Did the offender complete the programme? If not, why not?). Mechanisms for obtaining client feedback can also be introduced, enabling their views of the value and impact of the project to be collected on a systematic basis. Information of this kind can inform, from an early stage, the evolution of practice consistent with maximizing the effectiveness of services provided. Thinking about evaluation from the outset can also help to clarify and focus the objectives of a project by requiring that they be cast in operational/researchable terms.

Ideally, therefore, some basic but useful monitoring and evaluation should be undertaken from the start. A more focused and detailed evaluation, which addresses both the process of intervention and its outcomes, can then be conducted once the project has had time to settle down and initial practical issues have been resolved. Subsequent evaluation may, however, be critically dependent upon information gathered earlier in the life of the project.

Resources

Undertaking evaluative research as a practitioner can demand a considerable amount of time and energy, especially if the information required for the evaluation is not routinely available through existing practice. It is important, therefore, to make a realistic assessment of how much of an investment of time will be required and, if necessary, to be more modest in your evaluative aspirations. If the task is clearly focused and manageable, it is more likely to be seen through to completion: many practitioners abandon their research projects because they realize, in retrospect, that they have taken on much more than they can realistically handle.

Elicting the support of colleagues and managers is crucial. Colleagues may be required to take on some of your existing commitments to enable you to create the time and space necessary for conducting the evaluation. Sharing responsibility for the evaluation with a colleague, or embarking upon evaluation as a team effort, can help to spread the workload and limit the demands upon any individual worker. It may also be appropriate to recruit additional assistance from colleagues not closely involved with your project: for example, to interview clients or co-workers who might feel inhibited about expressing their views honestly and openly to someone with whom they are familiar and whom they know to have a personal interest in the project.

Managers have an essential role to play in ensuring that other demands do not infringe upon the time set aside for research. If time is not carefully negotiated and protected, practitioners are likely to find it virtually impossible to complete their evaluative studies while keeping on top of other aspects of their work and initial enthusiasm and commitment can quickly subside. Many managers do not, unfortunately, regard evaluation as an integral component of practice: the Social Work Research Centre's experience of advising practitioner researchers has shown than many complete their projects despite the lack of management support.

Access

It is necessary, too, to identify the types of access that will be required to conduct an evaluative study. Will it be necessary, for example, to interview colleagues within your agency? Will the co-operation of other agencies, such as the courts, be required? Are there formal procedures within your own or other organizations for negotiating access to records or to people you need to interview in connection with your research? These may appear to be rather mundane considerations, but if researchers fall foul of protocol then they may find themselves denied access to important types or sources of information that they require. If access to a particular source is denied, then it may be possible to obtain the necessary information through other means.

Confidentiality

Confidentiality is another aspect of research that can be given insufficient attention or even overlooked. When you give a guarantee of confidentiality to colleagues, to clients or to others whose views you have drawn upon in your evaluation what does it really mean? Is it enough to anonymize clients or sources of information? Even if an individual or agency is not named in any resulting report, could they nevertheless be identified by someone familiar with the project or its parent organization? Bald assurances may, therefore, not be enough: it will be necessary to spell out clearly the implications of participating in the evaluation and the extent to which the confidentiality of the views that are expressed can be guaranteed.

A related issue, which can pose particular problems for the practitioner researcher, concerns how to respond if professional/personal conflicts are unearthed in the course of the evaluation or, more worryingly, if poor or potentially damaging practice is uncovered. There are no easy answers: the manner in which important practice issues or professional conflicts are addressed will depend very much upon the climate in an agency and the manner in which colleagues and managers are likely to respond. It is, however, necessary to give some thought beforehand to how, as a practitioner, and perhaps as a manager, issues such as these may be aired and resolved.

Finding an Advisor

In her workbook for practitioner researchers, Carole Addison stresses the importance of finding a research advisor who can assist with the design and execution of a study and provide, where necessary, moral and practical support. She suggests that:

> Two qualities are essential in a research advisor: the ability to advise on the technicalities of undertaking your project, and the ability to be objective in carrying it out. He or she should also be sympathetic to the idea of workers undertaking research, and able to advise on how to conduct a small-scale project without sacrificing research integrity. (Addison, 1988: 31).

Addison (1988) suggests that while a knowledge of probation practice might be useful, there can also be benefits in having to convey clearly to someone outside the profession your working philosophy and aims and the objectives of your evaluation.

Departmental researchers and researchers in academic institutions will often be happy to offer practitioner researchers the necessary guidance while completing evaluative projects. They may also be well placed to offer advice about how to deal with worrying information about practice that is disclosed by the evaluation or with professional or personal conflicts that are unearthed.

GETTING THE MESSAGE ACROSS

Having completed a study the final, but by no means least important, step involves disseminating the results. Dissemination, which need not be confined exclusively to the final stages of the evaluation, can serve a number of purposes. The format in which reports of the evaluation are presented will be influenced to a significant extent by the audience for whom and purposes for which it is intended.

Feedback to participants. Researchers have an obligation to provided feedback to individuals and agencies who have participated in the evaluation and who are likely to be influenced by conclusions and recommendations flowing from it. In addition to providing participants with a copy of the findings it will often be appropriate to consult them at an earlier stage (that is, prior to the production of a finalized report) to ensure that their views have been accurately represented and to seek their assistance, if necessary, in explaining and interpreting results.

Influencing service provision. Dissemination of your findings can be a means of influencing policy makers, service managers and other agencies in order that improvements can be made in practice and in service delivery. The evaluation may be instrumental in securing the continued funding of a project; it may highlight the need for additional resources or for redeployment of existing resources; and it may identify other gaps in locally available services. Short summary reports (such as the ones produced by participants in the Social Work Research Centre's (1991) practitioner research programme) will often be the most effective way of conveying concisely to those who can directly influence service provision the implications of your findings for future policy and practice.

Promoting effective practice. Wider dissemination (via reports or articles in professional or academic journals) can contribute to an enhanced understanding among the profession of what constitutes effective practice with offenders. In this way practitioners who engage in the evaluation of their own work can contribute to the wider debate about what works and can positively influence the development both locally and elsewhere of effective responses to offending behaviour.

CONCLUDING COMMENTS

Evaluation requires skills—such as problem-solving, negotiation, effective interviewing and planning—which are already possessed by probation officers and which can, with a little advice and support, be readily applied in assessing the effectiveness of their work. Evaluation can draw upon a range of existing data and the collection of other types of information can often readily be incorporated into day-to-day practice. The support of colleagues and managers is, however, crucial and unless evaluation is accepted as a valid and essential aspect of practice, it is likely to make additional, perhaps even considerable, demands upon practitioners' time. The reality of practitioner research has perhaps been best summed up by Addison in the introductory section of her workbook:

> All the evidence suggests that only a minority of practitioners who begin investigative projects actually complete them. Fewer still go on to publish their results. Those who do finish their projects generally have some special personal reason which keeps them going. It might be a burning interest in some aspect of human behaviour or social work practice, or a desire for professional advancement, or the wish to raise funds for a particular piece of work. Some rare individuals are content to pursue knowledge for its own sake, but most of us need a 'pay-off' of some kind to justify the effort involved in carrying out a research project in addition to a full-time job. You need to ask yourself what your pay-off will be, and whether it will compensate you for all the hard work that lies ahead. (Addison, 1988: 5).

Practitioner evaluation can be immensely rewarding and fulfilling. It is less likely to be experienced as a difficult and lonely endeavour in an organization that promotes the concept of evaluation as practice and that actively encourages and supports practitioners in their attempts to improve, through evaluation, the quality and effectiveness of the services they provide.

REFERENCES

Addison, C. (1988). *Planning Investigative Projects: A Workbook for Social Services Practitioners*. London: National Institute for Social Work.

Brody, S. R. (1976). *The Effectiveness of Sentencing: A Review of the Literature*. Home Office Research Study No. 35. London: HMSO.

Cheetham, J., Fuller, R., McIvor, G. & Petch, A. (1992). *Evaluating Social Work Effectiveness*. Milton Keynes: Open University Press.

Collett, S. & Hook, R. (1991). Evaluating group care: Should we leave it to the experts? *Practice*, **5**, 111–120.

Everitt, A., Hardiker, P., Littlewood, J. & Mullender, A. (1992). *Applied Research for Better Practice*. BASW/Macmillan.

Jenkins, S. (1987). The limited domain of effectiveness research. *British Journal of Social Work*, **17**, 586–594.

Jupp, V. (1989). *Methods of Criminological Research*, London: Unwin Hyman.

Lishman, J. (Ed.) (1984). *Research Highlights 8: Evaluation*. Aberdeen: University of Aberdeen/Jessica Kingsley.

Mair, G. (1991). Difference, disparity, discrimination: Ethnic monitoring and its limitations. In *Developing Effective Practice: Managing an Informed Approach*. Oxford: Midlands Regional Staff Development Unit/University of Oxford.

Martinson, R. (1974). 'What works? Questions and answers about prison reform'. *The Public Interest*, **10**, 22–54.

McGuire, J. (1991a). 'Things to do to make your programme work'. In *What Works: Effective Methods to Reduce Re-offending. Conference Proceedings.* Manchester: Greater Manchester Probation Service.

McGuire, J. (1991b). The single case design: Implications of research for effective practice. In: C. Roberts (Ed.). *Developing Effective Practice: Managing an Informed Approach.* Birmingham: Midland Regional Staff Development Unit/University of Oxford.

Morley, S. (1989). Single case research. In G. Parry & F. N. Watts (Eds). *Behavioural and Mental Health Research: A Handbook of Skills and Methods.* London: Lawrence Erlbaum Associates.

Robson, C. (1993). *Real World Research: A Resource for Social Scientists and Practitioner-Researchers.* Oxford: Blackwell.

Sechrest, L., White, S. O. & Brown, E. D. (1979). *The Rehabilitation of Criminal Offenders: Problems and Prospects.* Washington: National Academy of Sciences.

Sheldon, B. (1983). The use of single case designs in the evaluation of social work. *British Journal of Social Work,* **13,** 477–500.

Sheldon, B. (1987). Implementing findings from social work effectiveness research. *British Journal of Social Work,* **17,** 573–586.

Sheldon, B. (1994). Social work effectiveness research: implications for proba-tion and juvenile justice services. *Howard Journal of Criminal Justice,* **33,** 218–235.

Social Work Research Centre (1991). *Practitioner Research Programme: Summary Reports.* Stirling: Social Work Research Centre, University of Stirling.

Stecher, B. M. & Davis, W. A. (1987). *How to Focus an Evaluation.* Newbury Park: Sage.

CHAPTER 12

Effective Practice and Service Delivery

Colin Roberts
Green College, University of Oxford, UK

Paul Gendreau and Robert Ross, in the conclusion to their 1987 review of evidence of effective rehabilitation programmes, stated:

> It is downright ridiculous to say 'nothing works'. This review attests that much is going on to indicate that offender rehabilitation has been, can be, and will be achieved. The principles underlying effective rehabilitation generalise across far too many intervention strategies and offender samples to be considered anything other than of great significance. Over the last decade we have mistaken the issue. It is this—how do we translate our ever developing behavioural technology so it is readily available to those in need? We are absolutely amateurish at implementing and maintaining our successful experimentally demonstrative programmes within the delivery systems provided routinely. This is what doesn't work! We have made only very tentative progress in examining the conditions under which the principles of effective intervention can be implemented and maintained successfully . . . (Gendreau & Ross, 1987:395).

This is the subject I want to review in this concluding chapter, because I take the view that however good and appropriate are the programmes you are using, or are planning to use, with offenders, they will have little chance of success unless particular attention is given to all aspects of the delivery and organization of such programmes—whether in probation services, social work and juvenile justice departments, prison establishments, health units or voluntary agencies.

There are of course many different aspects of service delivery for

What Works: Reducing Reoffending—Guidelines from Research and Practice.
Edited by J. McGuire. © 1995 John Wiley & Sons Ltd.

programmes for offenders, and some will clearly reflect the quite different settings in which programmes are delivered. Prisons and secure hospitals pose some different problems to probation day centres, hostels or community-based projects, not solely concerning the availability of offenders but also the different organizational and institutional objectives and demands made on both staff and offenders by the different settings.

What I want to review here, however, are the general principles and the range of issues influence and affect the delivery of effective practice across different organizational settings and agencies. Not all settings will be able or permitted in law to be directly involved in all aspects of effective service delivery, but even if a particular setting such as a prison cannot involve itself in all aspects of community-based provision and support for offenders once released, staff in prisons need to be aware and take account of the importance of such provision and the likely success of a programme started with offenders while in custody. Similarly, staff working in community-based provision need to be aware of the content of prison-based programmes, to ensure appropriate reinforcement and intervention before and after release.

There are three levels at which one can consider general issues concerning effective service delivery.

1. At the first level there is the need to consider an overall organizational plan or design, to locate the range and type of provision which a service might reasonably be expected to provide for effective work with offenders and sometimes with significant others (e.g. parents, partners, etc).
2. At the second level there is the need to have a clear framework for understanding the sequential order and processes involved in delivering, monitoring and evaluating effective practice. These plans are often largely determined by some existing organizational and statutory arrangements.
3. At the third level there is the need to have a clear framework to address the availability, knowledge and competency of staff to deliver effective practice. This should include work with and by other professionals and agencies, knowledge and skill development in staff, staff supervision and management, and other aids to enable staff to develop, deliver and sustain all elements of effective practice.

OVERALL ORGANIZATIONAL PLAN AND DESIGN OF PROVISION

There is a need in all settings for a clear overall organizational plan or design for the range and type of provision to be provided for offenders.

This requires clear and precise definitions not only of the range of programmes and provision to be provided, but also of which practitioners and which agencies or resources would manage and deliver the various elements. One model for such a plan is presented in Figure 12.1. It is based on a triangle with an 'individual offender focus' at its apex and a 'community focus' at the base of provision.

This particular model gives a picture of the range of provision that a typical probation division (or large team) might provide. At each level and in respect of each element, there needs to be not only a clear definition of the content and form of each element, but also precise details of where the primary responsibility rests for the delivery of each element. At the top for instance, a 'Reasoning and Cognition' course may be managed and taught by specified probation officers, as may some of the specific offending courses available, but the alcohol- or drug-abuse programmes may be run jointly with the specialist agency or solely run by such an agency on behalf of the probation service. A 'violence and aggression' course may be jointly run with staff from a local Regional Secure Unit, or again may be provided by a specialist group of probation service staff. In relation to probation service provision, as you move down the triangle there is a greater probability that elements will be either jointly run with other agencies or professionals, with some increasingly being provided by other agencies on a contractual basis. Literacy and numeracy courses (including special provision for offenders with dyslexia) are likely to be best provided by trained teachers, specializing in this field, probably based in colleges of further education. At the bottom level the provision is not solely for offenders, and will usually be completely provided by other agencies and organizations, possibly supported financially by a probation service or other statutory agency (Roberts, 1992a).

Such models (not necessarily triangular in shape, as this may for some situations overemphasize a hierarchy of provision) can be drawn by middle managers in relation to their existing local provision, whether in a community team, hostel or prison. Even a simple model of this type will quickly assist in identifying the gaps in provision or the lack of information about what is available locally. To develop and fill in the details of each element will require specificity about roles and responsibilities, both within an agency and between other agencies and professionals.

Such an organizational model is based on the research evidence that any specific provision focusing on offending will have greater impact upon an offender's lifestyle and criminal behaviour, if his or her underlying problems and needs have also been addressed. In addition, assisting offenders to reintegrate into a local community where they can find their own local support network, and activities and resources, which will provide them with opportunities to meet their personal and social needs.

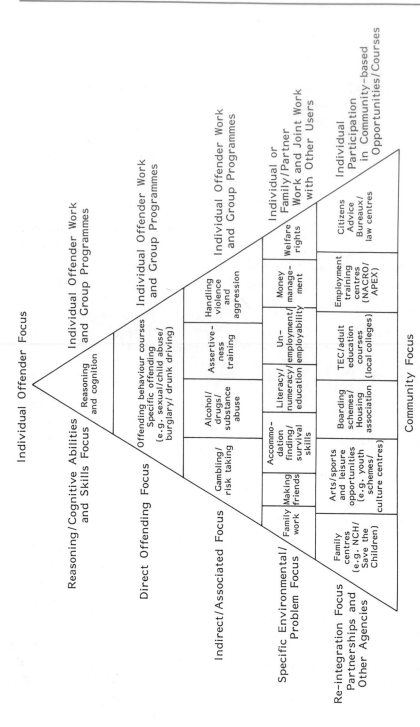

Figure 12.1. Model to show an organizational plan for provision for offenders.

NEED FOR CLEAR FRAMEWORK FOR THE SEQUENTIAL ORDER AND PROCESS INVOLVED IN DELIVERING EFFECTIVE PRACTICE

At this second level there are three stages which need careful planning and critical appraisal.

1. Selection, assessment and allocation of offenders.
2. On-going maintenance of quality and consistency of provision.
3. Procedures for the evaluation of inputs, processes and outcomes.

Selection, Assessment and Allocation

From some of the evidence we now have about effective programmes we know how critical it is to get a proper fit between the content and methods employed and the needs of the offender or offenders. Effective targeting requires the development of rigorous and systematic forms of selection, assessment and allocation.

Some practitioners and agencies have no, or very limited, influence in the initial decisions about which offenders receive which disposals. However, most agencies have some influence at the court stage and have considerable responsibility for selection and allocation once in the agency or institution. Pre-Sentencing Reports (in England and Wales) and Social Enquiry Reports (Scotland and Northern Ireland) still provide an important source of advice to sentencers, about the suitability of offenders for particular disposals. They serve an important gate-keeping function, and help to limit the range of offenders made subject to supervisory disposals, as well as in the process enabling some offenders to give informed consent to the possible forms of supervision they will receive. The specific issue of 'conditions' or additional requirements in Probation and Combination orders needs careful consideration, particularly in the light of recent evidence of its association with effectiveness (e.g. Mendelson, 1992).

The most detailed and precise assessment can usually only be done if the offender is either remanded for a reasonable period of time (which in itself is usually not desirable for reasons of justice and other factors), or at the beginning of a period of supervision or a custodial sentence. While the broad parameters of a disposal will already have been determined by the Court (with or without the offender's consent depending on the sentence), there is almost always still considerable discretion in the allocation to and provision of different programmes within a sentence (whether community- prison- or sometimes hospital-based), so at this stage it should be possible for a thorough assessment to be undertaken of each individual offender. There is a clear need for the use of more rigorous and

systematic forms of assessment, possibly making greater use of well validated schedules and tests, and thereby ensuring that the individual idio-
syncrasies of practitioners are reduced to a minimum.

I would suggest that, for offenders subject to community-based supervision or preparing for conditional release from custody, the following areas
could be covered in such an assessment:

(a) *Social circumstances*: assessing the offender's situation, coping and
     satisfaction with accommodation and living arrangements; finances;
     employment or occupation; family/domestic relationships; leisure
     activities and social associates.

(b) *Health/mental disorder*: assessing the offender's access to health,
     dental and other medical services; identifying any disabilities, serious
     health conditions or psychiatric treatment; using validated sched-
     ules to detect mental disorder (e.g. General Health Questionnaire).

(c) *Addictions*: assessing the offender's self-reported use of alcohol, drugs
     and solvents, possibly using validated schedules (e.g. Short Alcohol
     Dependence Data (SADD) Questionnaire). Also assessing the offend-
     er's involvement in gambling and fruit machine use by self-reporting.

(d) *Educational skill and ability*: assessing the offender's intellectual
     ability (possibly by use of intelligence tests) and competence in literacy
     and numeracy, by use of standard tests. Testing for dyslexia using
     tests designed for use by professional ss workers other than educa-
     tional or clinical psychologists (e.g. The Bangor Dyslexia Test).
     Assessing the offender's motivation to improve educational compe-
     tence.

(e) *Self-efficacy and self-control*: there are a wide range of possible
     elements of self-image and temperamental traits. Assessment of social
     and interpersonal skills, (e.g. Hudson, (1982) and anger and provo-
     cation (e.g. the Novaco Provocation Inventory (NPI) or Novaco Anger
     Scale (NAS (Novaco, 1994)), would appear to provide a useful starting
     point.

(f) *Offending behaviour*: this would include critical and detailed analysis
     of current or recent offending (e.g. using an ABC analysis), crim-
     inal career assessment, and attitude and motivation to future
     offending (e.g. Walters, 1990). Offence-specific assessments can also
     be undertaken (e.g. burglary, car theft, sex offences; see Cornish &
     Clarke (1986), Maletzky (1991) and Weiner & Wolfgang (1989)).

Behavioural and cognitive assessments are clearly required to examine
offending behaviour.

Only after such assessments can proper decisions be made by both
offender and practitioners about the specific kinds of programmes and

interventions which could be followed during a period of supervision. Such a plan can then be written into an agreement or contract, clarifying the obligations and responsibilities for not only the offender but also the practitioner and the agency. Such clarity will then improve appropriate allocation to groups or individual programmes for offenders who are most likely to benefit from those particular forms of intervention.

A recent vivid and worrying example of the need for more rigorous and consistent assessments is provided by Macdonald's study (1993) of the probation caseload of one team in a small southern probation service. She did a detailed audit of all the cases being supervised by a team of ten probation officers—a total of 168 probationers (25 women, 143 men) aged 17 years and over. She looked in detail at all the cases, in respect of information available in the probation records as to their offences, previous convictions and social circumstances. She also analysed PSRs and on-going records and interviewed all the probation officers about each case, to determine in particular the officers' assessments of what factors were associated with each offender's (recent or current) offending behaviour. There was an even distribution of offenders by offences, previous convictions and the range of types of social problems and circumstances (recorded by the officers). The individual caseloads were considered reasonably manageable, with an average of less than 20 probation order cases per officer (the highest single number being 24 cases).

Macdonald, however, found marked differences between officers in their perceptions of factors associated with offending in the offenders, which in turn was directly and strongly associated with substantial differences in the context of their assessments, and in the range and type of methods being employed in the supervision of the offenders.

Some officers viewed offending behaviour of clients as being influenced by a number of social, behavioural and cognitive factors, but others tended to select only social factors and with some a narrow range of social factors. Only one officer (but in several cases) mentioned mental disorder as being an associated factor, which seems statistically highly improbable (see Hudson et al., 1993).

It is particularly worrying that there is a large number of cases in which no behavioural difficulties and/or cognitive problems were mentioned. It seems most unlikely that these factors play *no* part in so many offenders. These apparent differences in assessment were also directly associated with differences in the range and types of interventions employed. Only three of the ten officers regularly assessed clients in behavioural and cognitive ways and these three were the only ones to employ behavioural methods, and were internally also the only three to employ task-centred methods in respect of social factors and problems.

Quality and Consistency of Provision

Hollin (this volume, Chapter 10) has emphasized the importance of the integrity of programmes and has provided indications as to how this can be assessed. The point bears repetition: successful programmes are those that give particular attention to ensuring consistency and quality. This applies not only to individual elements but to the whole range of provision provided. Even before the Citizens' Charter was written, it was not difficult to identify that one of the weaknesses of work with offenders in all criminal justice agencies in the UK, was the inconsistency of provision, not only from place to place but also across time and the constant failure to provide what had often been promised both to offenders and courts. Quality has undoubtedly been overdependent on the individual opinions and interests of practitioners. One of the keys to better quality and greater consistency has to be more accountability—from clear standards about the amount and quality of service provided under the Citizens Charter and National Standards, to professional accountability within and between agencies, and at colleague, supervisory and managerial levels. The past Chair of the Association of Chief Officers of Probation said recently:

> Accountability to the consumer brings demands that are not dissimilar to those required to demonstrate effectiveness. Setting and achieving published standards and objectives both require a cascade approach, to ensure that the efforts of all in the organization are as far as possible integrated. Systems which help to secure quality and consistency will need to be adjusted—appraisals, inspections, auditing and gate-keeping, consumer surveys. A proper complaints procedure must be operating and well publicised. Those we supervise are often too complacent about what they get from us—a higher level of dissatisfaction might be healthy. (Roberts, 1992c).

Evaluation—Measuring Process and Outcomes

As with the previous elements, the crucial importance of evaluating outcomes of programmes has already been emphasized in this volume. It is not solely a matter of evaluating the differential outcomes achieved by different programmes with different offenders that is required: it is equally important to monitor and evaluate the content and process in programmes themselves, otherwise differences in outcomes can be wrongly ascribed to programmes that are presumed to be similar but may in fact have distinctly different elements or features. The present evaluation being done in the Mid-Glamorgan Probation Service by Peter Raynor and Maurice Vanstone, has put considerable effort and time into not only evaluating the outcomes of the use of the *Reasoning and Rehabilitation* Programme, but also of evaluating the actual delivery of the programme by probation officers.

What is needed is a commitment and acceptance on the part of all practitioners that evaluation is in itself a critical and inseparable part of being an effective practitioner. Sheldon (1987) has advocated this principle for some years, and McIvor (this volume, Chapter 11) demonstrates how such forms of evaluation can be undertaken by those working in institutions or in the field. The use of single-case design methods (McGuire, 1991a) can be another important aid to achieving this.

Also, if more systematic and rigorous assessments are used consistently, then process and outline evaluation can be related to the data identified at the assessment stage, to measure movement or change over specified periods of time on a wide range of different dimensions, not simply or solely those of reconvictions or reincarcerations.

STAFF, KNOWLEDGE AND SKILLS: WORKING WITH OTHER PROFESSIONALS AND AGENCIES, STAFF SUPERVISION AND SUPPORT

Changing Supervision and Culture

One of the most obvious consequences of an emphasis on effective practice is the challenge that it poses for much of the custom and practice of one-to-one 'casework' in probation and social work agencies. This practice culture in probation clearly has its origins in the religious and philosophical ideals described by McWilliams (1983), 'Saving souls through divine grace', as being distinctly embraced by the original Police Court Missions. Today, work done by individual practitioners with individual offenders has often developed into presumed permission to practise some personally selected forms of social work. However well intentioned many practitioners are, one of the often unintended consequences of such individualistic practice can be discriminatory and biased outcomes for offenders. A focus on effective practice does not in itself remove the need for the use of individualized or of one-to-one methods of work, but it does require planned intervention, with specific objectives, and more rigorous monitoring and evaluation. Individual and group-based programmes will have to be more accountable and open to scrutiny not only to meet the National Standards and Local Standards/Guidelines, but also need to be open and accessible to supervision and examination to ensure the proper application of effective methods.

Existing facilities, even if well planned and resource-intensive, are not however always fully accessible to those for whom they are provided. This applies, for example, to probation centres and hostels, which are often dependent on referrals from only a minority of the probation officers working in a local area. A specific example is the Beaver Employment Workshop which has been in operation in Nottingham since 1977. This offers a two-stage programme which is attended voluntarily (i.e. not as a condition of a Probation Order), and which has a proven track record of helping offenders to improve their employability and obtain jobs. From careful monitoring of referrals over 15 years, it has been shown that at no time have more than 40% of the probation staff in the area made referrals to the Workshop. This is despite the fact that studies of offenders' work prospects in the locality have indicated high levels of unemployment or patterns of unstable job-holding. To put it crudely, your chances as an offender of being referred to a helpful resource seemed largely to be determined by who your supervising officer happened to be. Extrapolating this, it is likely that there are special projects or services in most probation services in which offenders are being denied access to differential forms of help and supervision.

There is in my opinion a need for a significant cultural change in the practice of staff in all criminal justice agencies, not just probation. The requirements for case management and purchaser–provider skills demanded by recent legislative, organizational and financial changes in social services, health and criminal justice require a reassessment of supervision roles and tasks in work with offenders. A focus on effectiveness itself provides an equally strong need to re-assess the kind of tasks and skills which practitioners need, to deliver appropriate group and individual programmes.

Only a practice culture change which fully embraces the need for clear objectives and plans for supervision, the use of empirically sound methods and content, in the approach to offenders, colleagues and other professionals, and an ongoing evaluation of work and its effects, will produce the environment in which effective programmes can be delivered (in the community or in institutions).

Interprofessional and Interagency Working

Another aspect of the evidence on effective practice is that no professional group can claim a monopoly of effective outcomes. Prison officers, clinical psychologists, teachers, nurses, social workers, psychiatrists, police officers, probation officers and even volunteers, can and have been successful implementers of effective programmes. What is needed is a recognition of respective skills and competencies, and the consequent better matching of different skills and experience, and to use them co-operatively to deliver the most appropriate programmes available. Certainly some social workers and probation officers have at times claimed a monopoly of values about clients and offenders. This itself leads to them precluding themselves from working with, for example, prison officers. At times professional notions of superiority, professional jealousies and exclusivity, have precluded interprofessional co-operative work. As well as practice professions, this can also apply to work with researchers, whether from within or from outside agencies or institutions.

There is a need to promote more active interagency work in which traditional boundaries are reviewed at both practitioner and managerial levels. Questions about who can best do what, rather than who has traditionally done what, need to be addressed in a wide range of settings, not just institutional ones, but community-based ones also. At times legislative and existing financial barriers may have prevented such work, but now with an emphasis on cash limits and cost effectiveness, there are real incentives for the wider development of interagency programmes and projects.

All this means that greater attention must be given at practitioner and managerial level to co-ordination and partnership. Working with other professionals, including researchers, and other agencies, and even sometimes other colleagues seems sometimes to be even more challenging and difficult than the direct work with offenders. In many instances individual practitioners or some agencies, cannot be the primary provider of programmes, facilities or provision. But they can and should be able to negotiate and act as brokers for the most appropriate provision for specific offenders. It is not always easy to ensure that such provision is available, but each practitioner and agency should at least be able to ensure that their own attitudes towards sharing those who are supervised are not a major obstacle to getting them the right help or provision.

Evidence from research on effective intervention shows that a diversity of practice is required to achieve the most successful outcomes. Success is most likely to be achieved through the careful matching of offenders to those interventions which are best able to address the issues that underlie offending behaviour, and which are consistent with the offenders' learning abilities. Given the complexity of offending behaviour, plans will need to be tailored to individual offenders' abilities and needs. Effective supervision involves the development of programmes which draw upon a wide variety of methods of intervention. Diversity of provision within a geographical area is also necessary to ensure that the range of services provided and available to a probation service or social work department are such that the personal, social and family problems which may contribute to offending behaviour can be addressed and different resources can be targeted at those offenders who are most likely to benefit from them.

Partnership does not, however, work unless there is a proper level of confidence and trust between partners, whether they are individual practitioners or agencies. Undoubtedly in the present political and financial context, working with other statutory and voluntary agencies can help to broaden the resource base available to offenders in the community, far beyond what any single agency may be able to provide itself.

Knowledge Development and Appropriate Staff Training

We know that one of the key elements in successful programmes is having staff who clearly understand both the theoretical basis of any work and have the skills necessary for competent practice. There are many other examples of the need for knowledge and understanding (Andrews et al., 1990).

Practitioners must have a sound theoretical and intellectual understanding of the basis for the programmes that are being used. As long ago as 1978 the Inner London Probation Services Differential Treatment Unit (Goldberg & Stanley, 1985) was demonstrating that one of the critical factors in providing effective task-centred casework for offenders, was that the most effective probation officers could be distinguished in terms of their greater knowledge of task-centred theory and methods, and their level of enthusiasm and commitment to the use of the method.

This means that staff in different agencies require sound basic education and training in the range of theory, skills and competencies that are required to deliver effective programmes. It is notable that in neither the Central Council for Education and Training requirements (CCETSW(1991)) for the new Diploma in Social Work qualification, nor more specifically in the joint Home Office and CCETSW requirements for probation training in the Diploma in Social Work is there any reference to teaching the range of theoretical and conceptual knowledge needed to undertake the sort of programmes that are effective with offenders. Staff however also need ongoing in-service and postqualifying training appropriate to what is likely to be effective. This commitment to on-going professional knowledge development requires not only formal training, but also commitment on the part of practitioners and managers, to keep themselves up to date by regular reference to relevant journals and publications.

Unless staff and managers are well informed about both the conceptual base of any programme, and the skills and competencies required to deliver it, then well intentioned provision may at best be less effective than it could have been. Sound understanding and knowledge of theoretical and methodological issues is also essential for the evaluation of programmes and their modification and improvement.

Staff Supervision and Support

One of the clear consequences for practitioners of working individually, jointly or in groups with high-risk offenders is the effects on their own motivation and commitment to such work. Inevitably, challenging situations, allied to high levels of apparent failure, can test the resolve of staff to maintain the quality of work undertaken with offenders. A freshness and enthusiasm for work can only too easily be replaced by strategies to survive and cope with the pressure of work. This means that appropriate, consistent and reliable forms of support for staff have to be built into provision. Middle management provision, properly resourced and available regularly, may be sufficient in many instances, but consideration may have to be given to the provision of external supervision, counselling and support for staff.

Less individual autonomy for work with offenders and more collective responsibility also demand explicit recognition of inter-colleague, supervisory and inter-agency systems of appropriate support and accountability. The debriefing of programmes and ongoing evaluation processes also require specific support, supervision and management. In all respects, the need for support, supervision and staff management which is geared to the needs of staff and which ensures high levels of accountability, quality control and ongoing evaluation, all require specific knowledge and expertise on the part of the managers who are expected to undertake them. Sometimes this can only be provided by using outside consultants to support such work.

Not only do staff need appropriate supervision and support, but projects and programmes themselves also need specific management inputs. Practice methods which need to be sustained and to be predictable in both their availability and their quality, require specific management attention. Consistency in practice and in the inspection and evaluation of practice and programmes also require specific management attention.

CONCLUSION

It is clearly apparent from the wide range of literature and research that is now available that no single approach is likely to be effective with all offenders in terms of reducing subsequent rates of recidivism. Indeed, as Lösel (1993: 18) highlights, even with some 'rather promising results, we are still far from a conclusive answer with respect to what works best, with whom and under what conditions . . . offender treatment research is still in its infancy'. The evidence that we already have, that offenders with differing histories and behaviours tend to respond differentially to various forms of rehabilitative programmes, clearly establishes the need for a wide range of clearly defined, interconnected and well managed services, targeted towards those most likely to benefit from them. Alongside this, if further evidence of the kind presented in this book is to accumulate, it is essential that agencies such as probation services which are responsible for provision of such programmes, systematically evaluate their effectiveness as rigorously as possible, using information of a variety of kinds to learn what is associated with successful outcomes.

REFERENCES

Andrews, D. et al. (1990). Does correctional treatment work? A clinically relevant and psychologically informed meta-analysis. *Criminology*, **28**, 369–404.

CCETSW (1991). *Rules and Requirements for the Diploma in Social Work, Second Edition. CCETSW Paper 30*. London: CCETSW.

Cornish, D. & Clarke, R. (1986). *The Reasoning Criminal*. New York: Springer-Verlag.

Gendreau, P. & Ross, R. (1987). Revivication of rehabilitation: evidence from the 1980's. *Justice Quarterly*, **4**, 349–407.

Goldberg, M. & Stanley, S. (1985). Task-centred casework in a probation setting: In Goldberg, M. et al. *Problems, Tasks and Outcomes. The Evaluation of Task-Centred Casework in Three Settings*. London: Allen & Unwin.

Hudson, B., Cullen, R. & Roberts, C. (1993). *Training for Work with Mentally Disordered Offenders*. London: CCETSW.

Hudson, W. (1982). *The Clinical Measurement Package: A Fieldwork Manual*. Illinois: Dorsey Press.

Lösel, F. (1993). *Evaluating psychosocial interventions in prison and other penal contexts*. Paper presented to the 20th Criminological Research Conference, Council of Europe. Strasbourg: Council of Europe.

Macdonald, G. (1993). Implementing the findings of effectiveness research in probation. In C. Roberts (Ed.). *Improving Practice: Towards a Partnership between Information, Research and Practice: Proceedings of 9th Annual Probation Research and Information Conference*. Birmingham: MPTC.

Maletzky, B. (1991). *Treating the Sexual Offender*. London: Sage Publications.

McGuire, J. (1991a). The single case design: implications of research for effective practice. In C. Roberts (Ed.). *Developing Effective Practice, Managing an Informed Approach. Conference Proceedings*. Birmingham: Midlands RSD Unit and University of Oxford.

McWilliams, W. (1983). The Mission to the English Police Courts, 1976–1936. *The Howard Journal*, **12**, 129–147.

Mendelson, E. (1992). A survey of practice in a regional forensic service: what do forensic psychiatrists do? Parts I and II. *British Journal of Psychiatry*, **160**, 769–776.

Novaco, R. (1994). Anger as a risk factor for violence. In J. Monahan & H. Steadman (Eds). *Violence and Medical Disorder Developments in Risk Assessment*. Chicago: University of Chicago Press.

Roberts, C. (1992a). What works—using social work methods to reduce re-offending in serious and persistent offenders. In *Proceedings of the ACOP Annual*

Conference. University of York, 1991. Wakefield: Association of Chief Officers of Probation.

Roberts, C. (1992b). *The Criminal Justice Act 1991: its roots and relationship to probation practice*. Wakefield: Association of Chief Officers of Probation.

Roberts, J. (1992c). Probation practice after the Criminal Justice Act 1991: a management viewpoint. In *Proceedings of the Joint Centre Professional Conference, Sheffield Polytechnic, 1992*. Sheffield: Sheffield Polytechnic.

Sheldon, B. (1987). Implementing findings from social work effectiveness research. *British Journal of Social Work*, **17**, 573–586.

Walters, G. (1990). *The Criminal Lifestyle*. London: Sage Publications.

Weiner, N. & Wolfgang, M. (1989). *Pathways to Criminal Violence*. Newbury Park: Sage Publications.

FURTHER READING

Brown, A. & Caddick, B. (1993). *Groupwork with Offenders*. London: Whiting & Bush.

Clare, A. et al. (1984). Social adjustment: the design and use of an instrument for social work and social work research. *British Journal of Social Work*, **14**, 323–336.

Doel, M. & Marsh, P. (1992). *Task-Centred Social Work*. Ashgate: Gower.

Frude, N., Toness, T. & Maguire, M. (1990). *Crime-pics: a measure of an individual's inclination to commit an offence*. Cardiff: Michael & Associates.

Goldberg, D. (1984). The recognition of psychiatric illness by non-psychiatrists. *Australian and New Zealand Journal of Psychiatry*, **18**, 128–134.

Goldberg, D. (1986). Use of the general health questionnaire in clinical work. *British Medical Journal*, **293**, 1188–1189.

Hutchings, J. (1986). *Dyslexia, Crime and the Probation Service*. London: Inner London Probation Service.

Klofas, J., Stojkovic, S. & Kalinich, D. (1990). *Criminal Justice Organizations: Administration and Management*. Carmel: Brooks/Cole.

Loowenstein, P. (Ed.), Marshall, K. & Weaver, P. (1991). *Targets for Change: Focused One-to-One Work With Offenders*. Nottingham: Nottinghamshire Probation Service.

Macdonald, G., Sheldon, B. & Gillespie, J. (1992). Contemporary studies of the effectiveness of social work. *British Journal of Social Work*, **22**, 615–643.

McGuire, J. (1991b). Things to do to make four programme work. In *What Works, Effective Methods to Reduce Re-Offending. Conference Proceedings*. Manchester: Greater Manchester Probation Service.

McIvor, G. (1991). *Effectiveness Research: Implications for the Provision of Social Work Services in the Criminal Justice System*. Stirling: Social Work Research Centre, University of Stirling.

McIvor, G. & Roberts, C. (1991). Towards effective policy and practice. Supplement to: *The National Objectives and Standards for Social Work Services in the Criminal Justice System*. Edinburgh: The Scottish Office, Social Work Services Group.

McMurran, M. & Hollin, C. (1989). The Short Alcohol Dependence Data (SADD) Questionnaire: norms and reliability data for male young offenders. *British Journal of Addictions*, **84**, 315–318.

McMurran, M. & Hollin, C. (1989). Drinking and delinquency. *British Journal of Criminology*. **29**, 386–394.

Miles, T. (1983). *Dyslexia: The Pattern of Difficulties*. St Albans: Granada Publishing.

Monahan, J. (1981). *Predicting Violent Behaviour: An Assessment of Clinical Techniques*. Newbury Park: Sage Publications

Petersilia, J. (1990). Conditions that permit intensive supervision programs to survive. *Crime and Delinquency*. **36**, 126–145.

Pitts, J. (1992). The end of an era. *The Howard Journal*, **31**, 133–149.

Stanjkovic, S. et al. (1990). *The Administration and Management of Criminal Justice Organisations: A Book of Readings*. Illinois: Waveland Press.

Statham, R. & Whitehead, P. (1992). *Managing the Probation Service*. London: Longman.

Willis, A. (1993). *Talking tough to offenders: letting the client speak and its implications for effective supervision*. Paper presented at the What Works Conference, University of Salford, September 1992.

Index